S0-AAC-062

3 1668 01707 1181

FORT WORTH
PUBLIC LIBRARY

FORT WORTH
PUBLIC LIBRARY
FORT WORTH
TEXAS 76102

MAR 2 3 1992

641.59597 D
DUONG, BINH.
THE SIMPLE ART OF VIETNAMESE
COOKING/

Simple Art of Vietnamese Cooking

Simple Art of Vietnamese Cooking

BINH DUONG
AND MARCIA KIESEL

Foreword by Jacques Pépin
Photography by Becky Luigart-Stayner

PRENTICE
HALL
PRESS

NEW YORK LONDON TORONTO
SYDNEY TOKYO SINGAPORE

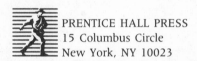 PRENTICE HALL PRESS
15 Columbus Circle
New York, NY 10023

Text Copyright © 1991 by Binh Duong and Marcia Kiesel
Photographs Copyright © 1991 by Becky Luigart-Stayner

Library of Congress Cataloging-in-Publication Data

Duong, Binh.
    Simple art of Vietnamese cooking / by Binh Duong and Marcia Kiesel.
        p.   cm.
    Includes index.
    ISBN 0-13-812124-9
    1. Cookery, Vietnamese.   I. Kiesel, Marcia.   II. Title.
TX724.5.V5D86   1991
641.59597—dc20   91-31156
                                                                      CIP

Designed by Barbara Cohen Aronica

Manufactured in the United States of America

10 9 8 7 6 5 4 3 2 1

First Edition

We wish to dedicate
this book to our mothers:
Mrs. Duong Van Thanh
and
Margaret S. Kiesel

Acknowledgments

Binh would like to thank his family and is especially grateful to Trai Thi Duong and Luy Nguyen for their help with the recipes.

A special thank-you to Jacques and Gloria Pépin, Ben and Gloria Zimmerman, Linda Guica, Robert Zemmel, Mr. and Mrs. James Sandler, and Charlie Mokriski for their support and encouragement.

Marcia thanks the Kiesels and the Gebhardts for being terrific. A big thank-you to Tina Ujlaki for her support and friendship. And to Jim Standard whose sensibilities impress me. Appreciation goes to Ann Altman, Peggy Cullen, Susy Davidson, Jonathan Dickenson, Cassandra, Barbara and LaPrial, Derrick R. Lambert, David, Paul and Martha Mullins, Ochiishi, Mike Weinman, Eric Weiss, and David Wollos. And everyone at *Food & Wine* magazine.

We both want to thank our editor Toula Polygalaktos for her patience and care. Evie Righter for her delightful enthusiasm. Elise Goodman who believed in us. Susie Kiesel and Carl Getchell who helped. Thanks to the people who introduced us to each other and Vietnamese food to *Food & Wine:* Ila Stanger, W. Peter Prescott, Catherine Bigwood, and Susan Wyler; Becky Luigart-Stayner who was a genuine pleasure to work with and to Claire Cavanagh. Thank you to Ruth Lingen for her handmade paper, Bob Chambers for his pottery, and to Alessandra Brunialti for her silks.

Contents

Foreword

There is a certain finesse, a certain quality to Vietnamese cooking that sets it apart from other types of oriental food: Clean, clear sauces; a minimum of fat; an abundance of vegetables; and very distinctive flavors, the most dominant of which are the famous *nuoc mam* fish sauce, used both as a flavoring and a seasoning, and the intensely aromatic lemongrass, which is infused in soups and used to flavor meat, fish patties, and other mixtures.

It is difficult to truly feel and understand a cuisine unless one is born in the country where that cuisine originates. Binh was born in Vietnam, where he was nurtured on his mother's home cooking and became immersed in the flavors unique to Vietnamese cooking. He is also blessed with an artistic temperament, sensitivity, feel, and touch, and these qualities, in combination with a thorough understanding of the cuisine, make him particularly apt at reproducing it faithfully while at the same time enhancing it with his own personal imprint.

Escaping the war in Vietnam, Binh came to America while he was still a teen, young enough to adapt to the American way of life. His entire family went into the restaurant business in order to earn a living, certainly, but also as a means of retaining their own identity and culture. Today, his sister runs a restaurant in Stockbridge, Massachusetts, and Binh has just opened a new restaurant in Boca Raton, Florida.

It was as a patron of Binh's restaurant, Truc Orient Express in Hartford, Connecticut, that I first came to know this personable young man and partake of his wonderful food. Binh's American business acumen and his deep knowledge of Vietnamese cuisine make him a particularly good practitioner and distinguish his family's restaurants and food.

In his own way, Binh will guide you here through the intricacies and refinement of that special cuisine, and at the same time show you how to simplify and adapt it to the American home kitchen. His youth and enthusiasm shine through on every page of this straightforward book from the heart. Extremely generous by nature, he dispenses his knowledge with eagerness and total sincerity.

Enter into the gentle, fragrant, comforting world of Binh and you will make as many people happy as I do when I cook Binh's food for my family and friends.

—Jacques Pépin

Introduction

While the cooking of Vietnam does not, as a rule, involve numerous complicated steps, as do so many of the other refined cuisines of the world, it takes the intuition and creativeness of a person like Binh Duong to capture its truths—its secrets—if you will. Up until the age of fourteen Binh lived with his eleven brothers and sisters, his mother, his father, and assorted relatives in Nha Trang, a small village on the coast of Viet Nam about 8 hours away over circuitous winding roads from Saigon, now called Ho Chi Minh City. Binh's father was an engineer, a man with the uncanny ability of being able to look at a machine and then build it. His father worked for the government, which was too poor to purchase much machinery; his talents were appreciated; his efforts remunerated. The family lived well by comparison to other Vietnamese, in a two-story house. Binh's mother was the cook of the family, a superb one, as was Binh's aunt. Early on, Binh's mother recognized that Binh had a fascination with cooking and an instinctive knowledge of how dishes were made. By the age of six, Binh, with his mother's encouragement, was watching her cook, learning the Vietnamese way of preparation, their subtle traditions and methods. He was also going to the market every day—a ritual in Viet Nam—and observing firsthand the extraordinary wealth of fruits and vegetables grown in his land. He was also honing his already masterful skills at bartering and haggling and negotiating, the only way to really get what you want at a Vietnamese open-air market.

I would meet Binh many years after that, in 1988, in the test kitchens of *Food & Wine* magazine in New York City, where I work, as the test kitchen associate director. Binh was visiting the magazine at the invitation of editor Peter Prescott, who had heard exceptional reports about Binh's cooking in his restaurant, Truc Orient Express. In hindsight, it now strikes me that fate must have had something to do with that chance meeting. For several years, I had been nurturing a fascination with Vietnamese food made unforgettable to me by a meal I had had in a restaurant called The Lotus in Memphis, Tennessee. As Binh passed through the kitchen, I mentioned to him my abiding interest in the cooking of his country. He responded enthusiastically, then asked if, by any chance, I would have any chicken wings around! It so happened, I did. He immediately took to the task of showing me the most amazing way of boning them. It struck me almost as magic, sleight of hand, he was so quick and so deft at it. (See our Stuffed Chicken Wings recipe to learn how to do it yourself!)

Shortly after that meeting, *Food & Wine* decided to launch a new column in the magazine called "The Ethnic Kitchen." Everyone was so taken with Binh, it was decided that the first article should be on his Vietnamese cooking. I was assigned to write it. Unlike many talented chefs who do not want to be bothered with the details of recipe-writing, Binh measured ingredients perfectly. He has a remarkably true and uncompromised sense of taste. His food was simple and unforgettably fine. We tested and developed recipes together and began to work as a team. In time, the idea of a book occurred to each of us. The rest is collaborative history—the *Simple Art of Vietnamese Cooking*, which I would also learn from Binh—is simple only if you appreciate how pure the food is.

Binh is a born teacher and a very generous man, and from him I learned of the history of his country—some of the factors that indirectly, or directly, had influenced Vietnamese culture, its cooking being just one of those components. China had ruled Viet Nam for more than 1,000 years, until A.D. 900. During the seventeenth and eighteenth centuries, political division—a recurring problem in the evolution of Viet Nam— would continue. Then the French arrived, gaining control of the country in the late 1800s and 1884 actually incorporating it into the French empire. With them they brought possibly their most substantial and long-lasting culinary contribution to Vietnam—French bread. The Japanese would occupy Viet Nam during World War II. For some time a Communist presence had been organizing itself under the leadership of a man whose name is now familiar to us all—Ho Chi Minh. Fighting between the Vietnamese Communists and the French broke out in 1946, in a bloody civil war, and in 1954 the Geneva Conference decided to divide Viet Nam: The Communists would get control of the North; the non-Communists control of the South. In 1957, the Communists from both the North and the South tried to take control of the South.

Beginning in 1961, Vietnam became a part of the history of the United States. The war in Viet Nam raged on until a peace agreement was concluded on January 27, 1973. But the Communists continued to send troops to South Viet Nam, pushing farther and farther south. Saigon would fall in April, 1975 and thousands of Vietnamese would flee the country, including Binh Duong.

Binh has returned to his homeland several times since 1975. And in January 1990, we would go there together, for Tet, the New Year.

Nothing could have prepared me for that journey, not even my almost uncontainable enthusiasm. After thirty hours in transit, another galaxy might have been our next scheduled stop, so far removed did I feel. As we were approaching Saigon, getting ready to land suddenly, everyone on the plane began to sing in Vietnamese, their enlivened voices filling the air. We then deplaned at the airport in Saigon, in blazing sun, and it was teeming with Vietnamese there to meet family and friends. When excited, which they all were, the Vietnamese scream. The most astonishing cacophony of overwhelming joy again filled the air.

Binh's mother, a small, very dignified, self-contained woman, was there to meet us. Over the next two weeks I would see how close her relationship was to her son, an indication of the remarkable strength of the Vietnamese family and the abiding belief that the Vietnamese reserve for relatives. This fact of life evinces itself time and time again, in the home, at the Vietnamese table—occasions where family ties are recognized and reknotted on a daily basis.

We stayed in Saigon, another world to me entirely, for about six days. Binh showed me the sights, not the least of which was the open-air market, which we visited and then visited again, always early in the morning, before it got too hot or late in the day, when life had cooled down however much it was going to that day. The aisles bulged and dripped with fruits and vegetables and flowers and herbs and spices and people, all knowing what they wanted and getting it. Beautiful produce, most of it grown in the nearby mountains of Da-Lat, was weighed on cumbersome, lumbering old scales. There were animals—cages of chickens, which would be killed to order, bled, and feathered before one's very eyes. Meat is butchered to order from behemoth cuts that lie ready, without refrigeration. There was produce I did not recognize and smells that delighted and repulsed me at the same time: roasting coffee, incense, overripe fruit, dried blood. A Vietnamese open market is not for the faint of heart. Nor is Vietnam, for that matter, particularly for an American.

Many of the side streets of Saigon have a smoky aroma to them, reason being that the Vietnamese cook over small charcoal braziers, which they set up on the sidewalks of the city. They then bring out tiny stools, which they sit down upon. It amazed me that anyone could balance on those stools, so tiny were they in size. I was thinking as a Westerner, though; obviously dinner on the street is a custom, a common and entrancing occurrence there.

The best place to eat, though, if one has the money, and there is not very much extra money for most people in Vietnam, are the food stalls in the open-air market. The atmosphere is convivial; the food as pure and fresh as it can be made. Life throbs by in the market.

From Saigon, a city of hustle and bustle, motorscooters and traffic, and an alive, thriving, and greedy black market, Binh and I drove about seven hours north to Da-Lat. Perched in the mountains, this tiny spot with its cool temperatures, pine forests, and rosy-cheeked inhabitants bears almost no resemblance to the rebuilt, sophisticated stifling hub from which we had just come. We stayed at a remarkable old French colonial hotel, a former famous retreat for the French officers. It was off-season and the hotel had been opened just for us.

To Nha Trang, Binh's birthplace, it was another daylong drive over torturous dirt roads through a mountain range. We had rented a van in Saigon, with a driver who had brought his young daughter along for the ride. Even the child was quiet as we laboriously teetered around hairpin turns and through mountain passes. My relief at arriving safe and sound in Nha Trang was heartfelt and I believe had something to do with being back at sea level, Nha Trang being on the ocean.

There I would stay in a hotel while Binh stayed at his family home. I would take my meals with his family. His mother and sisters outdid themselves cooking for us. For each lunch and dinner there would always be the table salad, a fixture on the Vietnamese table, replete with rice papers and dipping sauces. Either seafood or grilled meat would accompany the salad. Then poultry (or meat), boiled or fried, would be presented with a vegetable stir-fry, rice, and finally, for dessert, a dazzling selection of fresh fruits. Binh's mother, understandably, treated me as a guest, not allowing me to assist in the cooking or in the preparation of a meal in any way. It wasn't until the last day of my visit in Nha Trang that I was welcomed into the kitchen at Binh's family home and actually had the chance to watch Binh's sister make silver dollar cakes in a clay brazier. The cakes, which she would sort of sandwich together, were delicious. Better even than the cakes though, was that I got to squat on the floor with them and eat by the burner.

The experience of going to Vietnam, enigmatic, mysterious, mystical country that it is, cannot, nor should it be, related in detail here. Suffice it to say that its sights and smells and sounds are etched in my memory and that I would go back in an instant should the opportunity allow. Until then, I am reminded of its many captivating ways by my friendship with Binh Duong and the cooking of his homeland, which I have only really just embarked upon learning about from him. I know that the basic flavors of this cooking are clean, clear, tart, and sweet. It has adopted outside influences, from China, for example, but it is very much its own cuisine. There are only a few basic ingredients in Vietnamese cooking, but they are vital ones: *nuoc mam*, or fish sauce, lemongrass, a handful of unusual herbs, rice paper, and rice flour. What makes Vietnamese cooking special, of course, resides in how these basic ingredients are combined. Binh and I hope you will take this journey with us to find out.

A little window in a low, low hut.
No lordly mansion this—a hermit's den.
On the blue stream you idly cast your line.
Beneath green trees, in silence you read books.
Rain stops—hushed hills stand peeking in the door.
Wind blows—white waves come dancing to the sill.
Noonlight shines through a window clear of dust—
a leisured heart at one with the Great Void.

—NGUYEN TRAI

The Vietnamese Kitchen

EQUIPMENT

Houses are tiny in Vietnam and the kitchen isn't a separate room but a small area of the house that expands to include the outdoors. In a tropical climate, open-air cooking in the light of day makes the most sense. Vietnamese cooks are able to prepare a variety of foods with only the bare essentials. The preparation centers around the source of heat—a charcoal brazier. The brazier has three rests on top to accommodate pots and pans over the fire. Even before braziers were invented, the Vietnamese used three stones, or clay blocks, as a hearth. These three stones are called the three kitchen gods and serve as a reminder of family fidelity as described in an old tale about a merchant and his wife. For years, the merchant failed to return home, so his wife remarried. Finally the merchant did come back, but the wife hid him under a pile of straw from her new husband. The new husband arrived with a deer he planned to roast. Setting the straw on fire, he started to cook the deer, killing his wife's former mate. The wife, blaming herself for the tragedy, threw herself into the fire. The new husband then threw himself in, unable to live without her. Petrified in death, they became the three stone martyrs, the heart of the kitchen.

Another threesome defines the kitchen work area. The charcoal cooker, along with the mortar and pestle, and the chopping block form a triangular cooking station. With just these three basic pieces of equipment, the Vietnamese cook can prepare a multi-course spread that can feed the large families of this culture. A charcoal or gas outdoor grill is perfect for grilling Vietnamese food and an oven broiler also works well. Electric rice cookers are also present in most kitchens, but electricity isn't very reliable and tends to shut down regularly, while charcoal remains plentiful and affordable. Other equipment includes woks, saucepans, bowls, colanders, a sheet grater with fine, sharp holes for long vegetable shreds, and a bamboo steamer. You can cook the recipes that follow with basic tools like regular and nonstick skillets, saucepans, sharp knives, a grater, and a steamer basket. Listed below are a few items you might also find useful.

AEBLESKIVER OR MUNK'S PAN. This cast-iron pan with rounded depressions is most commonly used in Scandinavian cooking for small sweet pancakes. A version of the pan is common in Asian cooking as well and is used for a type of mini-rice pancake. You can find these pans at specialty cookware stores and at some Asian markets. Those made in Taiwan come with a tin lid, but any lid or covering will work.

BAMBOO STEAMER. This is useful because, unlike the stainless-steel steamer basket, it provides a wide, uninterrupted space in which to steam food like special rice, noodle cakes, banana leaf cakes, even a large, plated fish, or small bowls of meatballs in broth. Its rustic bamboo beauty lends itself both to cooking and presentation at the table. A metal steamer basket will perform most steaming functions. If you like professional equipment, a large, stainless-steel steaming pot with a removable steaming plate is available at Asian appliance stores.

CHARCOAL BRAZIER. This is basically a heavy, deep clay charcoal cooker with three rests on top to accommodate a wok and other pans. Grilling is done either on a metal rack fitted on top or with skewers that balance across the top. You may find braziers in some specialty Vietnamese and Thai stores. They're often forced into tin buckets with handles for easy carrying.

CHOPSTICKS. Just as we use spoons and forks to maneuver food while cooking, the Vietnamese find chopsticks handy for stir-frying, tossing noodles, flipping deep-fried foods, and mixing batters and sauces. Eating with chopsticks may be a struggle for some Westerners, and, if that is the case, the important thing is to relax. A low, pinched grip on chopsticks results in awkward food handling. If you hold them farther up, your hands will perform more gracefully. Don't think of using them in an up- and -down fashion. Approach the food more from the side, with the chopsticks resting horizontally between your thumb and forefinger. The wide ends should be almost flush with your hand at this point, with your thumb holding the chopsticks in place. Your middle and ring finger perform most of the action and your forefinger is used secondarily.

CLEAVER. A heavy meat cleaver is useful if you like the way Asians hack cooked chickens and ducks into flavorful morsels of meat, bone, skin, fat, and gristle. A cleaver allows you to separate spareribs individually and cut them crosswise into desirable bite-sized pieces. A Chinese vegetable cleaver, lighter and thinner-bladed than the meat cleaver, is an excellent chopping and slicing knife.

COCONUT GRATER. This is a very sharp, metal grating disk attached to a small wooden bench. One sits on the bench and scrapes the inside of a coconut half over the teeth of the disk, the grated meat falling into a bowl below. This is the quickest, most practical way to grate coconut and doesn't involve breaking the coconut into small pieces, peeling the pieces, and then grating them on a box or in a food processor. You can find these graters at Asian and Latin markets. Sometimes the metal disk is sold alone (perhaps as a replacement). Then you must attach it to a board yourself.

GRATERS. To obtain the long, thin julienne strips of vegetables so desirable in Vietnamese salads, try a grating box. This is a compact plastic box complete with an assortment of blades and grating disks that are inserted on top, with the cut food falling into the box below. Those you find at Asian markets are inexpensive and well made. Binh and I use a box called The Kitchen Wonder, found in many Asian stores for around $5.00. There are many other types of graters available, from Japan, Taiwan, America, and Germany. A French *mandoline* and other *mandoline*-type instruments found in specialty cookware stores give the same cuts with excellent results. *Mandolines* are much more expensive. Otherwise, use the thin grating disk of a food processor. Or a plain sheet grater will do. If you are extremely dextrous and have good, sharp knives, all the work can also be done by hand.

MINI-CHOP. This relatively new mini-food processor is a chopping device especially handy for the herb and flavoring mixtures that are the base of Vietnamese marinades and dipping sauces. You can use a mini-chop in place of a mortar and pestle, but you may want to cut back on the amount of garlic in the recipe, as the finer chop of the metal blades makes it much more pungent than the mortar does and may bring out some bitterness.

MORTAR AND PESTLE. Once you start using this ancient piece of equipment, you will realize how efficient and time-saving it is. You are spared from having to separately mince each ingredient that make up the flavorful pastes for marinades and sauces. The mortar and pestle keeps the combination contained until ready to use and does not require intricate assembly, like a food processor. And it is simple to clean. Its most important contribution to cooking, though, is the way it renders gentle flavors from highly aromatic and pungent foods like garlic, shallots, ginger, and chiles. And when sugar, fish sauce, and lime juice are added, the mortar blends the whole into a glossy, viscous mass unobtainable by any other means.

There are many interesting and beautiful types of mortars and pestles: carved granite ones from Thailand; craggy, mysterious ones from Mexico; and textured pottery mortars from Japan. White porcelain mortars from France are fine, but be sure they are large and wide. Wooden mortars work well but retain oil and garlic residues.

RICE STEAMER. If you eat a lot of rice, the electric cooker is one modern device we wholeheartedly recommend. There is no guesswork involved, you simply fill it, cover it, and press the button. Reasonably priced, compact and quiet, it will hold cooked rice in prime condition for hours. Rice steamers come in many sizes from 4- to 24-cup capacity. They can be found at Asian markets, appliance stores, and through mail-order sources (see pages 317 and 318).

TRADITIONAL VIETNAMESE RICE PANCAKE COOKER. The Vietnamese use another type of clay-pot cooker just for Silver Dollar Cakes (see page 142). It has a special disk with many holes in it that fits on the top. Small, shallow saucers fit into the holes and each saucer has its own knobbed lid. When well-seasoned, these cookers produce rice cakes that have a hard, crunchy crust. These cookers may be difficult to find, but most Vietnamese and Thai specialty stores should carry them.

WOK. The wok is a bowl-shaped, thin-gauged metal fry pan the Vietnamese have adopted from the Chinese to use for stir-frying and deep-frying. In Vietnam they are made of aluminum. Woks are widely available at specialty cookware shops as well as at most department stores.

SHOPPING

It's the marketplaces of the world that divulge a country's culture. What farmers grow and how they display their produce can reveal many mysteries. The marketplace is where all good cooking begins, of course. In Vietnam, as in many parts of the world, it is this spot that is still the hub the community. On the streets, as the breakfast soup pots are simmering, one can see merchants cycling to the market while it is still dark, their wares and produce crammed onto the sides of their bicycles. One wonders how far they had come and how long and hard they had peddled to reach the market. Carts pulled by donkeys are packed with fruits, vegetables and as many passengers as can hang onto the sides of the vehicle. Walking through the thoroughly packed, very narrow aisles that create a vast maze around, and to the interior of the market, it can get claustrophobic, especially with the hot sun beating down. But the smell of cooking food and burning incense and especially the beautiful displays of such abundant produce provide an abrupt distraction. Around the outer reaches of the market, goods are displayed on the ground. It is here, where a Westerner with bright blue running shoes is immediately noticed, since your feet are the first thing the sellers can see of you. This can start off a chain reaction of yelling and bantering that goes on amongst the merchants throughout the day. As you get closer to the heart of the market, usually enclosed like a small arena, sit-down meals, dry goods, and equipment are sold on a series of platforms. Merchants are perched on the tiniest stools behind scales, where they will squat all day, crowded in by their wares. The talk is lively and the market can now be seen as the great community center it is. Beggars, some prodding children in front of them, latch onto you and you must be prepared to give or assert yourself. At times, the almost impassable aisles become overloaded and a people-jam occurs. Before you know it, you are stuck in a mass of heat and confusion. And just when you think you can't stand another second of being a sardine in a can, somehow, a motor scooter will buzz by or a delivery man with a large order will plow through and everyone's moving again. But these instances are a natural part of living in a densely populated, Asian country.

The Vietnamese go to the marketplace to socialize. They shop there everyday. It is not uncommon for them to shop twice a day, in fact, as Binh was sent to do when he was growing up. His sense of quality and good value and street smarts, the art of bargaining, all were refined at the marketplace.

It is also in the markets of Vietnam that one can eat very well, in most cases, better than in restaurants. The food stalls are usually located in the very center of the market. There, at low, tiled counters on tiny stools is where a breakfast bowl of soup or steamed dumplings can be eaten before shopping and where in the middle of the day one can enjoy a quick lunch of spring rolls, happy pancakes, and noodle dishes. There are booths that specialize in meat pâtés and sausages, vegetarian dishes, and sweets and candied fruits. And it is where you can see every side of life. How rare and fascinating to be able to observe a culture that has remained virtually unchanged for hundreds of years.

When Binh shops, whether it is in Vietnam or Chinatown, there is no object too trivial not to bargain over, and I've watched him dicker a good five minutes just to get ten cents knocked off some oranges. For good reason, because the next time he goes to the market, the merchants will remember to offer their best, knowing what he will not settle for. If you shop at open-air markets, look closely at the prices of the produce. As you move from stall to stall you may see significant price differences. The mangoes at the first stall might be a dollar each, and farther down they're only fifty cents. But then you must look closely and decide are the fifty-cent ones in good shape, overripe, underripe, bruised, bad? Which is the better buy?

Though many people do not have access to an Asian community and marketplace, in today's supermarkets it is possible to find a wide range of exotic fruits and vegetables from many cultures as well as some basic imported prepared seasonings and condiments through mail-order sources (page 317).

Key Ingredients

Shopping at an Asian market can be overwhelming—trying to decipher what's what among the plethora of packaged and canned goods, some marked, some unmarked, some unreadable. It almost seems fruitless to give advice on how to shop for many items are mislabeled or have a number of different names to them, some that are meaningless.

Fortunately, you can make wonderful Vietnamese food with very little in the way of special ingredients and that is the glory of this food. Fish sauce, rice paper, noodles, and flour; lemongrass, fresh coriander, and chiles are about as exotic as you need to be. After you get a taste for these, then move on and explore the more adventurous ingredients. Our best advice is to begin by shopping for things you are familiar with or have a good idea about. If there is an ingredient you cannot find, it's likely that it is something you can probably do without, like dried pork skin or carrot powder. We've included below many of the Southeast Asian and Vietnamese ingredients that set Vietnamese cooking apart from all others. You will also find foodstuffs mentioned that are standard to Chinese and Latin and American cooking. We offer our advice and preferences on how and what to buy.

ANNATTO SEEDS (HOT DIEU). These orange-red seeds are common in Latin American cooking as well as Asian cooking. They impart a very mild flavor and are used here for their color, which is more orange than red. When the seeds are cooked in oil, that oil is used as a coloring agent. You can buy annatto seeds in cellophane packages in Asian and Latin markets.

BANANA LEAVES (LA CHUOI). These large, broad leaves are available fresh, folded into square bundles in ethnic markets. They are also widely available frozen, in one-pound bags. Because the leaves are sturdy and pliable, they can be folded into different shapes for steaming dumplings, fish, bananas, and coconut rice and are good for lining steamers when preparing loose rice or dumplings. They impart a gentle, floral taste. Whatever doesn't get used can be refolded and put back in the freezer.

BEAN CURD, DRIED (TAU HU KY). Soybean milk is brought to a simmer, and as skin forms on top, it is skimmed off and set to dry in thin sheets. Dried bean curd sheets are sold in plastic packets or colorful paper packages and are sometimes labeled "bean sticks." Check for whole, unbroken sheets.

Dried bean curd can be used a number of ways: fried as is until very crisp or softened in water, then simmered in a stew or sautéed in oil.

BEAN CURD, FRESH (DAU KHUON). Commonly called by its Japanese name, tofu, this is coagulated soybean milk curds that have been pressed and formed into "cakes." Some cakes are soft and delicate, others firm and tight. Use the freshest you can find. Usually the kind in Asian markets, sold free-floating in large tubs are the freshest. Tofu should be odorless with a delicate feel on the tongue, almost tasteless. Considered a vital protein source by vegetarians, it is cut into chunks for soups and sautés, mashed into fillings for spring rolls, fried and sliced for salads and stews.

BEAN CURD, FRIED (DAU KHUON CHIEN). These prefried tofu cubes are specially good filled and simmered in a flavorful stew. They come in 2-ounce packages that hold 10 cubes.

BEAN CURD, RED (CHAO). A spicy, wine-fermented tofu that imparts a reddish-brown luster and rich flavor to marinades. It is also called preserved bean curd and "wet" bean curd. The better-quality red bean curd comes in glass jars and some in small crocks.

BEAN THREADS (MIEN). These glassy, thin noodles are made from the paste of mung beans. They are also called cellophane noodles. Individual 1.8-ounce packets are the most practical for these recipes. You can deep-fry these as is and they will puff up into an airy, crisp nest of noodles. Otherwise they must be soaked in water before using, then they are often cut into smaller lengths before cooking.

CABBAGE, PRESERVED (CU CAI HU). Available in red clay pots from China and labeled Tientsin Preserved Vegetables, preserved cabbage also comes in small plastic tubs from Thailand, where it is called Chou Conserve. It can be found in most Oriental or Asia markets. Covered and refrigerated, it keeps indefinitely. No need to rinse preserved cabbage, its character is in its sharpness. To use, chop into small pieces and add sparingly.

CELLOPHANE NOODLES. Made from mung beans, these very fine, dried strands are also called bean threads or glass noodles. They turn translucent when reconstituted and cooked, and are added to fillings and braises, or they can be deep-fried from the package to make a crunchy base for stir fries. They come in packages that range from 3½ ounces to 8 ounces.

CHILES (OT). Though many varieties of chiles are grown in Vietnam, the tiny green and red ones, often called bird or Thai chiles, are the most popular in Vietnamese and Southeast Asian cooking. People living in hot climates enjoy the intense heat of chiles. They believe that chiles warm your stomach while eating and help regulate the appetite and digest food. The factor in the vegetable that produces the heat is capsaicin, which is concentrated in the chile placenta. It reacts in the human body by quickening the flow of blood to the skin, making the inside of the body cool down significantly. Eating spicy food is also believed to sharpen the mind: even when you're full, you feel alert. Chilies are also high in vitamins A and C.

The Thai, or bird, chile is the chile of choice here and luckily requires no special precautions or directions. As long as your fingers stay dry and avoid the juice of a cut chile, there is little chance that you will burn yourself. Using these chiles is very simple and straightforward: just chop them as they are, adding them, seeds and all, to a recipe. A little goes a long way and usually one or two, finely chopped, is plenty for one preparation. Discard what you don't use, keeping your exposure to the cut chile as minimal as possible. With a small paring knife, push the chopped chile onto the chopping knife, then scrape it into whatever you're making.

Your fingers never have to touch the chile. Even simpler and a little more primitive is the way Binh, when rushed, adds chile to soup or a dipping sauce. While holding the chile by the stem on a small plate, he tears off little pieces with the tip of a spoon. Then he scoops them up with the spoon, ready to use. At Asian markets you'll find small plastic bags of these chiles. For most Americans who cook Asian food a few times a month, or a week for that matter, one of these bags will last for at least ten, if not twenty, recipes, depending on your tolerance. (And the chiles will keep in the refrigerator for up to one month.) Be sure to discard any rotten chiles in the bag as one can contaminate the others. Green and red chiles can be used interchangably. However, there is a slight flavor difference: The unripe green is sharp and tart; and the red is sweeter and a shade cooler.

Dried Chiles (Ot Kho). Dried red Chinese chiles, whole or in flakes, are a perfectly good substitute for fresh chiles and are preferred in some recipes. Whole chiles are available in a few varieties. Most are of a cayenne type; others might be serrano, japonese, pequin, and de arbol. Chile flakes, or crushed red pepper, can be used as a substitute for dried whole chiles. Buy those that are in prime condition. The dried pods and flakes should be bright, glossy red and a bit pliable, not too brittle. Dried chile flakes are preferred for flavoring oil as they have better keeping quality in oil than fresh chiles do. Sate-Chile Oil, a potent condiment, is made with the dried flakes and much garlic (see page 58).

Chile Sauces (Tuong Ot). Prepared chile sauce, such as Sriracha, is a very popular condiment in Vietnamese cuisine. Basically a chile purée that is sharpened with vinegar and flavored with garlic, each brand has its own piquancy. I prefer the mellower Shark brand Sriracha, Binh likes the stronger one called Tuong Ot Vietnam. The chunky version with seeds, called Tuong Ot Toi Vietnam is made in California. For mail-order sources see pages 317 and 318.

COCONUT (DUA). Immature, green coconuts, freshly tapped, with a straw poking out of the center are a common sight in the markets and on the beach in Vietnam. The reason: Their young juice, or water, is a very popular beverage. It is very mild and pleasantly sweet and is also used as a stewing liquid in place of water or stock. (Since the coconuts found here do not contain as much juice, Binh uses coconut soda—a mild, sweet carbonated soft drink—found in Latin and Caribbean markets, as a substitute for this liquid. Coco Rico brand from Puerto Rico is easy to find in Asian and Latin markets.) As the coconut matures, the abundant water and jellylike portion of flesh turns to the rich, white meat we're familiar with as coconut. It is this flesh that yields the coconut milk used in cooking. Soaked in hot water, the meat is then strained to produce a thick "cream," that, in turn, enriches and slightly thickens curry dishes, vegetarian stews, steamed rice, and rice desserts. The meat is soaked a second time and this produces a thinner "milk" that makes a desirable simmering liquid for stews and sautés.

Look for coconuts in Asian, Caribbean, and Latin markets. To test for freshness shake one, you should hear a heavy sloshing of water. If you hear nothing or just a faint splash, don't buy it.

To break open a fresh coconut is an easy task that takes seconds to perform. Work over a sink and hold the coconut sideways in your hand, with the ends facing out. With the back of a heavy cleaver or a hammer, whack it dead center. Turn the coconut and hit it again in the center. Keep rotating and hitting the coconut, forming a ring around it, until the coconut splits apart, spilling its water into the sink and forming two halves. On a work surface, whack the halves into large pieces and with a dull butter knife, pry off the hard outer husk. With a swivel blade peeler, remove the thin brown skin from the white flesh. It is now ready for grating. This can be done with a box or sheet grater or in a food processor. We don't recommend baking a coconut to crack it open, for the heat of the oven removes freshness.

Once split in half, the Vietnamese don't break up and peel a coconut, for they have their own grating device. It's a grating bench, and this device, often carved into animal shapes, is used extensively throughout Southeast Asia, Africa, and the Pacific.

COCONUT MILK, UNSWEETENED (NUOC COT DUA). Canned unsweetened coconut milk can be very good and makes a better choice if very fresh coconut milk is not available. Look for Chaokoh and Chef's Choice from Thailand which come in 14-ounce cans. Coconut milk usually separates in the can, and you may want to whisk it into a bowl to emulsify it before using. Uncanned coconut milk will keep in the refrigerator for about 1 week.

CURRY SPICES (CA-RI). India's presence in much of the south of Vietnam long ago left its imprint on the cuisine with the use of the fragrant spice mixture called *ca-ri*. Usually a blend of freshly ground coriander, cardamom, fennel seed, cumin seed, cloves, and turmeric, among many others, these spices are usually used sparingly in Vietnamese cooking, sautéed with meat or seafood and simmered in coconut milk.

Jarred curry pastes from India are superior to commercial powdered blends because they don't have the rough taste frequently found in ground mixes. This fragrant paste is well rounded and retains its aroma and taste for a long time, especially when kept in the refrigerator. Daw Sen brand, made in Calcutta, is excellent as is Golden Bell brand from California.

Curry powder is produced by numerous spice companies and each one is slightly different from the next. Use one that pleases you and purchase it in small amounts from an Indian grocer if you can. Javin brand, a Madras-type curry blend from India is acceptable and readily available.

FIVE SPICE POWDER (NGU VI HUONG). This Chinese spice blend usually contains finely ground cloves, fennel seed, cinnamon, star anise, and licorice root. It is a very strong seasoning and should be used sparingly. Five spice powder often comes in large cellophane bags, far too much for average consumption. Look for the smallest amount you can find and store it in a jar.

FLOUR (BOT). The following are some flours commonly used in Vietnamese cooking.

Potato Flour (Bot Khoai Tay). This starch, most commonly used as a binder for pâtés and meatballs, lends a crunchy consistency to ground meat preparations. You can find potato starch in European grocery stores and in Asian markets. Be sure you don't make the mistake of buying sweet potato flour. Use cornstarch as a substitute if you can't find potato flour.

Rice Flour (Bot Gao). One of the most important staples of the Vietnamese diet, this is a highly digestible flour made from ground white rice. It is used in making rice noodles, *banh pho*. Batter made of rice flour is used to make Happy Pancakes (page 108); and rice flour comprises the dough for certain dumplings. Besides Asian markets, you may find rice flour in specialty food stores that carry French ingredients. Rice flour from Thailand is the most common and comes in 1-pound bags. The Erawan brand is recommended. Check the label to make sure you don't buy sweet rice flour, which is glutinous.

Tapioca Flour (Bot Binh Tinh). Made from powdered cassava root, this flour is used in dumpling dough to add chewiness as in the Hue Dumpling Flowers (page 148). When mixed with other flours, tapioca flour also produces a soft crepe with a bit of resiliency. We prefer the brand Up as it renders a finer texture than other brands. Erawan makes a good tapioca flour as well.

GINGER (GUNG). A member of the tuber family (along with turmeric and galingale), this plant captures the Asian spirit—spicy and sweet, restorative and soothing. Chopped, it is often pounded with garlic, shallot, chiles, lime, fish sauce, and herbs to form the base for many Vietnamese marinades and dipping sauces. Sometimes a Vietnamese stock will include a piece of ginger that has first been singed over a flame to warm it and give a roasted flavor.

Fresh tubers or "hands" of ginger are now readily available in supermarkets all over the country. Most come from Hawaii, but Jamaican ginger is the liveliest. Buy ginger that is very firm and heavy with juice, not shriveled and dry. Try to find moderately sized pieces, as very large, older ginger may be tough, stringy, and unusually hot. Taste ginger before adding it to a dish and adjust the quality if it's too pungent.

HERBS (RAU). The tangy herbs of Southeast Asia perk up delicate dishes, cool off fiery ones, and refresh the palate. Part of the charm and vitality of Vietnamese food is the prospect of all the fresh herbs used, and the Vietnamese grow a variety that are distinctive and delicious. Coriander, mint, scallion, garlic chives, and basil are eaten in such abundance that their presence goes beyond taste and aroma to provide the same essential nutrients found in other leafy green vegetables. You will get to know perilla leaf, a type of *shiso* leaf common to Japanese cooking, and the saw-leaf herb, which is used in Japanese and Caribbean cooking. Some of these herbs have special uses. *Rau ram*, is always added to chicken salad, and *ngo om*, the rice paddy herb, is the proper garnish for chicken curry. They are easy to grow at home, though they may be found at Thai, Vietnamese, and some Chinese markets. Sprigs of fresh herbs are packed in unmarked plastic bags. With the descriptions below, ask the grocer for them and use the Vietnamese names. This way you will get to know and appreciate the special qualities they offer. What's more, when you buy these herbs fresh, you can then root the sprigs and grow them in pots. If you can't find the fresh herbs, there are mail-order sources given for seeds on page 318.

Basil (Rau Que). The Vietnamese grow a sharp-tasting basil often called Thai basil. Its leaves are long and narrow and tinged with bronze and its flowers are purple. Sold at Thai and Vietnamese markets, it is also easily grown at home. Substitute any mild basil of your choice if you can't find this variety.

Coriander (Ngo). A parsleylike herb common in Asian, Indian, Middle Eastern, and Latin cuisines, coriander is also called *cilantro*, or Chinese parsley. Its musty, minty, orange flavor fits in so well with the other pungent qualities of Vietnamese cuisine that it is hard to imagine this cooking without it. Coriander is commonly found in large bunches in the vegetable sections of supermarkets and ethnic markets. Its taste can act as a substitute for other unusual Vietnamese herbs, like *rau ram, ngo om,* and *ngo gai,* if they cannot be found.

Giap Ca. Mildly sour, *giap ca* is rich in iron and highly regarded as beneficial for women. Its wide, rounded leaves come to a sharp point at the tip. Its use is not as prevalent in Vietnamese cooking as the aforementioned herbs, but it is enjoyed occasionally in the Table Salad.

Garlic Chives (He). This is the flat-leaf member of the chive family. You'll see hefty bunches of them for sale in Chinese markets. The bladed leaves have a sharp, garlicky taste and the long strands are used to garnish clear, simple soups and as an ingredient to be wrapped up in rice paper for Table Salad. This beautiful perennial grows easily and abundantly, producing large, white flower heads, which are also edible. See page 318 for mail-order sources.

Mint (Rau Thom). Bunches of fresh mint are available almost year-round at most markets in the United States. We prefer light and sweet spearmint to the more powerful peppermint. It's easy enough to grown your own mint, but set it out where it won't take over other plants.

Ngo Gai. In Vietnamese, *ngo gai* means "thorny coriander." It is also called the "saw-leaf herb," because its leaves have serrated edges. Used in the cooking of the West Indies and Puerto Rico, it is known as Puerto Rican coriander as well. The taste is quite similar to that of ordinary coriander, but a bit stronger. It is customarily a garnish for the national dish Pho Bo (page 73).

Ngo Om. Called the "rice paddy herb," *ngo om* has small rounded, pale-green leaves with a sharp, refreshing citrusy taste. It's traditionally used with curry dishes and in hot and sour fish soup. A little goes a long way. You can buy it in small sprigs that are easily rooted at Thai or Vietnamese markets.

Perilla Leaf (Tia To). Also called beefsteak plant or *shiso*, perilla leaf is wide and deeply veined with a purple iridescence on the underside. (There is also a red *shiso*, the leaves of which are deep purple and more ruffled.) Perilla belongs to the same family as mint and has a faint lemon-mint taste. The large, broad leaves can be used as a wrapping for grilled meats, as a substitute for the *la-lot* leaf, or shredded into salads and noodle dishes. It is an easily grown, hardy annual that when left to seed, will appear again next year. Seeds are available from mail-order catalogs. You may also find the fresh leaves in Japanese markets.

Rau Ram. A pungent herb like coriander, but with its own unique taste, *rau ram* has narrow, pointed leaves and pale red stems. Small bunches packed in plastic bags are available. A mixture of half coriander and half mint makes a good substitute. Sprigs can be rooted and will grow profusely in a pot or garden.

JACKFRUIT (MIT). Only available in cans in this country, jackfruit is fragrant and naturally sweet. Its sections are packed in water or sugar syrup. You can find Newton and Filtaste brands in most Asian markets.

JICAMA (CU XAN). Usually thought of as a Mexican vegetable, jicama is a tuber common in Southeast Asia as well. Its availability and character make it a great substitute for fresh water chestnuts and the two can be used interchangeably. Jicama must be peeled before being used in a recipe.

LA-LOT LEAVES. Many types of vine and herbal leaves thrive in Southeast Asia's tropical climate. *La-lot* vine leaves, in particular, are highly nutritious and are put to all kinds of uses in Vietnamese cooking, as wrappers for meats and seafood and as a leafy green in soups and vegetable sautés. The leaves are large, round, and crinkled and have a very delicate flavor. They are seasonally available in Vietnamese and Thai markets, where they are sold usually on the stem in bundles or bags. They are sometimes called Pepper leaf, as they are a relative to the vine that produces black peppercorns. A good substitute is the *shiso*, or perilla leaf, available year round in Japanese and Korean markets. Grape leaves, fresh or packed in brine, can also be substituted; just be sure to rinse them well before using.

LEEKS (BA-RO). A relative to the onion, leeks are mild and sweet in flavor and are used mostly in the vegetarian cooking of the Vietnamese Buddhists. Look for firm, unwilted greens that have large white bulbs.

Before using leeks they must be cleaned. Split the leeks lengthwise and remove the tough, green leaves. Wash thoroughly between the sections to remove hidden dirt. Pickled leeks (Cu Kieu), very small bulbs that look like pale-pink garlic cloves, are a sharp and crunchy Vietnamese snack. You can find pickled leeks in cans and jars in Asian markets.

LEMONGRASS (XA). The cuisines of Southeast Asia are noted for a unique tartness as well as for subtle and captivating undertones of unusual flavor, and lemongrass contributes to this mystique. This member of the grass family to which citronella, a far stronger essence, also belongs has a tender and aromatic bulb at its base that is used for cooking. Lemons are not grown in most of Southeast Asia, so it is lemongrass that gives Vietnamese food its lemony taste. Lemongrass is used mainly as an indirect flavoring, like bay leaf, that simmers long enough to release its perfume.

To use, cut off the dried, leafy top section of the stalk where most of the green is and peel away any dry outer leaves until you can reach the inner core that looks moist and tender. Depending on the freshness of the lemongrass and how sharp your knife is, you can sometimes eat the inner core if it is finely shredded. In some recipes, however, it is smashed with the side of a knife and then cut into long pieces that, when served are not ingested but removed to the side of the plate. When buying lemongrass, look for stalks that still have a lot of green on the top. The tops will always seem somewhat dry, because the plant is fibrous, but the leaves and bulb should be tight, firm, and fragrant, not dessicated, brittle and brown. Trim off the tops and outer leaves and wrap in plastic.

Lemongrass freezes well. When you use frozen lemongrass, it will be softer and easier to cut up. Lemongrass that has been dried comes sliced in little cellophane packages and is not very effective as is but it can be pulverized in a spice grinder or blender. A tart, highly fragrant powder, different and more concentrated than fresh lemongrass results and is put to best use in marinades and fillings.

Powdered lemongrass is also available in cellophane packets from Thailand and in jars from Indonesia. A good substitute for lemongrass is fresh lemon balm, also known as Melissa, an easy herb to grow. A tender herb, it is added at the last moment to soups where sturdy lemongrass would have been simmering from the beginning. Lemongrass makes a beautiful and lush house and patio plant. The next time you buy some, take a stalk that bears visible roots and keep it in water for several weeks, until a number of new roots appear. Then plant it in rich, sandy soil and keep it in a very sunny and warm spot. In colder climates, bring it indoors for the winter. It will grow, the bulbs will multiply, forming a large, tightly knit tuft. Pick the lemongrass as the stalks grow fat and tall; mature stalks tend to rot if not harvested and picking will also make room for more growth.

LIME LEAVES (LA CHANH). In Southeast Asia, these tough, citrusy leaves of the lime tree are often finely shredded and eaten. This is an acquired taste; we've found that the leaves are best used whole as an aromatic addition, like bay leaves. Fresh, frozen, and dried lime leaves are available in Asian markets and any of these can be used successfully. If you can't find lime leaves, substitute a small amount of grated lime zest with some lime juice.

MELON, BITTER (KHO-QUA). This vegetable is favored by the Vietnamese and the Chinese for its healthful benefits. True to its name, this looks like a lumpy cucumber that has a watery crispness and intense bitter sting. Bitter melon is easily found in Chinese and Asian markets. Look for firm, green melons about 5 to 6 inches long with no yellow or orange (age) spots.

MUNG BEANS (DAU XANH). Yellow mung beans are just peeled and dried green mung beans. Usually soaked and added to batters or steamed with rice, yellow mung beans provide a subtle flavor and slight crunchiness. They come in one-pound packages and go by the name Peeled Mung Beans.

MUSHROOMS (NAM). Here are a few of the mushrooms most commonly used in Vietnamese cooking.

Dried White Fungus (Nam Trang). Sometimes called silver fungus, white fungus is a relative of the tree ear and looks like feathery, yellow sponges. When reconstituted, white fungus turns shiny and translucent. Vegetarians regard it especially for its healthful properties. White fungus has little taste, but adds a delightful crunchiness to soups and salads. You can buy it loose or in plastic boxes or packages. Be sure the white fungus is whole with no shades of brown to it. To use, the fungus must first be soaked and trimmed of any hard knobs.

Shiitake, Dried (Nam Dong Co). Sometimes these are called dried black mushrooms. Shiitake mushrooms must be soaked in water and the stems trimmed before being used in other preparations where they lend a smoky essence. They come in plastic packages of all sizes and are found in Asian, Japanese, and specialty food stores.

Tree Ears. An ancient food regarded by the Chinese as valuable in medicinal properties, tree ears are a growth or fungus that sticks out from the tree trunk like flappy ears. Available dried in this country, tree ears when reconstituted have a resilient crunchy texture and very little taste. They constitute a fine filling and stir-fry ingredient as they do not compete in flavor. Tree ears are sold in most Asian markets, and a small amount goes a long way. You may want to buy the smaller bags.

NOODLES (BANH PHO, BUN). Made from rice flour and water, these dried noodles usually come in 1-pound packages and will keep indefinitely. These noodles should be soaked in cold water before using. Depending on how thick they are, the noodles are soaked 20 to 40 minutes to take away the brittleness and make them pliable. It takes just seconds to complete the cooking, as they should always retain some chewiness. Rice noodles come in many widths from fine vermicelli to medium or extra wide. Chinese rice noodles are called *Mei Fun.* Erewan and Three Elephant from Thailand are good brands and so is the Chinese Three Swallow brand.

PANDAN LEAVES. Also called screw pine or vanilla leaves, pandan leaves have a pleasant, sweet aroma. Sometimes a leaf is added to steaming rice to perfume it, or the leaves can be pulverized to obtain their green juice to flavor and color sweet rice preparations. Fresh or frozen, loosely packaged pandan leaves can be found in Southeast Asian markets. Canned pandan leaves from Thailand are available too, but are not as fragrant. Pandan paste, potently green colored, comes in small plastic tubes from Thailand and is very fragrant, so use sparingly.

PAPAYA, GREEN. A large, immature cousin of the yellow, sweet variety, green, or salad, papaya grow to great proportions with flesh that is crisp and mild, like underripe honeydew melon. Green papaya is sporadically available in Asian, Vietnamese, and Thai groceries. Be sure they are very firm with no bruises.

PEPPER, BLACK AND WHITE. Vietnam is a premier pepper producer and unfortunately the Western world is missing out on some of the finest pepper grown. Black pepper is the green, underripe berry that has been dried. Its smooth spiciness works best in marinades and fillings. The white pepper is the ripened, dried berry that has had its outer coating removed. The white pepper of Vietnam is uncommonly rich flavored, but all white pepper is hotter than the black. Because it is sharper, white pepper is preferred for seasoning soups. Always use whole peppercorns and grind them just before using. Try one of the many different types of black pepper available in specialty food stores such as Tellicherry, Malabar, and Lampong. Unfortunately, white pepper varieties are rarely available.

PORK SKIN THREADS. These are finely cut dried cooked pork rinds. When reconstituted, pork skin threads have little flavor but a crunchiness that is prized. They can be found in most Asian markets sold in large cellophane bags marked Dried Pork Skin or Dried Pork Threads and sometimes called by their Vietnamese name Bi.

PRESERVED PRUNES (XI MUI). Usually labeled preserved prunes, these are salted, preserved plums that have been coated with sugar and dried. To bite into one will pucker up your mouth—it is as salty as it is sweet and sour. When simmered in water, these candied plums add a unique flowery tartness to sauces and marinades. They come in plastic packages from China and are found in Asian and specialty food markets. Be sure to read the label before purchasing as some plums are licorice coated. Happiness Red Brand is particularly good.

RICE PAPER (BANH TRANG). Uniquely Vietnamese, rice paper is a curious and ingenious product which, when raw, appears to be made of plastic, but is actually made of cooked rice, mashed into a dough, then machine-rolled paper thin. The sticky dough is then cut into rounds and placed on bamboo mats to which it immediately adheres. After drying in the sun, the rounds are popped off the mats, leaving a woven, bamboo imprint. Glassy and brittle when dry, they become translucent and pleasantly chewy after being moistened with water.

You can also brush raw rice papers with beaten egg, then fill and fry them. This produces crisp, practically grease-free snacks. Rice paper wrappers are an integral part of a Vietnamese meal as part of the Table Salad (see page 32), like the flat breads of other lands: the Mexican *tortilla*, Indian *chapata*, and Middle Eastern *pita* (see the Vietnamese Table, page 31).

Dried rice paper comes in small and large rounds for the Table Salad and in a triangular cut, which is used for the less bulky spring rolls that make Vietnamese food so popular. You'll find rice paper at some Chinese grocers and at Thai and Vietnamese stores. Be sure to check the packages to see that the rice papers are whole, not chipped or broken.

ROCK SUGAR (DUONG PHEN). Also called crystallized sugar, this is liquid cane sugar that has been hardened into glassy chunks. The Vietnamese pound it in a mortar and the coarse crystals season and add crunch to forcemeats and pâtés. Sometimes rock sugar is added to a stock or sauce, giving it a special glossiness. Clear rock sugar is called for in this book and can be bought in Asian and other specialty food stores.

SAUCES. There are a variety of bottled (prepared) sauces commonly used in Vietnamese cooking. Here are some of the most essential.

Anchovy Sauce (mam nem). Not to be confused with fish sauce, this is a bottled mixture of ground anchovies, salt, and water. When properly combined with other ingredients, it is a delectable and savory condiment. Buy the higher-priced brands found in Thai and Asian markets. Upon opening, keep in the refrigerator for up to 6 months. Italian and French prepared anchovy paste can be substituted here, just thin it with water to a consistency similar to buttermilk.

Fish Sauce (nuoc mam). In many cuisines, cured or fermented small fish, like anchovies, act as an important food enhancer. The Vietnamese version of this is a salty but subtle amber liquid made from fermented anchovies, which is highly nutritious and rich in B vitamins and protein. Called *nuoc mam*, it is the soul seasoning of Vietnamese cooking. Although its presence is not detectable in Vietnamese dishes, were it to be left out, its rich depth of flavor would most definitely be missed. It is the one ingredient that cannot be substituted and is vitally important. It is used in place of salt except in most beef dishes where, due to Chinese influence, soy sauce is preferred.

In Nha Trang, Binh brought me to the home of a local fish sauce maker. As we walked the back alley to the house, I knew we were getting close because the smell, even from fifty feet away, was strong. A warm, friendly man by the name of Thieu Pham showed us his sauce works from beginning to end. Afterward, we sat in his front room, drank tea, and ate sweet cake, trying hard not to notice the fish smell that permeated the house. He was very proud of his product, for it was of the highest quality and a rarity. The distributor, he said, would dilute it with caramel water.

The process of making fish sauce, as we observed it, goes like this. First, tiny anchovies are set out in the sun to dry slightly and begin the first fermentation. After a few hours, the fish are layered with salt in large, wooden vats where they will sit for three days. What happens next is very similar to the making of cabbage into sauerkraut. The salt draws liquid from the fish and after three days the liquid is poured off and reserved. Then the fish are very firmly weighted, and the reserved liquid is poured on top to completely cover them. Now the fish will sit and ferment more. A spigot is opened at the bottom of the vat, just a crack to allow the liquid to very slowly drain off. When all the liquid has been collected, after about six months, it is poured into ceramic urns. These urns are covered with an earthenware lid and set in the sun for one month to further ferment and develop flavor.

Always buy fish sauce in glass bottles, a sign of high quality. Try to find Phu Quoc, a special, extra high quality fish sauce, just for dipping sauces. For cooking, buy either Squid, Golden Boy, or Lobster brands from Thailand, which are more available and also excellent. The Indonesian brands of fish sauce, or gravy, as they call it, come in plastic bottles and are inferior, too harsh.

Hoisin (Tuong Ngot). From China, hoisin is made from soybean paste, garlic, sugar, and spices. Quality, taste, and thickness vary significantly with each brand. Koon Chun brand is a good choice.

Oyster (Dau Hao). This sauce, acquired from the Chinese as an enrichment to stir-fries, is made of ground oysters, water, and salt, the whole often sweetened and thickened with cornstarch. Buy the more expensive brands and you'll get a much higher quality product. Lee Kum Kee and Hop Sing Lung Oyster Sauce are very good.

Vietnamese Bean (Tuong Cu Da). In its purest form, this sauce is simply ground or roughly chopped soybeans. Mixed with cooked rice and water, it makes a mellow but creamy sauce. This is thinner than Chinese versions, though both can be used interchangeably. Bean sauce is used in vegetarian cooking for enrichment. Huong-Viet *tuong bac* is made in California. Koon Chun brand from China is widely available; just thin it slightly before using.

SAUSAGES, CHINESE STYLE (LAP XUONG). These sweet and savory hard sausages must be steamed or simmered before using. They are usually made of pork and pork fat, though some are made with liver or beef. Our favorite is a packaged Vietnamese variety made by Viet-Hung Paris in California. While this variety doesn't have the desirable large bits of fat, we find the smoother texture appealing. Other good Chinese sausages are found at most Asian grocers. Look for the kind sold loosely and tied together with string.

SESAME OIL (DAU ME). This oil, pressed from dark browned sesame seeds, is a potent seasoning and is used sparingly in Vietnamese cooking, just enough so that it blends in with the other ingredients to add a hint of its nuttiness. Buy in a small bottle to keep it fresh and store in the refrigerator. Japanese brands such as Kame, Kadoya, and Red Dragon are very good.

SHALLOTS (HANH HUONG). A sophisticated member of the onion family, shallots are used in the marinades that season most Vietnamese meat and seafood. They are also fried until crisp and sprinkled on soups and salads. The small, purple shallots are preferred, and you can find them sold loosely or in net bags in most vegetable markets. Look for hard, smooth ones with no signs of sprouting. Prepared fried shallots, found in Asian markets are tasty, if a bit greasy. They're labeled Fried Red Onion and come from Thailand. See the recipe for Fried Shallots (page 62) to make your own.

SHRIMP, DRIED (TOM KHO). Used sparingly, dried shrimp act as a seasoning and their chewiness contributes texture to dishes. The Vietnamese also like to shred dried shrimp to a coarse powder to sprinkle over finished preparations. Good dried shrimp should be moist and springy to the touch, with a clean coral color, not brittle and brown. Choose the larger and brighter ones. You'll find them sold loose or in plastic packages, sometimes in the refrigerated section of an Asian grocer. For details on preparing pulverized dried shrimp see page 142.

SHRIMP CHIPS (BANH PHONG TOM). These hard, translucent chips are made of finely ground shrimp and egg whites. It is the whites that help the mixture dry completely and puff up to almost three times its size when dropped in hot oil. What results is a lighter than air, crispy chip that disappears in your mouth, leaving a pleasantly mild shrimp taste. The chips come in various shapes, mostly round or rectangular, and are sometimes called prawn crackers. In Vietnam, you can find fancy cut shrimp chips that when fried, curl up into a shape they call the Saigon Twist. They can be eaten plain, as an hors d'oeuvre, or with a salad. Brands vary in quality. Keep in mind that they shouldn't have a strong fishy taste, and by all means, avoid colored shrimp chips. Sa-Giang is an excellent brand, though hard to find. Pigeon and Pearl River brands are acceptable.

SHRIMP PASTE (MAM TOM). This is a dense mixture of fermented ground shrimp. In Vietnam as well as throughout Asia, you will see mounds of shrimp and seafood pastes for sale in varying shades of muddy red, purple, tan, and brown, the colors indicative of the way the pastes were cured and the length of their fermentations in the sun. The pungency of shrimp paste is a prized flavoring. In these recipes it is used in very small amounts, like anchovy paste, for enrichment. Price should be your guide in selecting shrimp paste; the more expensive, the better the quality. Lee Kum Kee from China and Shrimp and Boy brand from Malaysia are particularly good.

SOY SAUCE (XI DAN). Soy sauce is used a good deal in Vietnam, especially by the vegetarian Buddhists, who do not eat fish sauce. Soy sauce is favored for beef preparations over fish sauce, a taste acquired from the Chinese. Japanese soy sauces are light, pleasant, and well suited to Vietnamese cooking. Chinese soy sauces tend to be salty and strong. Kikkoman brand is very good. The 1-quart cans are a good buy.

STAR ANISE (HOI). These pretty, star-shaped pods are the flower of an evergreen tree. Their pleasing licorice fragrance infuses long-simmered dishes and is especially becoming to beef. You'll find star anise sold loose in plastic packages in Asian and specialty markets where it is often labeled dried aniseed. Look for pods that are not broken.

STARFRUIT (MIT). Star apple as it is commonly called, when cut forms slices in the shape of a star. It comes in two varieties, sweet and sour. Most of what is grown in this country comes from Florida and is the sweet variety, which unfortunately lacks the flavor and tang of sour starfruit. Most of the sour starfruit doesn't leave Florida as there is no great demand for it by the American public. It's the sour variety, however, that is popular in Vietnam. Its tartness makes it a refreshing part of the Table Salad. It's difficult to discern sour from sweet starfruit, so ask your grocer. If you can't find either, slices of tart apple such as Granny Smith, Winesap, or Greening can be used instead.

SQUID, DRIED (MUC KHO). All over Asia, people appreciate chewy and tasty dried squid as a snack. In Vietnam little carts offer it along with fresh pineapple. Drying squid gives it a unique taste and texture, much different from the blandness of fresh. The salt content concentrates in drying, so if you're trying it for the first time soak it first. Dried squid is eaten as is or can be simmered in a soup or stew to add a smoky, salty flavor the way a ham hock does. You'll find dried squid in Asian markets, sold in plastic packages, where it is sometimes called cuttlefish. It comes in many sizes but try to buy the 7-inch-long variety.

SUGAR CANE (MIA). Sugar cane is an important crop in Vietnam and is available in the markets in varying degrees of refinement: sticky tan pastes, thick, black caramel syrups, dark brown bricks, and ultra-refined white granules. On the streets of Vietnam, there are sugar cane juice stands where freshly cut stalks are passed through wringing machines to extract the green juice. Served on ice, this juice makes an interesting drink with a watery sweetness. The Vietnamese also like to chew on small sticks of peeled sugar cane as a snack. Or the stalks are peeled and split to use as skewers for grilling fish and shrimp pastes (see page 112 for recipe). In large Asian markets, you may find relatively fresh sugar cane in two-to-six-foot lengths. We recommend using fresh sugar cane only if it appears moist and heavy with juice. Avoid the plastic wrapped small pieces found in gourmet sections of many supermarkets, as they are likely to be old and dry. A fine alternative is canned sugar cane in syrup. Chao-koh brand from Thailand comes in 20-ounce cans containing about six good-sized stalks that are juicy and sweet. Leftover sugar cane in its syrup will last for weeks in a covered container in the refrigerator.

SWEET OR GLUTINOUS RICE (GAO NEP). Also known as sticky rice, this type has a higher starch content and a solid, creamy white color that is notice-ably different from the translucency of regular long-grain rice. It is favored by the Vietnamese as a comfort food, sometimes eaten for breakfast but generally reserved for ceremonial rites (such as throwing at the bride and groom at weddings), and holidays. It is usually cooked in a bamboo steamer on a banana leaf, arranged free form. When cooked, it forms a sticky mass. Glutinous rice is meant to be shared; it is cooked in large amounts to feed big families at gatherings and weddings and to bring in the New Year. Sweet rice is available in short and long-grain varieties.

SWEET POTATOES (KHOAI LANG). The sweet potato is a popular food in Asia, the Pacific, and the Caribbean. In Vietnam, sweet potatoes come in many varieties and colors, including purple, red, yellow, orange, and white. Use orange sweet potatoes for these recipes since they're the sweetest.

TAMARIND PULP (ME). Tamarind trees grow abundantly throughout South Vietnam, sometimes lining long avenues, their feathery leaves giving speckled shade and their fat, fuzzy brown pods hanging low as they ripen. The pulp, which surrounds the large seeds in these pods has an intensely sour and faintly floral sweetness that is a treasured and unusual tart condiment. It is most widely known for its use in the Vietnamese hot and sour fish soup, which has as many versions as the number of cooks who make it. The pulp heavily coats the large seeds and when sold in this state is a sign that it is good quality and will have to be soaked and strained before using. Be sure the pulp isn't dried out and feels moist when pressed. Try to find brands that don't have added sugar, though some salt is fine. Tamarind pulp comes in small packages. Erawan and Roland brands are good. Kept tightly wrapped in plastic, it keeps many months in the refrigerator.

TAPIOCA SHREDS (HU TIEU UOT). These are a kind of noodle made from tapioca flour and water and have a ridged cut. With little flavor but a pleasing chewiness, tapioca shreds are appreciated for the texture they add to a dish. They are made in China and come in 1-pound packages labeled Dried Tapioca Shreds, often with no specific brand name.

TARO ROOT (KHOAI MON). Taro root is a bland, starchy vegetable used like a potato, adding soothing heartiness to soups and stews. It is sometimes fried in cubes or shreds. This vegetable comes in many sizes: from small golf ball-sized knobs called baby taro to the average-sized taro to almost football-sized ones. All are covered with a coarse, dark skin that must first be peeled off, and have creamy-colored flesh with reddish-brown specks. Peel and cut just before using as taro root discolors quickly. Taro is a common vegetable found in most Asian markets.

TIGER LILY BUDS (KIM CHAM). A standard ingredient in Chinese cooking is the dried, unopened bud of a day lily. The Vietnamese like to use them too for dishes that are Chinese influenced, like the Steamed Whole Bass with Tiger Lilies (see page 200). They come loosely packaged. Be sure they are dry but pliable, not brittle. Golden Dragon is a good brand. When reconstituted in water, tiger lily buds have a subtle tanginess and firm texture, even when cooked.

TURMERIC (NGHE). A relative of ginger, this small tuber with ribbed skin is most usually found in dried, ground form, although the fresh is also used in Vietnamese cooking sliced and added to stir-fries to lend a mild, slightly metallic taste. It is not eaten, however, but pushed to the side of the plate. Ground dried turmeric, a common curry spice, is used to add color, and is frequently a component in fish marinades, batters, and doughs. Medicinally, turmeric is thought to clear the skin and prevent scarring from measles and chicken pox. You may find fresh turmeric in Thai or Vietnamese markets. Ground, dried turmeric is available in Asian markets. Try some of the Thai varieties. The flavor is never strong but it may be more aromatic than generic ground turmeric.

WATER SPINACH (KAU MUONG). A water-growing vine that has arrowhead-shaped leaves and hollow, reedlike stems, water spinach has a mild, tangy flavor and when cooked an interesting textural contrast between the tender leaves and crunchy stems. You can buy large bunches of it in Asian markets. Trim off the lower, tough part of the stems, tear the leaves off with some of the tenderer stems attached, and chop the remaining stems. This highly nutritious vegetable can be stir-fried or wilted into soups. The Vietnamese especially like the curled stems in salads and as a garnish for soups.

YELLOW MUNG BEANS (DAU XANH). These are peeled and split dried green mung beans. They are usually soaked and added to batters or steamed with rice, giving a subtle sweetness and slight crunchiness. Yellow mung beans come in 1-pound packages, called Peeled Mung Beans, Yellow Mung Beans, or Green Mung Beans.

THE VIETNAMESE TABLE

There is always an interesting assortment of different dishes on the Vietnamese table to feed the typically large family. A bowl, a set of chopsticks, and a small saucer for dipping sauce is the place setting for each family member or guest. All of the dishes are presented at once and as soon as the big bowl of hot rice is brought in, the commotion begins. Each platter of food is passed around and everyone takes a modest amount as it goes by. Rice is eaten with stir-fried, stewed, and braised dishes. Grilled meats and seafood and little fried appetizers are eaten out of hand after being wrapped in the assortment of herbs, sliced vegetables, lettuce leaves, and sheets of moist rice paper arranged on a platter that is called the Table Salad. After wrapping, the bundle is dipped into *Nuoc Cham* Dipping Sauce that has also been passed around and ladled into each saucer. It is this process of wrapping and dipping that is so refreshing to the palate and so distinctly Vietnamese. Second and third helpings are encouraged, so when your bowl is empty, the food is passed around again. Such a variety of foods and busy eating encourages a long, leisurely visit with family and friends, and the Vietnamese meal always seems like a special occasion.

TABLE SALAD *(Sa Lach Dia)*

MAKES ENOUGH TO SERVE 6 TO 8

This integral part of the Vietnamese meal, also makes a beautiful centerpiece for the table. Use whatever selection of ingredients listed below you can find or have on hand. Adjust the amounts according to the number of people you are expecting. The herbs, sliced fruit, and vegetables can all be replenished in a flash; so the only items you will need to have ready in advance are the moistened rice papers and rinsed lettuce leaves.

24 rice papers, either small 6-inch circles or triangles (page 22)
1 large or 2 small heads Boston lettuce, leaves separated
1 bunch mint, separated into small tender sprigs and large leaves
1 bunch coriander, separated into large sprigs
1 cucumber, peeled and seeded, if desired, and sliced crosswise or cut into
    wide sticks
1 bunch scallion greens, cut into 3-inch lengths
2 cups mung bean sprouts, optional
2 sour starfruit, or 1 tart apple, thinly sliced, optional
18 to 24 perilla or shiso *leaves, optional*
Small bunch garlic chives, optional
Noodle Cakes, optional (page 66)

1. Dampen the rice papers by taking a small stack of them at a time and running under cold water, making sure to let the water run between the layers. Give the papers a shake and let stand on a plate for about 3 minutes. They will become translucent and stretchy.

2. Rinse the lettuce leaves and herbs. Prepare the optional fruits or vegetables you are using.

3. On a large platter, arrange the lettuce leaves, herb sprigs, bean sprouts, and sliced garnishes. Pull the rice papers from the plate they are softening on and put them on the platter along with the vermicelli if desired.

4. To serve, place the platter in the center of the table. Each guest will peel a rice paper from the pile (they are quite resilient), put it on their plate, and start layering it with the lettuce and other garnishes. Top with the grilled meat, seafood, or fried appetizer that requires the Table Salad and roll up the bundle. Dip the roll into the dipping sauce and eat.

   For some dishes, it's not necessary to include both the rice paper and the lettuce leaves. The recipe will indicate.

THE RICE RECIPE

MAKES ENOUGH TO SERVE 6 TO 8

The following recipe may seem to yield a large quantity of rice, but Asians can eat incredible amounts of it, probably twice as much as the average American. It's as though Asians wash down their food with mouthfuls of rice. For Americans, the following recipe will yield enough for 6 to 8 hearty servings to accompany a main dish. The measurements below apply to both the saucepan and the electric rice cooker, one modern appliance we wholeheartedly recommend. It takes no space on the stove. Just add the water and rice, plug it in and forget it. When all the water is absorbed, it will automatically shut off and keep the rice hot and in perfect condition for hours. It is quiet, dependable, and not expensive. Wash the rice many times (this removes much of the surface starch that can interfere with proper cooking and good, fluffy results), drain, then cover with water by one knuckle or one inch. Simple.

It's important when cooking rice in a pan, to choose one that is narrow and deep. This ensures that the water will cover the rice and cook it more effectively. A medium-size, heavy gauge, stainless steel, copper-lined, or aluminum saucepan with a tight-fitting lid is ideal for the amount specified in this recipe. As you become more comfortable cooking rice, you won't need to measure with cups, but, like the Vietnamese, do it with your finger. What is most important is the method, one that works with any amount of rice.

3 cups long-grain rice, preferably Jasmine or Indian Basmati (see Note)
2½ cups water
Yield: 9 to 10 cups cooked rice

Saucepan Method

1. Put the rice in the saucepan and wash it several times with cold water, swishing the rice with your fingers, until the water runs clear. Drain well and cover with the water. Smooth the rice into

an even layer. Stick your finger in the water so the tip just touches the top of the rice. The water should come up to your first knuckle, about 1 inch.

2. Put the saucepan over high heat and bring to a rolling boil. Cover tightly and reduce the heat to as low as possible. If you have an electric stove or a burner that runs hot, you may want to place the pan slightly off the burner, keeping it from tilting. Set the timer for 20 minutes and no peeking is allowed. After 20 minutes, remove from the burner and let stand, covered, for another 5 minutes. This ensures that the remaining heat dries the excess moisture while separating the rice grains. You can let the rice stand longer if needed. Then, remove the lid, and, with a large spoon, stir the rice lightly to fluff it up, but don't stir too much. Serve at once.

Electric Rice Cooker Method

1. Put the rice in the bowl of the machine and repeat step 1 of the saucepan method. Put the bowl in the rice cooker, cover, and press the button. When the rice is done, the cooker will shut off automatically and will keep the rice hot as long as the lid is left on. When ready to serve, uncover and stir the rice briefly to fluff it up.

NOTE: Jasmine rice is preferred for these recipes. It is highly aromatic and delicious and a pleasure to cook. It is available in Chinese, Thai, Vietnamese, and some Middle Eastern and Indian markets. Indian Basmati is an excellent substitute and is available at specialty food stores and Indian markets. Or try Texmati, a delicious American-grown rice which is a cross between Texas long grain and Indian Basmati (mail-order sources on page 317).

NUOC CHAM DIPPING SAUCE *(Nuoc Mam Cham)*

MAKES ABOUT 2½ CUPS

Every Vietnamese cook has his or her own recipe for this most essential sauce. Here is Binh's *Nuoc Cham*—one of the best. The shredded carrot adds color and crunch but isn't absolutely necessary.

1 to 2 small red chiles, minced, or 1 to 2 teaspoons dried chile flakes
1 tablespoon white vinegar, heated
½ cup bottled fish sauce (nuoc mam)
¼ cup fresh lime juice
1 small carrot, finely shredded, rinsed, and squeezed dry
2 cloves garlic, minced
½ cup sugar

1. If using dried chile flakes, soak them in the vinegar in a medium bowl for about 2 minutes.

2. In the bowl with the chiles, add the bottled fish sauce, lime juice, carrot, garlic, and sugar. Stir in 1½ cups warm water until the sugar is dissolved. Serve at room temperature. Store in a jar in the refrigerator for up to 3 days.

Dipping Sauces and Condiments

Sauces and condiments are the essence of Vietnamese cooking. Tart and sweet, hot and cooling ingredients are blended, usually in a mortar and pestle, though you can use a food processor, mini-chop, or a knife, to make the base for these lively enhancers. We suggest the mortar for the truest flavors. Most Vietnamese sauces combine garlic, chiles, lime juice, sugar, fish sauce, and sometimes ginger. Pounding the components by hand, you can feel, smell, and see their transformation into a glossy liquid. These pungent flavors are expertly balanced so that the sauce itself is well rounded and satisfying.

Dipping sauces unify and embellish assorted parts of a meal, such as fried appetizers, fine rice noodles, and grilled meats wrapped in lettuce and rice paper. A dipping sauce is just what's needed to encourage you to polish off the last of the rice, lettuce, and herbs of the Table Salad. Nuoc Cham, the most well-known and commonly served Vietnamese dipping sauce, sets the standard for all. Multifaceted yet deceptively simple looking, it sparkles with lime juice and explodes on the tongue.

As to some of the other sauces we've included, you will find two coriander combinations, one fiery and tart, the other creamy and smooth. Our ginger sauce is sweet, hot, and extra-spicy. When you make Pineapple Chile Sauce with an unusual touch of anchovy sauce you will understand how it's possible to correctly blend two extremely different foods with certain essences and extracts to produce an exquisite taste, one you may never have experienced otherwise. This particular sauce is especially good with beef. There are two peanut sauces, one closer to a soup, served warm and eaten with a spoon, and the other thick and spicy. There is a second version of Nuoc Cham, called Light Nuoc Cham Dipping Sauce, which does not contain lime juice and garlic and has its own uses. Dipping sauces develop their flavors completely within a few hours, so they are usually made shortly before a meal.

Many of the little tastes that underscore each bite of Vietnamese food, keeping it interesting and ever-changing, come from condiments like roasted rice powder, pulverized dried shrimp, and shredded salt-cooked pork. Fried, crispy shallots and pork rinds are scattered generously over noodles and soups. Sharp, crunchy vegetables of all sorts are pickled in Vietnam. Once brined, they are perfect to have on hand to add yet another colorful dish to a buffet table. Simple vinegar- and sugar-brined vegetables like Cauliflower and Carrot Pickles (page 63) stay fresh tasting as they remain quite nutritious. All these condiments keep if stored properly.

There are other dressing and dipping sauce recipes in the chapter on vegetarian cooking (pages 294 to 296).

GINGER SAUCE *(Nuoc Mam Gung)*

MAKES ABOUT ½ CUP

This is my favorite sauce, good on its own with just rice. Though chiles add the sting, the ginger has a heat of its own, and the outcome can vary considerably with the amount of ginger used. Add half the amount, taste the sauce, then add more ginger as needed.

1 piece ginger, 2 inches by 1 inch, peeled and chopped
2 tablespoons sugar
2 small red chiles, chopped, or to taste, or ½ to 1 teaspoon dried chile flakes
2 cloves garlic, smashed
½ small lime, peeled and sectioned
2 tablespoons fish sauce

1. In a mortar, pound together the ginger, sugar, chiles, and garlic to form a somewhat syrupy sauce. Add the lime sections, pounding to blend them in, then stir in the fish sauce. Serve at room temperature. This sauce can be kept in a small jar in the refrigerator for up to 1 week.

LIGHT NUOC CHAM DIPPING SAUCE *(Nuoc Mam Lac)*

MAKES ABOUT 2 CUPS

This sauce is used with certain dishes like Silver Dollar Cakes (page 142) and Rice Noodles Tossed with Grilled Pork and Peanuts (page 246) when the acid in citrus fruits can interfere and a little extra sweetness is complimentary.

$\frac{1}{2}$ *cup sugar*
$\frac{1}{4}$ *cup plus 2 tablespoons bottled fish sauce* (nuoc mam)
3 to 4 fresh chiles, crushed in a mortar, or finely chopped

1. In a small saucepan over high heat, combine the sugar with $1\frac{3}{4}$ cups water. Bring to a boil, then remove from the heat. Stir in the fish sauce. Allow to cool to room temperature and stir in the chiles. Serve at room temperature. Keep this in the refrigerator for up to 1 week.

CARAMEL SYRUP *(Nuoc Mau)*

MAKES ABOUT ¼ CUP

Sugar and water are cooked here to a bronze glaze, a teaspoon or two of which adds rich smoothness to a sauté or sauce. Stored in a ceramic jar, the syrup will keep for up to three months. In Vietnam, you can buy freshly made caramel syrup in tiny plastic bags, just enough for two or three uses.

> *¼ cup sugar*
> *¼ cup plus 1 tablespoon water*

1. In a small saucepan, combine the sugar and the ¼ cup water and bring to a boil over high heat. Continue to boil, swirling the pan a few times, until the mixture is colored a deep brown and is syrupy, about 3 minutes.

2. Remove the pan from the heat and very slowly pour in the remaining water, stirring briskly. Immediately pour the caramel into a small heat-proof ceramic dish to cool, then cover with a lid.

PINEAPPLE CHILE SAUCE *(Mam Nem)*

MAKES ABOUT ½ CUP

Don't be put off by this unusual combination of ingredients. It is a harmonious blend, beautifully suited to beef dishes.

1 to 2 small fresh red chiles, thinly sliced, or to taste
2 large cloves garlic
2 tablespoons sugar
2 heaping tablespoons finely chopped unsweetened pineapple, fresh or canned
1 tablespoon plus 1 teaspoon lime juice
2 tablespoons anchovy sauce (page 23)

1. In a mortar, combine the chiles, garlic, and sugar and pound to a paste. Stir in the pineapple, lime juice, and anchovy sauce. Set aside to develop flavor at room temperature for at least 20 minutes. This sauce can be made a day in advance and stored in the refrigerator. Be sure to bring to room temperature before serving.

SHRIMP AND PEANUT SAUCE *(Nuoc Leo)*

MAKES ABOUT 3½ CUPS

This chunky dipping sauce is light and flavorful. Generous portions are served in individual bowls with a spoon, and it is so good you'll be eating any remaining like soup. Thickening the sauce with prepared rice cakes, similar to thickening with bread crumbs, gives a subtle flavor while gently binding the other ingredients. This is good with Ninh Hoa Grilled Meatballs (page 152) and Silver Dollar Cakes (see page 142).

1 tablespoon vegetable oil
2 cloves garlic, minced
½ small onion, finely chopped
¼ pound ground pork
¼ pound medium shrimp, peeled, deveined, and cut into ½-inch pieces
½ teaspoon freshly ground black pepper
1 teaspoon salt
2 teaspoons tomato paste
1 tablespoon creamy peanut butter
1 teaspoon dried chile flakes
2 tablespoons sugar
1 tablespoon Vietnamese bean sauce (page 24) or Chinese unsweetened bean paste, thinned with water
3 cups water or chicken stock
2 plain puffed rice cakes, broken into very small pieces, or 1 teaspoon cornstarch dissolved in 1 teaspoon water

1. In a medium saucepan over high heat, combine the oil, garlic, and onion and cook, stirring, for 1 minute. Add the pork, shrimp, pepper, and salt and cook, stirring gently, for 2 minutes. Stir in the tomato paste and cook for 1 minute, until shiny.

2. Stir in the peanut butter, then the chile flakes, sugar, bean sauce, and water. Bring to a boil and cook for 2 minutes.

3. Stir in the rice cake crumbs. Reduce the heat to medium and cook, stirring frequently, until slightly thick and creamy, about 5 minutes. Serve hot or warm.

CORIANDER-CHILE SAUCE *(Nuoc Mam Ngo)*

MAKES ABOUT 1/3 CUP

Deep green and fragrant, this fresh-tasting dipping sauce has a wonderful silky consistency that comes from pounding the coriander leaves in a mortar, which releases the aromatic oils that help blend the sauce.

2 cloves garlic, chopped
1 to 2 minced red chiles, or to taste
2 tablespoons sugar
1/3 cup chopped coriander
3 large sections of 1 large lime
1 tablespoon fish sauce

1. In a mortar, pound the garlic and chiles to a coarse paste. Add the sugar and coriander and pound until smooth and emulsified. Add the lime sections and pound them into a pulpy liquid. Stir in the fish sauce. Allow to sit about 5 minutes to develop flavor. The sauce will keep in a jar in the refrigerator for up to 5 days.

CREAMY CORIANDER SAUCE *(Nuoc Sot Ngo)*

MAKES ABOUT 1 CUP

This aromatic sauce takes minutes to prepare and appears creamy because it is lightly thickened with puréed coriander. The combination is especially becoming on a delicate fish like Trout Stuffed with Shrimp and Scallops (page 191) or on any glisteningly fresh steamed fish. The flavors and consistency are best if the sauce is served soon after it's made. Should it separate, whirl it a few times in the blender to restore the emulsion.

1 teaspoon vegetable oil
1 teaspoon sesame oil
1 shallot, sliced
1 1-inch piece ginger, peeled and finely chopped
1 cup chicken stock
1 cup chopped coriander

1. In a small saucepan, heat the oils over high heat. Add the shallot and cook until fragrant, about 30 seconds. Add the ginger and cook, stirring, for about 1 minute. Add the chicken stock and bring to a boil. Boil over medium-high heat until reduced to $\frac{1}{2}$ cup, about 8 minutes. Remove from the heat and pour into a blender. Add the coriander and blend to a purée.

PEANUT SAUCE *(Nuoc Cham Dau Phung)*

MAKES ABOUT 1 CUP

This authentic peanut sauce is an interesting combination of cooked onion and garlic simmered with tomato paste, peanut butter, and chiles.

1 tablespoon vegetable oil
1 small onion, finely chopped
2 cloves garlic, minced
1 teaspoon tomato paste
1 teaspoon hoisin sauce, Vietnamese or Chinese unsweetened bean sauce
    (page 24)
$2^{1}/_{2}$ tablespoons creamy peanut butter
$^{1}/_{2}$ cup water
2 teaspoons sugar
$^{1}/_{2}$ teaspoon Sate-Chile Oil (page 58) or dried chile flakes

1. In a medium saucepan over high heat heat the oil until hot. Reduce the heat to low and add the onion and garlic. Cook, stirring, for about 3 minutes. Increase the heat to medium and stir in the remaining ingredients. Simmer, stirring, for about 3 minutes. Serve warm or at room temperature. The sauce will keep in a jar in the refrigerator for up to 1 week.

SHRIMP SAUCE *(Mam Tom)*

MAKES ABOUT $1/4$ CUP

Here's a strong but tasty sauce, used primarily for dipping.

$1/2$ *teaspoon Sate-Chile Oil (page 58)*
1 small clove garlic, crushed
$1/4$ *teaspoon grated orange zest*
1 teaspoon shrimp paste
3 tablespoons fresh orange juice

1. Prepare the Sate-Chile Oil and set aside.

2. In a mortar, pound the garlic, orange zest, and shrimp paste until smooth. Blend in the orange juice and chile oil. Allow to sit at room temperature for at least 20 minutes before serving.

PIQUANT BUTTER SAUCE *(Nuoc Bo)*

MAKES ABOUT ¼ CUP

This rich, tart sauce is used for the Mini Crab Cakes (page 128) and Fine Shrimp Paste on Asparagus (page 118), but you'll find it's wonderful just with steamed vegetables.

4 tablespoons butter
1½ tablespoons lemon juice
A few dashes chile sauce

1. In a small saucepan over medium heat, melt the butter. Turn off the heat, stir in the lemon juice and chile sauce. Rewarm just before serving.

SOY VINAIGRETTE *(Nuoc Xi Dau Giam)*

MAKES ABOUT ¾ CUP

A sophisticated salad dressing.

1 clove garlic, minced
½ teaspoon peeled and minced ginger
2 tablespoons sugar
3 tablespoons soy sauce
2 tablespoons red wine vinegar
½ tablespoon dry sherry
¼ cup water
¼ teaspoon freshly ground black pepper
2 tablespoons vegetable oil

1. In a jar, combine all the ingredients and shake well. The dressing will keep in the refrigerator for up to 2 weeks.

SOUR LIME SAUCE *(Nuoc Mam Chanh)*

MAKES ABOUT ½ CUP

This is a sparkling, citrusy sauce.

1 small red chile, chopped
3 tablespoons sugar
1 large lime, peeled and sectioned, any juice squeezed and reserved
2½ tablespoons fish sauce

1. In a mortar, pound the chile and sugar to a paste. Stir in the lime pulp and pound gently to make a coarse sauce. Stir in the lime juice and fish sauce. Allow to sit at least 10 minutes before serving. The sauce will keep in the refrigerator for up to 5 days.

SWEET AND SOUR SAUCE *(Sot Chua Ngot)*

MAKES ABOUT 4 CUPS

This may seem like a lot of sauce, but it's chunky and filled with cauliflower florettes. Use as a dipping sauce and as a vegetable relish accompaniment to fried appetizers.

1 small head cauliflower, cut into 1-inch florettes
3 cups water
$1/3$ cup white vinegar
1 tablespoon cornstarch
1 tablespoon vegetable oil
1 medium onion, finely chopped
3 cloves garlic, minced
2 tablespoons tomato paste
$1/4$ cup sugar
1 teaspoon salt
1 teaspoon freshly ground black pepper

1. In a large saucepan of boiling, salted water, cook the cauliflower until tender, about 3 minutes. Drain and set aside.

2. In a medium bowl, combine the water, vinegar, and cornstarch and stir to dissolve.

3. In a large saucepan, heat the oil over high heat and add the onion and garlic. Cook, stirring, for 1 minute. Add the tomato paste, sugar, and salt and cook for 1 minute. Bring to a boil and stir in the water mixture. Cook the sauce, stirring until thickened, about 2 minutes. Add the cauliflower and pepper and remove from the heat. Serve hot or at room temperature. The sauce will keep in the refrigerator for up to 2 weeks.

RICH BEAN SAUCE *(Nuoc Tuong Ngot)*

MAKES ABOUT ½ CUP

This sauce employs the pure Vietnamese bean sauce. The result is a mellow combination that will be swirled with hot chile sauce just before serving. A good substitute for the Vietnamese bean sauce is the light-colored, unsweetened Chinese bean paste, which is thicker and can be thinned with a little water.

2 teaspoons vegetable oil
1 clove garlic, minced
1 heaping tablespoon pure Vietnamese bean sauce or Chinese bean paste
2 tablespoons sugar
1 tablespoon chile sauce
Chopped peanuts for garnish

1. In a small saucepan over high heat, cook the oil and garlic together for 1 minute. Add the bean sauce, sugar, and 3 tablespoons water and cook stirring, until slightly thickened, about 1 minute. Remove from the heat and set aside to cool completely.

2. To serve, pour equal amounts into small dipping bowls and with chopsticks, swirl in some chile sauce to make a pretty pattern. Sprinkle the top with chopped peanuts.

PRESERVED PRUNE SAUCE *(Nuoc Xi Mui)*

MAKES ABOUT 2 CUPS

Serve this tangy, tart sauce with tempura vegetables, like Curly Fried Eggplant (page 136), or with grilled chicken, or other fowl.

5 dried preserved prunes
1 tablespoon vegetable oil
1 clove garlic, minced
Pinch dried chile flakes
$\frac{1}{4}$ cup hoisin sauce
1 teaspoon creamy peanut butter
1 tablespoon cornstarch
1 tablespoon water

1. In a small saucepan, cover the prunes with 2 cups water. Bring to a boil over high heat, reduce to low, and simmer until the prunes are soft, about 8 minutes. Reserving the water, remove the prunes with a slotted spoon and pit them. Chop the prunes finely and set aside.

2. In a small saucepan, heat the oil over medium heat. Add the garlic, prunes, and chile flakes. Cook, stirring, for 1 minute. Add the reserved prune water, hoisin sauce, and peanut butter and simmer for 1 minute. Mix the cornstarch with the 1 tablespoon water and stir into the sauce. Simmer, stirring, until thickened and smooth, about 1 minute. Serve hot or at room temperature.

ORANGE BRANDY SAUCE   *(Nuoc Sot Cam)*

MAKES ABOUT $\frac{1}{2}$ CUP

If you serve this sauce with roast chicken or Laque Duck, be sure to add a few tablespoons of the pan juices to it and cook it a little longer to reduce it slightly.

> 2 3-inch pieces lemon zest, cut into very thin strips
> 5 3-inch pieces orange zest, cut into very thin strips
> 1 tablespoon butter
> 1 clove garlic, minced
> 1 tablespoon brandy
> 1 tablespoon soy sauce
> 2 teaspoons honey
> $\frac{1}{3}$ cup fresh orange juice

1. In a small saucepan of boiling water, combine the zests and cook for 30 seconds. Drain and reserve.

2. In a small saucepan over medium-high heat, melt the butter, add the zests and garlic, and cook for 1 minute. Add the brandy, soy sauce, honey, and orange juice. Increase the heat to high and cook until slightly syrupy, about 2 minutes.

SPICED WINE *(Ruou Uop)*

MAKES ABOUT 5 CUPS

This lovely fragrant wine is a great addition to meat marinades. The wine keeps a very long time, up to 8 months, and as it sits develops further complexity from the carefully selected spice mixture in it.

1 cup Szechuan peppercorns
3 cinnamon sticks
1 cup fennel seeds
1 tablespoon whole cloves
4 whole star anise
5 cups dry white wine

1. To a large skillet over high heat, add all the spices and cook, stirring frequently, until very fragrant and evenly toasted, about 2 minutes. Place in a large bowl or glass jar and add the white wine. Keep at room temperature, covered, for at least 3 days before using.

SATE-CHILE OIL *(Tuong Ot)*

MAKES ABOUT 2 CUPS

This is a fiery, chile condiment, as common on the table as Sriracha chile sauce. For a more complex flavor, add one whole star anise as you simmer it. To use, spoon the oil from the top or stir the oil up and use flakes and oil.

$2/3$ *cup dried chile flakes*
$1^1/_2$ cups water
1 cup vegetable oil
10 cloves garlic, chopped
$1^1/_2$ tablespoons sugar
$1/_2$ teaspoon salt

1. In a small saucepan over high heat, cover the chile flakes with the water and bring to a boil. Reduce to medium-high heat and cook until the water boils completely away. Stir and cook briefly another minute to dry all the flakes. Remove from the heat.

2. In a medium saucepan over high heat, combine the oil, chile flakes, garlic, sugar, and salt. When hot, reduce the heat to medium and simmer, stirring occasionally, for 5 minutes. Cool, pour into a jar, and refrigerate. Keeps for months.

SCALLION OIL *(Mo Hanh)*

MAKES ABOUT ¾ CUP

This oniony oil is a staple sauce in Vietnamese cooking. The oil is great to have on hand to drizzle over grilled or steamed fish or to toss with noodles.

½ cup vegetable or peanut oil
6 large scallions, thinly sliced

1. In a medium saucepan, heat the oil over high heat. When a piece of scallion added to the pan sizzles furiously, add all the scallions. (They should swell or bloom after about 5 seconds.) Remove the pan from the heat and pour the oil into a small bowl. Use the scallion oil warm or at room temperature. It will keep in the refrigerator for up to 4 days. If you refrigerate it, be sure to warm it before serving.

ROASTED RICE POWDER *(Thinh)*

MAKES ABOUT 1 CUP

You'll find this toasty powder adds a pleasant flavor to salads and plain rice and acts as a binder to fillings such as those in Crab Farci (page 126), Stuffed Squid (page 192), and Shrimp Toasts (page 124).

1 cup long-grain rice

1. In a large skillet, preferably nonstick, cook the rice over medium-high heat until it starts to brown, about 3 minutes. Stirring the rice constantly, continue to cook it, shaking the pan, until all the grains are golden brown, 8 minutes. (You may have to remove the pan from the heat occasionally to cool it slightly to prevent the rice from burning.) Pour the rice onto a large plate and let it cool to room temperature. Put the rice in a blender or clean coffee grinder and pulverize it to a fine powder. Pass the powder through a sieve to remove any coarse granules. The powder will keep in an airtight container for up to 1 month.

COTTON PORK *(Thit Cha Bong)*

MAKES ABOUT 2 CUPS

Pork is simmered in salted water, then pulled into fine shreds to make this salty condiment. Pounding the shreds in a mortar makes them fluffy. Cotton pork can be used to flavor noodle dishes, salads, and plain rice. Steamed rice topped with cotton pork is a favorite comfort food of Binh's. He likes it when he is not feeling well and not very hungry. You can find cotton pork in Asian markets, but it often has MSG added.

1 10-ounce piece lean loin or shoulder of pork
2 teaspoons salt
1 tablespoon plus 2 teaspoons bottled fish sauce (nuoc mam)

1. In a medium saucepan of boiling water, simmer the pork with the salt until the meat is cooked through, about 30 minutes. Pour off the cooking water and fill the pan with cold water. Let the pork sit in the water about 1 minute. Drain.

2. Cut the pork into a few large pieces, then pull the meat apart into very thin shreds. Put these shreds in a mortar and pound to a fluffy, cotton-like consistency. Or, pulverize the meat in a food processor.

3. In a wok over medium-high heat, stir-fry the meat to dry it completely, about 2 minutes. Reduce the heat to medium and add the fish sauce. Stir-fry until fluffy and dry, about 3 minutes. The meat will keep in a jar in the refrigerator for up to 2 weeks.

FRIED SHALLOTS *(Hanh Phi)*

MAKES ABOUT 1 CUP

These sweet crunchy onions are indispensable as a garnish on Vietnamese soups and salads. Binh prefers the age-old method of drying the sliced shallots in the sun, which makes them crisp up better and cook very quickly. You can eliminate this step if you're short of time or if the sun doesn't shine for you that day. Just know that fresh-sliced shallots have more water in them and will take longer to brown. Fried shallots are delicious eaten just by themselves, so you may want to double or triple the recipe.

6 large shallots, thinly sliced
¼ cup vegetable oil

1. Put the shallots on a large baking sheet and put in a sunny place, preferably outdoors. Toss occasionally, until quite dried and curled. Depending on the day's humidity, this could take from 3 to 5 hours, or longer, if you wish.

2. In a large skillet heat the oil over medium heat until very hot. Add the shallots and cook, stirring occasionally, until brown and crisp, 4 to 5 minutes. Drain the shallots on paper towels, let cool completely, and store. The shallots will keep in an airtight container for 3 weeks.

CAULIFLOWER AND CARROT PICKLES *(Do Chua)*

MAKES ABOUT 4 CUPS

These tart, crunchy pickles make a great contribution to a buffet table or large dinner spread and are especially refreshing when eaten with fried foods.

1 head cauliflower, about 1½ pounds, cored and separated into florettes
2 teaspoons salt
2 large carrots, peeled and sliced ¼ inch thick
1¼ cups sugar
1½ cups white wine vinegar

1. In a medium bowl, cover the cauliflower with water and add 1 teaspoon of the salt. Soak for about 10 minutes. In a separate bowl, do the same with the carrots. Drain the vegetables and put them in a deep glass jar or ceramic container with a lid.

2. In a medium bowl, mix together the sugar, vinegar, and 1½ cups warm water and let the sugar dissolve. Pour over the vegetables and let them stand at room temperature for 3 days. The pickles will keep in the refrigerator for up to 1 month.

GINGER-SPICED CUCUMBER *(Dua Leo Dau Dam Gung)*

MAKES ENOUGH TO SERVE 4 TO 6

This is a great-looking vegetable condiment. The cucumber, while still in one piece, is cut to resemble an accordion, which is achieved by making a series of cuts on the top and bottom of it without cutting all the way through. The method of salting the cut cucumber softens it just enough to remove any bitterness while leaving in the fresh taste. The effect of the hot ginger sauce on the cool cucumber is a pleasant surprise to the palate.

1 European (hothouse) cucumber (about 1 pound)
$3/4$ teaspoon salt
1 teaspoon vegetable oil
1 teaspoon sesame oil
1 clove garlic, minced
1 $1^{1}/_{2}$-inch-long piece ginger, peeled and minced or grated
$1/3$ cup sugar
$1/3$ cup white or white wine vinegar

1. Rest the cucumber against the handle of a wooden spoon or chopstick and cut it on an angle into $1/4$-inch slices, allowing the tip of the knife to stop at the spoon so as not to cut all the way through. Turn the cucumber over and rest it against the spoon again, then cut straight down into $1/4$-inch slices, without cutting all the way through.

2. Sprinkle the cucumber all over and in between the slices with the salt. Wrap in a clean towel and refrigerate for at least 2 hours or overnight.

3. In a small saucepan, heat the vegetable and sesame oils over high heat. Add the garlic and ginger and cook, stirring, until fragrant, about 1 minute. Add the sugar and vinegar. Bring to a boil and cook, stirring, until the syrup is slightly reduced, to about $1/3$ cup, about 3 minutes.

4. Arrange the cucumber on a long platter, fan the slices slightly, and pour the ginger syrup over it.

SUGGESTIONS: The gingery sauce and crunchy cucumber of this dish would be delicious with Beef Grilled in La-Lot Leaves (page 158), Golden Pepper Steak (page 260), Grilled Curried Steak with Roasted Peppers (page 262), Laque Duck (page 219), or in Curried Grilled Jumbo Shrimp (page 184).

NOODLE CAKES *(Banh Hoi)*

MAKES FIVE 9-INCH CAKES

Presoaked rice vermicelli is tossed with cornstarch and steamed to form tender noodle cakes that are then cut into squares. These are easy to eat with chopsticks and good as a bed for many dishes, especially those with a sauce. You will need a wide flat surface to steam the cakes. Some steamer sets come equipped with such a tray, but an insertable steamer basket placed completely open in a large saucepan also works just fine. Be sure to remove the lid of the pan slowly and turn it away from you to avoid a blast of steam in your face. These cakes are part of a standard Vietnamese dish—Grilled Pork with Noodle Cakes (page 244).

1 7½-ounce package rice vermicelli
¼ cup cornstarch
Vegetable oil

1. In a large bowl, cover the vermicelli with hot water and let soak for about 7 minutes. Drain well, lifting the noodles with chopsticks to dry them. Put the noodles in a large bowl and toss with the cornstarch to coat completely.

2. Oil a flat steamer rack and add enough water to the steamer or a large saucepan to barely touch the rack. Bring the water to a boil, take a large handful of the noodles, and scatter them evenly over the rack to make a large, thin pancake. Cover and steam until the noodles form a soft cohesive cake, about 1 minute. Remove the cake with a rubber spatula to a work surface and repeat the procedure, making 4 more cakes. Cut the noodle cakes into 2-inch diamonds or squares and keep warm on a large plate.

SHRIMP CHIPS *(Banh Phong Tom)*

MAKES 24 TO 30 CHIPS

Shrimp chips take seconds to cook in properly heated oil, puffing up almost immediately on contact. They should be white to pale tan when done; try not to let them get brown as their delicate taste will diminish. Eat warm or at room temperature.

24 to 30 uncooked shrimp chips (page 25)
2 to 3 cups vegetable oil

1. In a medium saucepan with high sides, heat the oil over medium-high heat to 350 degrees on a deep-fry thermometer. Fry the shrimp chips, 5 or 6 at a time, until they expand fully and float on the surface, about 12 seconds. Adjust the heat as needed to maintain 350 degrees. Drain on paper towels before serving. Cooked and cooled shrimp chips can be stored in an airtight container for up to 2 days, depending on the humidity.

CRISPY PORK RINDS *(Top Mo)*

MAKES ABOUT 2 CUPS

A little different from our snack pack fried pork rinds, these have some meat to them and are more like mild bacon bits. Like fried shallots, they are great to have on hand to add to noodle dishes and soups.

1 pound very white pork fat with some skin and meat attached (from the leg of a fresh ham), cut into very thin short strips

1. In a large skillet over medium heat, cook the pork fat in a single layer, without stirring, until most of the fat has been rendered and the pieces are brown on one side, about 10 minutes. Turn and cook until the pieces are very crisp and dry, about 10 minutes more. Drain on paper towels and let cool completely. The rinds will keep in an airtight container at room temperature for about 2 weeks.

Soups

PHO: NOODLE SOUPS

A typical breakfast in Vietnam is a large bowl of noodle soup. These soups are meal-sized portions of broth, meat, and noodles, with many garnishes added at the last minute. *Pho*, or *bun*, as it is also called, translates to "your own bowl," meaning each person's meal is in his own bowl, very different from the other Vietnamese meals where all food is passed and shared.

Here's how the Vietnamese day begins: Hearty, fortifying noodle soup is the wake-up call for early morning Vietnam. In the dim light of its city streets, villages, and hamlets, a breakfast scene is being repeated throughout the land: burning fires, simmering pots of broth, and low tables being set for breakfast soup, as coffee drips into glasses and tea brews in kettles. Of all the foods from Vietnam, *pho*—noodle soup—with its contrasting hot and cold fresh ingredients, best demonstrates the uniqueness of this cuisine. The morning meal, based on meat broth, consists of rice or egg noodles nestled under a mound of bean sprouts and a tangle of herb sprigs, then embellished with pieces of chicken or pork, salty bits of preserved cabbage, crisp-fried onions, and bits of alarmingly hot chopped chiles. Soup for breakfast? In a hot and humid country like

Vietnam, the best time to consume such a dish, one that lies somewhere between a brothy stew and a warm salad, is in the cool comfort of the morning.

These soups are not, however, exclusive to breakfast. Any time of the day one can duck into a soup stall for a bowl of *pho*. This is soup made to order, put together as one wishes, and hastily consumed with both hands. You may decide on the size (thick or thin) and kind of noodle (egg or rice); the cut of meat; the combination of meat and/or seafood; and the preference for a regular soup or dry soup (meaning a bowl of the noodles and solids with the broth served separately on the side). Or, you may order one of the standard combinations. When the soup is placed in front of you, the fragrance of sesame oil and white pepper greets you. You choose a condiment or two, such as chile sauce, hoisin sauce, or fish sauce. A saucer is placed beside the soup bowl to hold the sauce or a swirl of several. Soup, like breakfast on any working day, is eaten hot and fast. This is busy eating, not meant for lingering. With chopsticks in your stronger hand and a Chinese soup spoon in your weaker one, the long noodles are lifted out releasing the steam. And it's proper to slurp, a natural reaction to eating hot soup, for sucking in air cools the noodles just enough to make it possible to swallow them. Then large pieces of meat or seafood are plucked from the broth and dipped into the sauce. The whole is morning tonic—one that clears your head and, with the sting of chiles, clears your lungs. You are fully awakened; your spirits lifted.

Preparing noodle soups at home requires a lot of ingredients, which is why soup stalls are so common in Vietnam. However, soup from a vendor can never be as good as homemade. Here in America, most people aren't lucky enough to have a Vietnamese restaurant, let alone, a soup-house nearby, and I urge you to make one of these noodle soups for lunch or supper, just for the splendid feeling you will derive from it. To spare yourself from having to individually dress each soup with multiple garnishes, allow each guest to dress his or her own. Have chopsticks, soup spoons, and small dipping saucers as well as bottles of chile and hoisin sauce ready on the table. Arrange herb sprigs and bean sprouts on a platter. Put the chopped or sliced chiles, crispy shallots, lime wedges, and preserved cabbage pieces into their own small bowls. All that will remain to be done in the kitchen is to line up the soup bowls, cook the noodles, add the meat or seafood, and ladle the broth over all. Let the eating begin. Finally, breakfast, or meal soups, can be served in much smaller servings as a first course, if you wish, but because they call for a wide variety of last-minute additions, you may need extra help in the kitchen.

HANOI SOUP *(Pho Bo)*

MAKES 6 MAIN-COURSE SERVINGS

Originating from the north of Vietnam, this soup is probably the most favored of all the *phos*. Made with the Spiced Beef Stock, it is hauntingly fragrant with cinnamon, star anise, fresh basil, and if you can find it, *ngo gai*, the Japanese saw-leaf herb. Paper-thin slices of beef are added raw to each bowl, then hot broth cooks them. Pass the fish sauce separately.

10 cups Spiced Beef Stock (page 83)
1 pound rice vermicelli
1 pound lean beef, preferably the round, cut into paper-thin slices

ACCOMPANIMENTS
Lime wedges
Mung bean sprouts
Sprigs of coriander
Ngo gai, *chopped, optional*
Small leaves of basil
Chopped fresh chiles
Chopped scallions
Freshly ground black pepper
Bottled fish sauce (nuoc mam)

1. Prepare the Spiced Beef Stock.

2. In a large bowl, cover the rice noodles with cold water and soak until pliable, about 30 minutes. Drain.

3. In a large pan, bring the stock to a boil. Put a large handful of noodles in a strainer you can fit into the pan. Dip the strainer with the noodles in it into the hot stock and with chopsticks swirl them around until tender but still chewy, about 20 seconds. Shake the noodles dry and dump them into a soup bowl. Repeat with the remaining noodles. Put equal amounts of beef over the noodles and divide the hot stock among the bowls. Serve with the accompaniments, allowing each person to garnish the soup as desired.

FAMOUS HANOI CHICKEN SOUP *(Pho Ga)*

MAKES 6 TO 8 MAIN-COURSE SERVINGS

This ginger-infused soup is well known all over Vietnam, where versions vary with the local tastes and ingredients. A plain, more substantial soup is eaten up north, where they experience a significantly cooler winter and the use of fresh greens is limited. Binh's recipe is typical of the south: colorful with herbs and lively with chiles. This Vietnamese chicken soup is appreciated for its redeeming tonic qualities and delicious ginger-flavored chicken fat—a kind of spicy schmaltz—that tops off the soup at the last minute. You can use just broth in which to steep the crushed ginger if you like.

1 3-pound chicken
2½ pounds chicken wings, necks, or backs
1 tablespoon salt
1 teaspoon whole white peppercorns
5 ounces ginger, cut in 2 pieces
1 pound rice noodles

ACCOMPANIMENTS
1 small onion, thinly sliced
¼ cup chopped rau ram *(page 18), optional*
1 cup coriander sprigs
½ cup chopped scallion
1½ cups mung bean sprouts
3 to 4 small red chiles, chopped
6 to 8 lime wedges

1. In a large soup pot, cover the chicken and the wings with 14 cups cold water. Bring to a boil over high heat and add the salt and peppercorns. Reduce the heat to low and simmer, skimming the surface occasionally.

2. Put both of the ginger pieces directly over a high electric burner or low gas burner and, using tongs, turn them every minute or so to char

them on all sides. Rinse under water to remove the ash. Add one piece to the broth.

3. Coarsely chop the remaining piece of ginger, then pound it in a mortar or process it in a minichop to a paste. Put the paste in a medium bowl and set aside. Soak the rice noodles in a large bowl of cold water to cover until pliable, about 30 minutes.

4. After about 40 minutes, check the chicken for doneness. When it is cooked through and the juices run clear from the thigh, remove it to a large plate. Let cool slightly, then remove the skin and discard. Remove all the meat from the bones and discard them, then pull the meat into shreds or chop it into 2-inch pieces.

5. Skim off about ½ cup of the rendered chicken fat from the surface of the broth (or use a combination of fat and broth) and pour it over the ginger paste in the bowl. Set aside to develop flavor for at least 20 minutes.

6. Strain the broth and return it to the pot. Bring to a boil over medium-high heat and skim thoroughly. Drain the rice noodles. Bring a medium saucepan of water to a boil over high heat.

7. To serve, put a handful of chicken meat into each soup bowl. Take a handful of rice noodles and put them in a strainer that will fit into the saucepan of boiling water. Dip the strainer with the noodles in it into the boiling water and with chopsticks swirl them around; cook until opaque and slightly chewy, about 20 seconds. Shake the noodles dry and turn them into the soup bowl. Repeat with the remaining noodles. Then with a ladle fill the bowls ¾ full with broth. Spoon about 1½ tablespoons of the ginger liquid with some of the ginger over the top and serve. Bring the accompaniments to the table in small bowls, allowing each person to garnish the soup as desired.

HUE SOUP WITH PORK AND BEEF *(Bun Bo Hue)*

MAKES 6 TO 8 MAIN-COURSE SERVINGS

This is Binh's favorite soup and ambitiously he uses beef in it, which in the Vietnamese diet is usually prepared on its own. Pork, lemongrass, and shrimp paste are among the other savory ingredients.

$1\frac{1}{2}$ *pounds lean pork from the shoulder, loin, or ham, cut into 1-inch cubes*
2 large carrots
3 stalks lemongrass, flattened and cut into 2-inch lengths
1 1-pound piece beef round
1 tablespoon salt
2 to 3 tablespoons vegetable oil
1 tablespoon annatto seeds, optional
1 teaspoon dried chile flakes
1 medium onion, thinly sliced
$\frac{1}{2}$ *teaspoon shrimp paste*
3 tablespoons bottled fish sauce (nuoc mam)
1 pound medium-width rice noodles, soaked in cold water at least 45 minutes
Chopped scallions
Coriander sprigs
Mung bean sprouts
Lime wedges

1. In a large stockpot, cover the pork, carrots, and lemongrass with 14 cups water. Bring to a boil over high heat. Skim the surface and add the beef and salt. Reduce the heat to medium-low and simmer, skimming occasionally, until the beef is rare in the center, about 10 minutes. Remove the beef and set aside on a plate until ready to serve. Continue to simmer the soup until the pork is tender, about 15 minutes more. Remove the pork and simmer the soup, skimming often, for another 15 minutes or so.

2. Meanwhile, in a small saucepan, heat 1 tablespoon of the oil over medium-high heat. When hot, add the annatto seeds, if using, and allow to sizzle about 5 seconds. Remove from the heat and pour the oil into a small bowl, discarding the seeds. Put the pan back on medium-high heat and add another tablespoon of the oil. When hot, add the chile flakes. Allow them to sizzle about 5 seconds and pour the oil and chile flakes into the annatto oil. Set aside until ready to serve.

3. In a large skillet over medium-high heat, add the remaining tablespoon of oil and when hot, add the onion and cooked pork. Cook, stirring, for 1 minute. Add the shrimp paste and 2 tablespoons of the fish sauce and mix well. Cook, stirring, for another minute. Add this to the simmering stock along with the remaining tablespoon of fish sauce. Slice the beef very thin and set aside.

4. To serve the soup, have the remaining ingredients ready and the soup bowls out. Begin to cook the rice noodles: Bring a medium saucepan of water to a boil over high heat. Put a large handful of soaked noodles in a strainer you can fit into the saucepan. Dip the strainer with the noodles in it into the hot water and with chopsticks swirl the noodles. They will immediately wilt and shrink a bit. Cook, stirring, until the noodles are tender but firm, about 20 seconds. Do not overcook. Lift the strainer, shake the noodles dry and dump them into a soup bowl. Repeat with the remaining noodles. Put equal amounts of sliced beef in each bowl. Ladle the broth over the noodles and beef and include some pieces of pork, onion, and a chunk of carrot. Top the soup with equal amounts of the red chile oil, scallion, coriander, and bean sprouts and serve the lime wedges on the side. Eat with chopsticks and soup spoons.

SAIGON SOUP *(Hu Tieu)*

MAKES 8 MAIN-COURSE SERVINGS

Dried squid lends a subtle smoky flavor to this soup, which is popular all over the south of Vietnam. The *daikon* radish isn't meant to be eaten but simmers in the soup to absorb salt from the dried squid and to contribute a mild flavor.

1 medium dried squid, about 6 inches long
2½ pounds pork bones and/or chicken bones
1 1-pound piece lean pork, from the leg or shoulder
1½ tablespoons salt
1 5-inch piece daikon *radish, about ½ pound*
1 2-inch piece rock sugar
1 pound medium-width rice noodles
1 pound medium shrimp, peeled and deveined

ACCOMPANIMENTS
Bean sprouts
Chinese or garlic chives, cut into 2-inch lengths
Coriander sprigs
Preserved cabbage
Fried shallots (page 62)
Sliced chiles
Bottled fish sauce (nuoc mam)
Sesame oil, optional
Lime wedges

1. Remove any cartilage from the squid. Heat an electric burner to medium-high or a gas burner to low. Using tongs, put the squid directly over the gas or electric burner and scorch on both sides until lightly charred, about 1 minute per side. Rinse the squid briefly under running water, place in a medium bowl, and cover with cold water to soak for 1 hour.

2. In a large soup pot, cover the bones with 16 cups of water and bring to a boil over high heat. Reduce the heat to medium and simmer, skimming occasionally, for 30 minutes. Add the pork, salt, squid, *daikon*, and sugar. Simmer until the pork is cooked through, about 40 minutes. Remove the pork to a plate and continue to simmer the broth for another hour. Strain the broth and return it to the pot.

3. In a large bowl, cover the rice noodles with water and soak for at least 20 minutes. Drain. In a medium saucepan of boiling water, dump the shrimp and when the water returns to a boil remove from the heat and drain. Slice the cooked pork thinly.

4. Bring a medium saucepan of water to a boil. Put a large handful of the rice noodles in a steel mesh strainer with a handle. Dip the strainer with the noodles in it into the boiling water and with chopsticks swirl them around until they wilt. Cook until tender but still a bit chewy, about 30 seconds. Shake the noodles dry and dump them into a soup bowl. Repeat with the remaining noodles. Add to each bowl some pork slices and shrimp and pour the hot broth over all. Bring the accompaniments to the table and allow each person to garnish his or her soup.

CRAB DUMPLING AND NOODLE SOUP *(Bun Rieu)*

MAKES 4 TO 6 MAIN-COURSE SERVINGS

The preparation of this soup is elaborate and unusual, definitely from another world. The broth is made from crushed whole crabs. Then uncooked crab meat is pushed through a sieve, combined with water, and simmered with tomato and onion, during which time a thin raft of cooked meat forms on top. Hence, the word *"rieu,"* which means soft and foamy. Lastly, small dumplings, made with cooked crab meat and egg, are poached in the soup just before serving. Add the shrimp paste last as an enhancement. It's a very small amount and enriches the dish just enough. This soup, which comes from the north of Vietnam, is served as a special breakfast meal and is traditionally topped with finely shredded banana blossoms or curls of water spinach stems.

1 pound rice noodles
10 lively very large blue claw crabs
2 tablespoons vegetable oil
1 small onion, thinly sliced
1 tablespoon tomato paste
3 small tomatoes, cut into thin wedges
1 teaspoon freshly ground black pepper
1 whole scallion, thinly sliced, plus 1 white of scallion, minced
3 tablespoons plus 1 teaspoon bottled fish sauce (nuoc mam)
1 teaspoon sugar
$1/2$ teaspoon shrimp paste, optional
2 eggs, lightly beaten

ACCOMPANIMENTS
A few fresh chiles, chopped
Lime wedges
Sprigs of coriander and mint
Mung bean sprouts

1. Soak the rice noodles in a large bowl of cold water to cover while preparing the soup. Bring a medium saucepan of water to a boil over high heat. With tongs, grab 2 crabs and plunge them into the boiling water. Boil until they are bright orange all over and just cooked through, about 4 minutes. Drain, rinse briefly with cold water, and set aside until cool enough to handle. Crack the crabs open and remove all the meat. Set aside in a small bowl.

2. Next, stun the remaining 8 crabs. Pick up a crab with a pair of tongs and turn it on its back. Position a chopstick just below the crab's eyes and with the chopstick puncture the crab through the eyes. Lift the crab while it is still attached to the chopstick and shake it off into the sink. Repeat with the remaining crabs. When all the crabs have been stunned, tear the claws off first so they won't pinch you. Then remove the apron from the underside of each of the bodies and discard it. Pull the top shell off in one piece, and remove the spongy lung tissue from both sides of the crab. Discard the lungs and reserve the top shells for Crab Farci (page 126) if you wish. (Reserve the green coral or tomalley for later use.) Remove all the legs, break the bodies in half, and then in half again. Working in batches, smash the crab parts in a mortar and pestle, or use a food processor to pulverize them. Put all the pulverized meat and shell in a large strainer set over a large bowl. Starting with 2 cups of cold water, pour it over the crab. With your hands rub the crab, loosening the jellylike meat from the pieces of shell with the water. Pour 2 more cups of water over and swish the crab in the water to loosen more meat. Repeat this 3 more times, using a total of 6 more cups of water. After the last 2 cups of water have been used, press very hard on the crab to extract as much meat as possible. (A pestle or a potato masher works well for this.) With a rubber spatula, scrape the underside of the sieve to gain all the extracted meat.

3. Slowly pour the crab liquid from the bowl into a large saucepan. Stop pouring when you come to the grit on the bottom. Discard the grit with any remaining liquid.

(continued)

(continued)

4. Over medium-low heat, bring the crab liquid to a slow simmer and cook for about 12 minutes; small, foamy pillows of crab will rise to the surface.

5. Meanwhile, in a large skillet over medium-high heat, heat the oil. Add the onion and tomato paste and cook stirring until shiny, 1 minute. Add the tomatoes and reserved tomalley, if using, and cook 2 minutes. Season with ¾ teaspoon of the black pepper, the whole sliced scallion, 3 tablespoons of the fish sauce, and the sugar. Cook for 1 minute, then pour into the soup. In a small bowl, dilute the shrimp paste, if using, in 1 tablespoon of water and add to the soup.

6. Make the crab dumplings: With a spoon, mix the beaten eggs with the reserved cooked crab meat and the scallion white and season with the remaining ¼ teaspoon black pepper and 1 teaspoon fish sauce. With the soup simmering, drop in the crab mixture by tablespoonfuls and cook the dumplings until they just firm up, about 1 minute.

7. Bring a medium saucepan of water to a boil and drain the rice noodles. Put a large handful of the noodles, enough for one serving, in a steel mesh strainer that fits into the saucepan. Dip the strainer with the noodles in it into the boiling water and with chopsticks swirl them until they are translucent and tender but still a bit chewy, about 20 seconds or more. Shake the noodles dry and dump them into a large soup bowl. Ladle some of the crab broth, including a few dumplings, over them. Repeat with the remaining noodles and broth. Bring the bowls to the table with all the accompaniments and allow each person to garnish his own soup. Eat with chopsticks and spoons.

SPICED BEEF STOCK *(Nuoc Dung Bo)*

MAKES ABOUT 10 CUPS

Many Vietnamese consume great quantities of beef stock and cooks are finicky about the bones that go into making it. Oxtails are usually cut crosswise before they are sold. Look for those that have a good red color and no dark or brown marks. Some Vietnamese prefer to blanch the bones first, then proceed with the cooking of the stock.

3 pounds oxtail pieces or other lean meaty beef bones, such as shin or neck
1 3-inch piece ginger
1 medium onion
1 tablespoon salt
6 whole star anise
1½ cinnamon sticks
2 large bay leaves
4 whole cloves
1 1-inch piece rock sugar or 1 tablespoon sugar
2 teaspoons fennel seeds

1. In a very large stockpot, cover the oxtails with water and bring to a boil over high heat. Drain off the water, cover the oxtails with 14 cups fresh water, and add the salt. Bring to a boil again.

2. Meanwhile, using tongs, put the ginger and onion directly over a low gas burner or electric burner on medium-high heat and char them all over, about 4 minutes. Be careful not to burn yourself. Remove from the heat and rinse any ash from the ginger and onion. Add the ginger and onion to the stock.

3. Add the star anise, cinnamon sticks, bay leaves, cloves, and sugar to the stock. Put the fennel seeds in a tea ball and add to the stock. When the liquid comes to a boil, reduce the heat to low and simmer, skimming occasionally, for about 2½ hours. Strain. The stock will keep, covered, in the refrigerator for up to 3 days.

BEEF BALL SOUP *(Bo Vien)*

MAKES 6 MAIN-COURSE SERVINGS

This simple soup is eaten all over Vietnam. What makes it so special is its wonderful stock and the chewiness of its beef balls. Processing lean meat very fine gives it a very tight, dense texture. As a consequence the beef balls may be hard to hold between two chopsticks. It is easier to simply spear the balls with one chopstick. The beef balls are plain tasting on their own, but delectable when dipped in the chile hoisin sauce.

Spiced Beef Stock (page 83)
$1^1/_2$ pounds lean beef, top or bottom round
$3/_4$ teaspoon freshly ground white pepper
$2^1/_2$ tablespoons bottled fish sauce (nuoc mam)
2 teaspoons sugar
$1^1/_2$ teaspoons baking powder
2 teaspoons cornstarch
2 cloves garlic, minced
2 tablespoons water
1 tablespoon plus 1 teaspoon vegetable oil
1 teaspoon lime juice
Preserved cabbage
Coriander leaves
Ngo gai *leaves, the saw leaf herb, chopped, optional*
Hoisin sauce
Chile sauce

1. Prepare the Spiced Beef Stock.

2. In a food processor, chop the meat into small pieces. Put the meat in a large bowl and stir in the white pepper, fish sauce, sugar, baking powder, cornstarch, garlic, water, and 1 tablespoon of the oil. Mix well and chill in the freezer for about 20 minutes.

3. Return the meat mixture to the processor, add the lime juice, and grind the meat fine, about 30 seconds. Scrape down the sides of the bowl and grind again for about 1 minute, until very stiff. Shape the meat into 1-inch balls; you should have about 36.

4. In a large saucepan of boiling water over medium-high heat, boil the beef balls in batches until cooked through, about 3 minutes. Drain and set aside.

5. In a large soup pot, heat the Spiced Beef Stock to boiling. Reduce the heat to low, add the beef balls, and heat through.

6. To serve, into each of 6 large soup bowls put 6 beef balls along with some of the beef stock. Garnish with a few pieces of preserved cabbage and some coriander leaves, *ngo gai*, if you have it. On the side, in small shallow dipping saucers, serve the hoisin sauce. Add a swirl of chile sauce and use as a dipping sauce for the beef balls.

LIGHT PORK STOCK *(Nuoc Dung Heo)*

MAKES ABOUT 6 CUPS

Pork bones are considered cleaner and the bones used for making stock do not need to be blanched beforehand.

1 pound lean but meaty pork bones, from the neck or leg of a fresh ham
5 white peppercorns

1. In a large saucepan, combine the pork bones, the peppercorns, and 9 cups of water and bring to a boil over high heat. Reduce the heat to low and simmer, skimming occasionally, for 45 minutes. Strain the stock and reserve the meat to add to soup, if you wish. The stock will keep, covered, in the refrigerator for up to 3 days.

CHICKEN STOCK *(Nuoc Dung Ga)*

MAKES ABOUT 10 CUPS

3 pounds chicken wings, necks, and/or backs
1 teaspoon white peppercorns
1 1-inch piece ginger, flattened
1 tablespoon salt

1. In a large stockpot cover the chicken with 16 cups of water and bring to a boil over high heat. Reduce the heat to medium-low, add the peppercorns, ginger, and salt, and simmer, skimming occasionally, for 2 hours. Strain and skim the surface fat with a ladle. Or, chill the stock and remove the hardened fat from the surface with a spoon. The stock will keep, covered, in the refrigerator for up to 5 days or in the freezer for up to 3 months.

OTHER KINDS OF VIETNAMESE SOUPS

A *sup*, in general, is a nonnoodle soup, served in small portions as a first course and sometimes referred to as a "small" soup. It can be subtle and soothing, or tangy and tantalizing. Thin in body but layered in texture, a *sup* is best appreciated in small portions and will fit easily into any dinner menu.

A *canh* refers to "family," meaning this type of soup is served in one large bowl, family style. Divided into portions at the table and usually but not always served with rice, a *canh* can act as a light and lovely first course, an elegant prelude to a meal.

CRAB, SHRIMP, AND DRIED WHITE FUNGUS SOUP
(Sup Nam Trang)

MAKES 4 FIRST-COURSE SERVINGS

This is a pleasing, mild soup crunchy with reconstituted dried white fungus, a more attractive-looking relative of the brown tree ear. The last-minute addition of fresh coriander and chile sauce gives the soup a lift.

$1/2$ ounce dried white fungus, about $1/4$ cup, (page 273)
1 teaspoon vegetable oil
1 large shallot, thinly sliced
A few pinches white pepper
4 ounces medium shrimp, peeled and deveined
4 ounces cooked crab meat
3 cups Chicken Stock (page 86)
1 tablespoon plus $1/2$ teaspoon cornstarch dissolved in 2 tablespoons water
1 egg white, lightly beaten
Salt and freshly ground pepper to taste
1 tablespoon chopped coriander
Sriracha chile sauce

1. In a medium bowl, cover the dried white fungus with hot water and soak until fully expanded and soft, about 10 minutes. Drain and rinse. Cut off the hard knobs and chop the fungus coarse.

2. In a large saucepan heat the oil over medium-high heat. Cook the shallot with some white pepper for about 1 minute. Add the shrimp and cook, stirring until almost cooked through, about 1 minute. Add the crab, stock, and the white fungus and bring to a simmer. Stir in the cornstarch mixture and bring back to a simmer, stirring constantly. Then in a slow, steady stream, pour in the egg white, stirring constantly while it cooks to form delicate ribbons of white, about 10 seconds. Remove from the heat, season the soup with salt and pepper, and stir in the coriander. Serve hot with the chile sauce.

CRAB AND ASPARAGUS SOUP *(Sup Mang Tay)*

MAKES 6 FIRST-COURSE SERVINGS

The French planted asparagus when they occupied Vietnam, but it didn't grow with great success. Therefore, canned white asparagus was shipped over from France to satisfy their longing. As a result, the Vietnamese took a great liking to it, giving it their own name of western bamboo and creating a soup that combines it with crab meat, so abundant in their waters. Red wine vinegar, another French fillip, refreshes and enlivens the combination and is passed at the table to be added at the last moment.

> 5 cups Chicken Stock (page 86) or Vegetable Stock (page 272)
> 1 teaspoon vegetable oil
> $1/4$ pound cooked crab meat, preferably king or Dungeness, cut into $1/2$-inch chunks
> $1/4$ teaspoon salt
> $1/4$ teaspoon freshly ground black pepper
> 1 pound green or white asparagus, cut into $1/2$-inch pieces
> 1 tablespoon cornstarch
> 2 tablespoons water
> 1 egg white, lightly beaten
> 1 scallion, thinly sliced
> 2 tablespoons whole coriander leaves
> Red wine vinegar to taste

1. Prepare the Chicken Stock.

2. In a medium saucepan over high heat, heat the oil until hot. Add the crab meat, salt, and pepper and cook, stirring gently, for 1 minute. Add the stock and asparagus and bring to a boil. Reduce the heat to medium and cook, skimming occasionally, until the asparagus is tender, about 6 minutes.

3. In a small bowl, combine the cornstarch and water and add it to the simmering soup. Stir until slightly thickened, about 30 seconds.

4. Have the egg white ready in a small bowl. Using a fork and stirring the soup constantly, pour the egg white in a thin stream creating long cooked strands. Remove the soup from the heat and add the scallion and coriander leaves. Serve very hot and pass the vinegar and more black pepper at the table.

WATERCRESS-SHRIMP SOUP *(Canh Sa Lach Soan)*

MAKES 6 FIRST-COURSE SERVINGS

Before adding the shrimp to the soup, Binh pounds the flavorings into them which makes them slightly soft and very sweet. Although it will be more authentic to leave the watercress whole you can chop it into large pieces. Eat the soup with chopsticks in one hand, for the watercress and shrimp, and a spoon in the other, for the stock.

> 6 cups Light Pork Stock (page 85) or Chicken Stock (page 86)
> 1 small shallot, thinly sliced
> $1/4$ pound medium shrimp, peeled and deveined, shells reserved
> 2 tablespoons plus 1 teaspoon bottled fish sauce (**nuoc mam**)
> $1/8$ teaspoon freshly ground black pepper
> $1^1/2$ bunches watercress

1. Prepare the Light Pork Stock.

2. In a mortar, pound the shallot to a coarse paste. Add the shrimp, fish sauce, and pepper and pound lightly to incorporate the flavorings into the shrimp. The shrimp should look beaten up but still whole. Set aside.

3. In a large saucepan, bring the stock to a boil. Add the reserved shrimp shells, reduce the heat to medium-high, and cook for 5 minutes. With a slotted spoon, remove the shells. Increase the heat to high and add the shrimp mixture. Cook for 1 minute. Add the watercress and cook another minute, until the cress is wilted but still crunchy. Season with more black pepper and serve at once.

GARLIC CHIVE AND TOFU SOUP *(Canh Dau Khuon)*

MAKES 6 FIRST-COURSE SERVINGS

Tofu, highly prized even by nonvegetarians because it is so nutritious, picks up the flavors it's cooked with and takes on a smooth and unusual texture that is quite pleasant.

3 ounces lean shoulder or loin of pork, thinly sliced
$1/4$ pound medium shrimp, peeled, deveined, and cut into small pieces
$1/2$ teaspoon freshly ground black pepper
1 tablespoon plus 1 teaspoon bottled fish sauce (nuoc mam)
1 white of scallion, finely chopped
1 tablespoon vegetable oil
3 cups chicken, pork, or vegetable stock
3 3-ounce tofu cakes, cut into 2-inch pieces
$1/3$ cup garlic chives, cut into 2-inch lengths
Sate-Chile Oil (page 58), or chopped chiles to taste

1. In a large bowl, combine the pork, shrimp, pepper, 2 teaspoons of fish sauce, and the white of scallion. Mix well and set aside for 10 minutes.

2. In a large saucepan, heat the oil over high heat. Add the pork slices and cook, stirring for 1 minute. Add the shrimp mixture and cook for about 30 seconds. Add the stock and bring to a boil. Reduce the heat to medium and simmer, skimming the top, until the pork and shrimp are cooked, about 3 minutes. Add the tofu and remaining 2 teaspoons of fish sauce. Simmer briefly and remove from the heat. Stir in the garlic chives. Serve the soup with chile oil or the chiles on the side.

CABBAGE ROLL SOUP *(Canh Bap Su)*

MAKES 6 FIRST-COURSE SERVINGS

This is a pretty and popular first-course soup and takes little time to make. The stock and cabbage rolls can be prepared a day ahead; finish the soup shortly before serving, however.

> 6 cups Light Pork Stock (page 85) or Chicken Stock (page 86)
> 12 small, tender cabbage leaves, cut in half lengthwise, large ribs cut off
> 3 large scallions, whites very thinly sliced, greens left in long pieces
> 1 tablespoon dried tree ears
> $1/4$ pound ground pork
> $1/8$ teaspoon freshly ground black pepper plus more to taste
> 2 tablespoons plus 1 teaspoon bottled fish sauce (nuoc mam)

1. Prepare the Light Pork Stock.

2. In a large pot of boiling water, cook the cabbage leaves until wilted but bright green, about 2 minutes. Remove with tongs or a slotted spoon and drain in a colander. Add the scallion greens to the boiling water and cook about 10 seconds. Remove and refresh under running cold water. Gently tear the scallion greens lengthwise into 24 long strips and set aside.

3. In a small bowl, cover the tree ears with hot water and soak until inflated and soft, about 5 minutes. Drain, cut off any tough knobs, and rinse well. Chop coarse. In a medium bowl, combine the scallion whites, pork, tree ears, black pepper and 1 teaspoon of the fish sauce. Mix well with your hands.

4. Place a heaping teaspoon of the filling on each cabbage leaf, leaving a short flap at the bottom of the leaf nearest you. Fold the flap over the filling and bring the sides in, folding the package like an envelope. Tie the bundle with a piece of scallion green. Continue making rolls with the remaining leaves and filling until you have 24.

5. In a large saucepan, bring the stock to a boil and add the remaining 2 tablespoons fish sauce. Add the cabbage rolls, reduce the heat to medium, and simmer the soup until the cabbage is tender, about 20 minutes. Season to taste with black pepper and serve.

BITTER MELON SOUP *(Canh Kho Qua)*

MAKES 6 TO 8 FIRST-COURSE SERVINGS

Bitter melon is a bumpy squashlike vegetable not loved by all, but much appreciated by those who believe in its restorative qualities and fancy its astringent bite. This soup would make a surprising first course for adventurous eaters. Look for long green melons with no yellow or orange spots.

6 cups Chicken Stock (page 86) or Light Pork Stock (page 85)
Half a 1.8-ounce package cellophane noodles
4 medium bitter melons (1½ pounds)
½ pound ground pork
1 scallion, thinly sliced
½ teaspoon freshly ground black pepper
1 tablespoon plus 1 teaspoon bottled fish sauce (nuoc mam)
8 small sprigs coriander

1. Prepare the Chicken Stock.

2. Soak the cellophane noodles in a medium bowl of cold water to cover until pliable, about 3 minutes. Drain and with scissors cut the noodles into 2-inch lengths.

3. Cut both ends from the melons and with your fingers push the inner core of seeds to one end. With a chopstick, push the seeds all the way out. You should have a hollow channel ready for filling in each melon.

4. In a medium bowl, combine the pork, noodles, scallion, pepper, and 1 teaspoon of the fish sauce. Divide the mixture into 4 portions and stuff each of the melons snugly.

5. In a large saucepan, cover the melons with the chicken stock and bring to a boil over high heat. Reduce the heat to medium and simmer, skimming occasionally, until the melons are tender when pierced with a knife, about 10 minutes. Add the remaining fish sauce. Remove the melons and slice them crosswise into $1/4$-inch-thick stuffed rounds. Put the equivalent of half a melon into each soup bowl and ladle the stock over it. Top with the coriander sprigs and pass extra fish sauce and black pepper at the table.

HOT AND SOUR FISH SOUP (Canh Chua Ca)

MAKES 6 FIRST-COURSE OR 3 TO 4 MAIN-COURSE SERVINGS

This is one of the most popular dishes in Vietnam and every cook has his own version, some using thick halibut steak instead of a whole fish. The okra is cooked for only a few minutes so that it keeps its crunch.

Full rice recipe (page 34)
1 2-pound whole sea bass or red snapper, cleaned and gills removed; fillets
   removed, skinned, and cut into wide strips; head and bones reserved and
   rinsed
1 scallion, thinly sliced
$\frac{1}{2}$ teaspoon freshly ground black pepper
3 tablespoons fish sauce
$\frac{1}{3}$ cup packed tamarind pulp
$\frac{1}{3}$ cup hot water
2 teaspoons vegetable oil
$\frac{1}{4}$ teaspoon dried chile flakes
1 medium tomato, cut into thin wedges
2 small red chiles, thinly sliced, or to taste
$\frac{1}{4}$ pound okra
1 cup mung bean sprouts
$\frac{1}{4}$ cup chopped ngo om *or coriander*
Small lime wedges

1. Prepare the rice. In a large saucepan, cover the fish head and bones with 5 cups cold water. Bring to a simmer over medium heat and cook, skimming occasionally, for 20 minutes. Strain the broth, stopping to pour when you reach the solids on the bottom. Discard the solids and set the broth aside.

2. In a medium bowl, combine the scallion, black pepper, and 1 tablespoon of the fish sauce. Add the fish strips and coat well. Set aside to marinate for 20 minutes.

3. In a small bowl, cover the tamarind pulp with the hot water and set aside to soften about 5 minutes. Mash well with a fork and remove the seeds or pass the tamarind through a strainer.

4. In a small saucepan, heat the oil over high heat until hot. Add the chile flakes and when they sizzle remove from the heat. Set the chile oil aside.

5. In a large saucepan, bring the broth to a boil over high heat. Skim the surface a few times and stir in the tamarind, tomato, chiles, and remaining 2 tablespoons fish sauce. Simmer for 1 minute, then add the okra and fish. Cook until the fish is just cooked through, about 3 minutes. Remove from the heat and add the bean sprouts, *ngo om*, and the chile oil. Serve hot with the lime wedges and rice.

SHRIMP AND BABY TARO ROOT SOUP *(Canh Khoai Mon)*

MAKES 4 TO 6 FIRST-COURSE SERVINGS

This particular soup is a favorite of Binh's mother. In Asian markets, baby taro root is usually sold alongside the much larger ones; you will find it easier to peel and slice.

5 cups Light Pork Stock (page 85) or Chicken Stock (page 86)
Full rice recipe (page 34)
2 large whites of scallion, thinly sliced
$1/4$ teaspoon salt
$1/2$ teaspoon freshly ground black pepper
$1/2$ pound medium shrimp, peeled and deveined
1 tablespoon vegetable oil
$1^1/2$ pounds baby taro root (about 4) or yellow waxy potatoes, peeled and cut
    crosswise into $1/2$-inch-thick slices
2 tablespoons bottled fish sauce (nuoc mam)
2 tablespoons chopped coriander
2 tablespoons chopped scallion greens

1. Prepare the Light Pork Stock and the rice.

2. In a mortar, pound the scallion whites with the salt and pepper to a rough paste. In a bowl combine with the shrimp and mix well. Set aside for about 10 minutes.

3. In a large saucepan, heat the oil over high heat. Add the shrimp and cook, stirring, for 1 minute. Remove the shrimp to a plate and pour in the stock. Bring to a boil and add the taro slices and fish sauce. Bring to a simmer, reduce the heat to medium-low, and cook until the taro is tender, about 15 minutes. Return the shrimp to the pan and heat through. Serve hot, garnished with the coriander and scallion greens and rice.

HOT AND SOUR SHRIMP AND LEMONGRASS SOUP
(Canh Chua Tom)

MAKES 6 FIRST-COURSE OR 2 TO 3 MAIN-COURSE SERVINGS

If you can't find lime leaves make the soup with lime juice and add some grated peel.

$1/2$ teaspoon Sate-Chili Oil (page 58) or other chile oil
Half rice recipe (page 34)
$3/4$ pound medium shrimp, peeled and deveined, shells reserved
3 stalks lemongrass, green tops trimmed off and reserved, white bulb pounded
    flat and cut into 1-inch lengths
1 15-ounce can straw mushrooms, drained
5 lime leaves
1 small tomato, cut into thin wedges
1 large scallion, thinly sliced
$1^1/2$ cups mung bean sprouts
3 tablespoons plus 1 teaspoon lime juice
$1/4$ teaspoon freshly ground black pepper
$1/4$ cup bottled fish sauce (nuoc mam)
$1/4$ teaspoon dried chile flakes, or more to taste

1. Prepare the Sate-Chile Oil and rice and set aside.

2. In a medium saucepan, cover the reserved shrimp shells with 4 cups water. Add the reserved lemongrass tops and bring to a boil over high heat. Remove from the heat, strain the broth, and return it to the saucepan.

3. Add the straw mushrooms, lime leaves, lemongrass pieces, and tomato to the stock. Bring to a boil, reduce the heat to medium, and simmer for 4 minutes. Add the shrimp and simmer until opaque about 2 minutes. Remove from the heat and pour the soup into a tureen. Stir in the scallion, bean sprouts, lime juice, black pepper, fish sauce, chile flakes, and chile oil and serve at once with the rice.

LA-LOT BEEF SOUP *(Canh Thit Bo La-Lot)*

MAKES 6 FIRST-COURSE OR 3 TO 4 MAIN-COURSE SERVINGS

La-lot leaves have a freshwater taste with a pleasing sour bite, like sorrel. Because they're so tender, they are added to the soup just before serving. This soup, or *canh*, is meant to satisfy the family as a meal when enhanced with lots of rice. Without rice, it makes a tasty first course.

4 cups Chicken Stock (page 86) or Light Pork Stock (page 85)
$1\frac{1}{2}$ cups steamed rice (page 34)
2 whites of scallion, thinly sliced
$\frac{1}{2}$ teaspoon freshly ground black pepper
3 tablespoons bottled fish sauce (nuoc mam)
1 $\frac{1}{2}$-pound piece lean beef round, cut into very thin slices
3 tablespoons vegetable oil
$\frac{1}{2}$ teaspoon dried chile flakes, or to taste
2 stalks lemongrass, flattened with the side of a knife and cut into 2-inch lengths
2 medium tomatoes, cut into thin wedges
10 La-lot, sorrel, or Swiss chard leaves, cut into wide strips

1. Prepare the Chicken Stock and the rice.

2. In a large bowl, combine the scallion, black pepper, and 1 tablespoon of the fish sauce. Add the beef and toss to coat. Set aside to marinate for 10 minutes.

3. Put 1 tablespoon of the oil in a small saucepan over high heat. When a chile flake sizzles, drop in the rest and remove from the heat. Set the chile oil aside.

4. In a large saucepan, bring the stock and the lemongrass to a boil, reduce the heat to low, and simmer for 10 minutes.

5. Meanwhile, in a wok or large skillet over high heat, heat the remaining 2 tablespoons oil. When it starts to smoke, add the beef and brown it on both sides, stirring once or twice. Add the tomatoes and stir-fry until the beef is cooked, about 2 minutes. With a large spoon, add the beef and tomatoes to the soup. Bring the soup to a boil over high heat, add the remaining 2 tablespoons fish sauce, and the reserved chile oil. Remove from the heat and stir in the *la-lot* leaves. To serve, spoon rice into each soup bowl and ladle the soup over it. Eat with chopsticks and soup spoons.

DUCK SOUP WITH TOASTED RICE AND GINGER SAUCE
(Chao Vit)

MAKES 4 TO 6 MAIN-COURSE SERVINGS

Like many Vietnamese soups, this duck and cabbage one can be a pleasant undertaking to eat: one consumes the broth and rice with a spoon, then uses chopsticks to dip the duck and cabbage pieces into the ginger sauce. Toasting the rice first gives it extra flavor and keeps it chewy when cooked.

Ginger Sauce (page 40)
Fried Shallots (page 62)
1 teaspoon salt
1 2-inch piece ginger
1 whole duck, about 5 pounds
½ cup long-grain rice
1 tablespoon vegetable oil, optional
¼ teaspoon annatto seeds, optional
3 tablespoons bottled fish sauce (nuoc mam)
2 cups finely shredded cabbage
¼ cup chopped mint
¼ cup coriander leaves
Freshly ground black pepper

1. Prepare the Fried Shallots and Ginger Sauce and set aside.

2. To a large soup pot, add 14 cups water, the salt, and ginger. Bring to a boil over high heat, then add the duck. Reduce the heat to low and simmer gently, skimming the surface occasionally with a ladle. After about 45 minutes, turn the duck over and continue cooking and skimming, until tender, when a leg moves easily, another 45 minutes.

3. In a skillet over medium-high heat, toast the rice, tossing it frequently, until brown and speckled all over, about 4 minutes. Set aside.

4. In a small saucepan over high heat, heat the oil until smoking. Add the annatto seeds and cook, swirling the pan, for 30 seconds. Let cool, remove and discard the seeds with a fork, and set the oil aside.

5. When cooked, remove the duck from the liquid to a work surface. Let it cool slightly and with a boning knife remove all the skin from the breast and legs. Cut the meat into 2-inch pieces. Set aside.

6. Bring the broth to a boil over high heat and with a ladle skim off as much of the fat as possible. Reduce the heat to medium, add the toasted rice, and cook, skimming occasionally, until the rice is firm but tender, about 12 minutes. Just before serving, stir in the fish sauce and annatto oil. Divide the duck meat among soup bowls and add a handful of cabbage to each. Pour the hot broth over all and top with a generous amount of mint and coriander. At the table, pass the fried shallots, ginger sauce, and black pepper. Or serve the sauce in small dipping saucers on the side.

Appetizers

The dishes offered here as appetizers are called *do nhau* or "little bites." They are, for the most part, small, finger foods that in Vietnam are sold in the market places as snacks. On holidays and special occasions, treats like spring rolls, silver dollar cakes, French bread shrimp toasts, and crunchy sweet potato nests with shrimp are made at home. You can learn the dynamics of Vietnamese food, the juxtapositions of textures and temperatures and bursts of bright flavors, by starting with the preparation of their appetizers.

In this country, we are accustomed to a wide range of ethnic cuisines. When eating out, we often begin with a varied selection of appetizers, for it is the starters in many of these cultures that are the most interesting and festive. And this is as it should be. First tastes set the tone and build the momentum to a spectacular meal.

The selection of appetizers given here is an assortment of small tastes and individual tidbits. Many are deep fried or grilled, to be wrapped and dipped. Piles of lettuce leaves and rice papers serve as edible wrappers that refresh the palate as well. Foods familiar to us, like shrimp, asparagus, sweet potatoes, chicken wings, and spareribs are served in clever ways. You will learn how rice can yield various batters, and you can create two remarkably different pancakes: small, creamy in the center but crusty on the bottom Silver Dollar Cakes, and the large, crunchy rice crepes called

Happy Pancakes. You will taste grilled meatballs unlike any you've ever experienced. Lightened with potato starch, their puffy texture is indescribably good.

The uncommon ingredients of Vietnamese cooking you will get to know and especially appreciate in appetizer form. As you work with rice papers, either frying them to a shattering crispness or filling, then serving them in a soft, chewy state, you will be working with an ancient staple, highly digestible and nutritious. Sugar cane, another basic of the Vietnamese diet, has many uses besides the common sweetener. Adapting the cane as a skewer, you will learn of a new way to grill food, one that sprang from necessity. The Vietnamese are used to having to improvise in making tools and implements and this is a brilliant alternative to bamboo skewers. You will taste how lemongrass enhances barbecued spareribs. As you become comfortable with these simpler, straightforward dishes, you can move on to the dumpling doughs, and learn how rice, tapioca, and corn flours produce soft or very chewy results. The final note for these appetizers is the dipping sauce that brings everything together.

At home, many of these appetizers benefit from being made ahead. This is true of most of the deep-fried items, which can be reheated in a hot oven shortly before serving. In general the dishes taste better when eaten warm or at room temperature, as they are in Vietnam. The flavors are clearer than when served piping hot, and when wrapped and dunked in the zesty dipping sauces, they truly come alive. And some appetizers make more elegant first courses and should be eaten with a fork and knife. Happy Pancakes, Fine Shrimp Paste with Asparagus, Mini Crab Cakes, and Escargots Wrapped in Shrimp Mousse are best served hot and right away.

HAPPY PANCAKES *(Banh Xeo)*

MAKES ABOUT 10 PANCAKES

For those unitiated to Vietnamese food, I love to make these crunchy pancakes as a first taste. This Asian "crepe," folded like an omelette, then drizzled with vibrant, spicy Nuoc Cham, never fails to please. Maybe they're called Happy Pancakes because of the instant elation they arouse in people. They are, however, often found on Vietnamese restaurant menus by other less enthusiastic names, such as Salty Cake or *Banh Xeo. Banh* means rice dough and *xeo* describes the sizzling sound it makes as it cooks over a hot fire. Many restaurant versions I've had, though, have not lived up to the name, being soggy and greasy rounds.

The batter is very simple, just rice flour and water; the trick is in keeping the temperature constantly high throughout the cooking process. Covering the pancake as it cooks creates the distinctive hard crust on the bottom. And a nonstick skillet works best. You can speed things up if you use two skillets at the same time. In Vietnam, a well-seasoned flat pan of clay, similar to the Mexican *comal*, or a wide, very thin gauge aluminum wok is used. The *banh xeo* Binh and I ate in the food stalls in the markets of Saigon were plain, unadorned pancakes, simply filled with bean sprouts. However modest, they were remarkably thin and crisp and the size of big dinner plates. The recipe that follows is the version Binh serves at the restaurant. It is filled with browned onions, mushrooms, pork, and shrimp.

Nuoc Cham Dipping Sauce (page 36)
$1\frac{3}{4}$ cups rice flour
$\frac{1}{4}$ teaspoon turmeric
1 scallion, thinly sliced
$\frac{3}{4}$ cup plus 2 tablespoons vegetable oil
1 pound lean pork shoulder or loin, cut into slices $\frac{1}{4}$ inch thick
1 pound medium shrimp, peeled and deveined
1 small onion, thinly sliced
10 medium mushrooms, sliced
$1\frac{1}{4}$ teaspoons salt
$1\frac{1}{4}$ teaspoons freshly ground black pepper
$2\frac{1}{2}$ cups mung bean sprouts

1. Prepare the Nuoc Cham Dipping Sauce and set aside.

2. In a medium bowl, whisk together the rice flour and 2 cups water. Add the turmeric and scallion and mix well. Set the batter aside. The batter keeps, covered, in the refrigerator for up to 3 days.

3. In a large nonstick skillet, heat $1\frac{1}{2}$ tablespoons of the oil over high heat. Add 3 slices of pork, 3 shrimp, a few slices of onion, and 1 sliced mushroom. Season with salt and pepper and cook until the onion starts to brown lightly, about 1 minute. Stir the rice flour batter again and ladle $\frac{1}{3}$ cup of it into the pan. Tilt the pan to distribute the batter evenly. Keep the heat high, cover, and cook until the sides of the pancake turn deep brown and curl up, about 3 to 4 minutes. Scatter $\frac{1}{4}$ cup of the bean sprouts over the pancake, fold it in half, and slide it onto a warm platter. Keep warm in a low oven while you make pancakes with the remaining ingredients. Serve the pancakes with the Nuoc Cham on the side. Eat with a knife and fork.

SUGGESTIONS: Don't feel bound to using all the filling ingredients listed above, for this dish originated when there was actually not much food in the house. You can compose a plain happy pancake with just the browned onions, then fill it with bean sprouts, making a vegetarian combination.

(continued)

(continued)

Or, use only one protein, either pork or shrimp, if that's all you have.

The amount the batter makes and the step of keeping the pancakes in a warm oven until all are cooked is more to serve the needs of a dinner party. Even at a party, I often cook and serve the pancakes directly from the skillet, one by one, making a show of it.

SIMPLE SHRIMP ROLLS *(Cha Ram)*

MAKES ABOUT 40 ROLLS

Utterly delicious and incredibly easy to make, these rolls originate from Central Vietnam, where Binh's father was born. They were his favorite snack. Traditionally they are made with freshwater shrimp, which have soft thin shells. If you can find shrimp—fresh or saltwater—with thin shells, leave them on, and when cooked they'll be crisp and tasty. As with other deep-fried items, you can make these ahead and reheat them in a hot oven.

Nuoc Cham Dipping Sauce (page 36)
Table Salad for 6 to 8 (page 32)
1 pound medium shrimp, tails and legs trimmed off with scissors, left whole or
    shelled
1 teaspoon freshly ground black pepper
40 triangle rice paper wrappers
1 teaspoon vinegar
5 large scallions, cut in half lengthwise, then cut crosswise into 2-inch lengths
Peanut oil or vegetable oil for frying

1. Prepare the Nuoc Cham Dipping Sauce and set aside.

2. Put the shrimp in a large bowl and sprinkle them with the pepper. Take each shrimp and crack it slightly to straighten it.

3. In a small bowl, combine the vinegar with $\frac{1}{3}$ cup water. Brush about 10 rice paper wrappers with the vinegar-water mixture and lay them out on a work surface to soften for a few minutes. Gently peel the softened rice paper off the surface and with the point facing away from you, put a shrimp about $\frac{1}{2}$ inch from the bottom of the wrapper. Put a couple of scallion pieces next to the shrimp and bring the bottom flap up and over the shrimp, covering it snugly. Bring the sides in and fold tightly. Fold the roll up tightly like an envelope, ending with the point of the triangle. Repeat using the remaining rice paper and filling.

4. In a large skillet, heat $\frac{1}{3}$ inch of oil over medium-high heat to 350 degrees on a deep-fry thermometer. Fry the shrimp rolls in batches until golden brown, about 5 minutes per side. Adjust the heat accordingly to keep the oil at this moderate frying temperature or the rolls may burst. Drain on paper towels. Serve hot or at room temperature with the Nuoc Cham and Table Salad.

SHRIMP ON SUGAR CANE *(Chao Tom)*

MAKES 4 TO 5 APPETIZER SERVINGS

This appetizer is renowned for its ingenious use of raw sugar cane. Acting as a skewer, it imparts a sweetness to whatever is wrapped around it. Meat and shrimp pastes are perfectly suited to this preparation. If you can find it in good condition, use fresh sugar cane, but the canned sticks packed in syrup are also excellent. Hand-chopping the shrimp gives the best results, leaving it varied in texture, with chunky pieces as well as paste. And tiny cubes of fresh pork fat mixed in help to make this incredibly succulent.

Nuoc Cham Dipping Sauce (page 36)
1 pound medium shrimp, peeled and deveined
1 1-inch piece rock sugar
1 1-ounce piece fresh white pork fat
$\frac{1}{2}$ teaspoon baking powder
1 teaspoon cornstarch or potato starch
$\frac{1}{2}$ teaspoon freshly ground black pepper
$\frac{1}{2}$ teaspoon salt
1 large white of scallion, finely chopped
1 12-inch-long piece sugar cane, cut crosswise into 4 3-inch pieces, then split
    lengthwise in half and in half again (page 27), or 1 can sugar cane in
    syrup, pieces split once
Boston lettuce leaves
Mint sprigs
Cucumber slices

1. Prepare the Nuoc Cham Dipping Sauce and set aside.

2. Spread the shrimp out in an even layer on a baking sheet and freeze until very firm, about 10 minutes.

3. In a mortar, pound the rock sugar to a coarse powder. Set aside.

4. In a small saucepan of boiling water over high heat, cook the pork fat until translucent, about 2 minutes. Drain and cut into tiny dice.

5. Remove the shrimp from the freezer and with a large sharp knife chop them fine. Add the pork fat and continue chopping until a coarse paste forms, leaving some small pieces of shrimp. Put the mixture in a bowl and stir in the pounded sugar, baking powder, cornstarch, pepper, salt, and white of scallion until well blended.

6. With oiled hands, take about 3 tablespoons of the shrimp mixture and wrap it evenly around a piece of sugar cane, leaving about ½ inch exposed on both ends. Repeat with the remaining shrimp and sugar cane. You should have about 10 shrimp sticks.

7. Oil a steamer basket and place the shrimp sticks evenly apart on it. In a large saucepan bring 1 inch of water to a boil over high heat. Put in the basket, cover, and steam the shrimp sticks until almost cooked through, about 3 minutes. Preheat the broiler or grill.

8. Remove the steamer basket from the pan and if broiling, put the shrimp sticks on a baking sheet. Broil about 5 inches from the heat, turning often, until deep brown on all sides, about 3 minutes. Or grill the shrimp sticks over a hot fire, turning often. Serve hot. To eat, remove the shrimp from the cane, wrap it in lettuce with sprigs of mint and slices of cucumber, and dip it in the Nuoc Cham. Chew on the sugar cane if you like.

CRUNCHY SWEET POTATO NESTS WITH SHRIMP
(Khoai Lang Chien Voi Tom)

MAKES 18 APPETIZER SERVINGS

The great charm of this dish is how a Vietnamese cook can take three simple ingredients and transform them into a marvelous snack, one that is differently delicious and beautiful to behold. It's important that the shreds of sweet potato be very thin so that they hold together when fried. The nests can be made a day in advance, cooled, then refrigerated and reheated in a moderately hot oven. You can serve the Table Salad with this appetizer if you wish, but the nests have such fine flavor lettuce leaves are all that's needed.

Sour Lime Sauce (page 52)
1½ pounds orange sweet potatoes, peeled and cut into long, ⅛-inch thin sticks
*   2 to 3 inches long (use a Kitchen Wonder Grating Box if possible)*
¼ cup plus 1 tablespoon flour
18 medium shrimp (about ½ pound) peeled, deveined, and butterflied
Vegetable oil for frying
18 Boston lettuce leaves

1. Prepare the Sour Lime Sauce and set aside.

2. Put the shredded sweet potatoes in a colander and rinse well. Squeeze the potato firmly to remove as much water as possible. Sit the sweet potatoes in the colander to drain completely, then transfer them to a large bowl and toss them with ¼ cup flour.

3. Put the shrimp on a large plate and sprinkle them with the remaining 1 tablespoon flour.

4. In a large skillet over medium-high heat, heat ¼ inch oil. Start to form the nests. Take about ¼ cup of the sweet potato and press it into the palm of your hand, forming an oval shape about 2 inches wide. Add a shrimp and press it in slightly so it adheres. Continue making the nests in this manner and when the oil is hot and shimmering, add the nests, about 5 at a time. Fry until brown and crisp on one side, about 4 minutes. With a metal spatula, gently flip the nests and press them lightly against the bottom of the skillet. Cook until brown and crisp all over, another minute or so. Adjust the heat if the sweet potato browns too quickly. Drain on paper towels and repeat with the remaining potatoes and shrimp. Add more oil if necessary.

5. To serve, present the nests hot or warm on a platter with the lettuce leaves on a plate. Bring the lime sauce to the table in individual dipping bowls.

SPECIAL SHRIMP ROLLS *(Tom Tam Giac)*

MAKES 17 ROLLS

This version of spring rolls encases a whole shrimp and twice as much filling as *cha gio*, everyday spring rolls. Here the rolls are folded up to form triangles, which accommodate the shape of the shrimp and make for a neat and completely enclosed package. This is a specialty of Binh's hometown, Nha Trang.

> *Nuoc Cham Dipping Sauce (page 36)*
> *2 tablespoons dried tree ears*
> *1 1⅛-ounce package cellophane noodles*
> *1 pound ground pork*
> *1 small onion, minced*
> *½ cup finely shredded carrot (about 1 small), rinsed and squeezed dry*
> *3 ounces cooked crab meat*
> *½ teaspoon salt*
> *1 teaspoon freshly ground black pepper*
> *3 eggs*
> *1 cup mung bean sprouts*
> *6 12-inch round rice paper wrappers*
> *17 triangular rice paper wrappers*
> *17 medium shrimp, peeled, except for the tail sections, and deveined*
> *Peanut or vegetable oil for frying*

1. Prepare the Nuoc Cham Dipping Sauce and set aside.

2. In a small bowl, cover the tree ears with hot water and soak until soft and inflated, about 3 minutes. Drain, cut off any hard knobs, rinse, and chop coarse.

3. In a large bowl, cover the cellophane noodles with cold water and soak until pliable, about 3 minutes. Drain and with scissors cut them into 2-inch lengths.

4. In a medium bowl, combine the tree ears, cellophane noodles, pork, onion, carrot, crab, salt, pepper, and 1 egg and mix well, using your hands to thoroughly combine. Gently mix in the bean sprouts.

5. In a small bowl, beat the remaining 2 eggs and set aside. Stack 3 of the 12-inch round rice paper wrappers together and with scissors make a cut just to the center of the round. Move about 8 inches past the first cut and cut again to the center forming a triangular wedge shape. Set this wedge aside. Cut what remains of the stack in half, forming 2 more wedges, all the same size. Repeat this procedure with the remaining 12-inch wrappers.

6. To assemble: Working with a few at a time, brush some of the larger wedges you've just cut out on both sides with the beaten egg and lay them on a work surface with the points facing away from you. Brush the same number of the smaller triangular wedges with egg. To form each roll, take the smaller wrappers and center them on the larger wedges with the points facing up and the bottoms flush together.

7. Now put a tablespoon of filling about ½ inch from the bottom of the wedge, and shape conforming to the wedge shape of the wrapper. Put a shrimp over the filling with the tail facing the point. Put another tablespoon of filling on top and shape similarly. Take the bottom flap of rice paper and bring it up and onto the filling, pressing it snugly to contain the filling. Fold one of the side flaps over the filling, pulling tightly over so there are no air pockets; be sure to form a tight point over the shrimp tail. Fold the other side over the same way. Fold up the bottom and press to seal. Continue making rolls with the remaining rice paper wrappers and filling.

8. In a large skillet, heat ⅓ inch oil over medium-high heat to 350 degrees on a deep-fry thermometer. Fry the shrimp rolls in batches until golden brown, about 10 minutes per side. Adjust the heat, lowering it if necessary to maintain a steady temperature. Drain on paper towels. Serve hot or at room temperature with the Nuoc Cham.

FINE SHRIMP PASTE ON ASPARAGUS
(Chao Tom Cuon Mang Tay)

MAKES 2 TO 4 APPETIZER SERVINGS

This is lean, close-textured shrimp paste, without the customary fresh pork fat, and with ginger added. The butter sauce adds richness. You can just steam these bundles, but broiling or grilling them afterwards gives them an attractive and tasty outer coating. If you prefer, as I do, the pork enriched shrimp paste from Shrimp on Sugar Cane (page 112), use it here instead, but serve it with the Coriander-Chile Sauce (page 46) instead of the butter sauce. Its spiciness complements the richer version.

1 1-inch piece rock sugar
1 ¼-inch-thick slice ginger, peeled and chopped
2 whites of scallion, finely chopped
½ teaspoon freshly ground black pepper
1 teaspoon bottled fish sauce (nuoc mam)
1 teaspoon vegetable oil
1 pound medium shrimp, peeled and deveined
1 egg white
10 large spears asparagus, trimmed
Piquant Butter Sauce (page 50)

1. Put the rock sugar in a mortar and pestle or the bowl of a food processor or mini-chop and pound or grind to a coarse powder. Add the ginger and process to a paste. In a large bowl, combine the ginger sugar with the scallion, pepper, fish sauce, and oil. Stir in the shrimp and coat well. Put in the freezer to marinate and firm up, about 20 minutes.

2. Put the shrimp mixture in the bowl of the food processor and add the egg white. Process, scraping the sides of the bowl a few times, until smooth, about 30 seconds.

3. Oil a steamer basket, then your hands. Take about 2 tablespoons of the shrimp paste and wrap it around an asparagus spear, leaving about 1 inch exposed on either end. Put the wrapped spears in the steamer basket and repeat with the remaining shrimp paste and asparagus.

4. In a large saucepan, bring about 1 inch of water to a boil over high heat. Place the steamer basket in the saucepan, cover, and steam the spears for 1 minute. Remove the basket and set aside to cool slightly. Light a grill or preheat the broiler.

5. Make the butter sauce. Lightly brush the shrimp paste on the spears with oil. Grill or broil the spears, turning until browned and puffed all over, about 2 minutes per side. Pour the butter sauce over the spears and serve hot.

ESCARGOTS WRAPPED IN SHRIMP MOUSSE
(Chao Tom Don Oc)

MAKES 4 TO 6 APPETIZER SERVINGS

This dish is a specialty of Hanoi, where snails are more common than in other parts. Though escargot, as they are called in Vietnam, are eaten throughout the country, they are not everyday food. This particular preparation, in fact, is served at weddings. The Vietnamese also like to wrap these before steaming in fragrant leaves, like the tops of lemongrass or ginger leaves, but it's not necessary. These could be served with Nuoc Cham, but the Ginger Sauce outshines it by far.

Ginger Sauce (page 40)
1 pound medium shrimp, peeled and deveined
1 tablespoon vegetable oil
1 teaspoon bottled fish sauce (nuoc mam)
$1/4$ teaspoon freshly ground black pepper
1 teaspoon sugar
1 teaspoon cornstarch
$1/2$ teaspoon baking soda
1 large scallion, finely chopped
1 tablespoon finely grated ginger
$1^{1}/_{2}$ dozen canned snails, rinsed well

1. Prepare the Ginger Sauce and set aside.

2. In a medium bowl, combine the shrimp with the oil, fish sauce, pepper, sugar, cornstarch, baking soda, and 2 teaspoons cold water. Mix well and chill in the freezer until very cold and firm, about 15 minutes.

3. Put the shrimp mixture in the bowl of a food processor and grind to a fine paste, scraping down the sides of the bowl a few times. Add the scallion and ginger and process just to combine.

4. With oiled hands, take about 1 tablespoon of the shrimp paste and shape into a 2-inch round. Place a snail in the center and turn up the edges to enclose the snail and form a ball. Put each formed dumpling on an oiled plate.

5. Oil a steamer basket and arrange the dumplings on it in a single layer. In a large saucepan over 1 inch of boiling water put the basket, cover, and steam the dumplings until cooked through, about 12 minutes. Serve hot with the Ginger Sauce in dipping bowls on the side.

IMPERIAL SHRIMP ROLLS WITH CORIANDER AND PEANUTS *(Tom Tai Chanh)*

MAKES 8 ROLLS

The shrimp in this dish are soaked in vinegar, then "cooked" seviche style in lime marinade. Rolled in softened rice paper, these rolls are extra juicy and tasty.

½ recipe of Nuoc Cham Dipping Sauce (page 36)
1 pound medium shrimp, peeled, deveined, and cut in half lengthwise
½ cup white vinegar
Pinch salt
1 small onion, thinly sliced
1 clove garlic, minced
¼ teaspoon dried chile flakes
¼ teaspoon sugar
2 teaspoons bottled fish sauce (nuoc mam)
1 tablespoon lime juice
8 round rice paper wrappers, 8½ inches in diameter
1 tablespoon plus 1 teaspoon chopped peanuts
2 tablespoons plus 2 teaspoons chopped coriander
2 tablespoons plus 2 teaspoons chopped mint

1. Prepare the Nuoc Cham Dipping Sauce and set aside.

2. In a medium bowl, combine the shrimp with the vinegar and salt and let soak for 5 minutes. Remove the shrimp and squeeze to remove any excess vinegar. Discard the vinegar and return the shrimp to the bowl. Add the onion, garlic, chile flakes, sugar, fish sauce, and lime juice. Toss to mix well. Cover and marinate in the refrigerator until the shrimp are almost opaque throughout, about 2 hours.

3. When the shrimp are ready, prepare the rice paper wrappers. Using a pastry brush, generously brush both sides of each wrapper with warm water and set aside in a single layer until softened and pliable, about 2 minutes. (If parts of the wrappers are clear and hard, brush with additional water.)

4. Place $\frac{1}{3}$ cup of the shrimp mixture along the lower edge of a prepared rice paper wrapper about 1 inch in from the edge. Sprinkle the shrimp with $\frac{1}{2}$ teaspoon of the peanuts and 1 teaspoon each of the coriander and mint. Fold the bottom of the paper up snugly over the shrimp mixture and fold in both sides. Roll up into a compact cylinder about 5 inches long. Repeat with the remaining shrimp mixture and rice paper wrappers. Serve, cut in half, soon after with the Nuoc Cham on the side.

SHRIMP TOASTS *(Banh Mi Chien)*

MAKES ABOUT 24 TOASTS

Bread slices are first oven-toasted on both sides so that the outsides stay crunchy. Only the filling side will be briefly fried, rendering them far less greasy than other versions. Eat plain or with lime wedges.

> *1 large loaf Italian or French bread (not a baguette), cut crosswise into 24*
> *   3-inch-wide slices*
> *$\frac{1}{2}$ pound medium shrimp, peeled, deveined, and coarsely chopped*
> *$\frac{1}{2}$ pound ground pork*
> *1 small onion, minced*
> *2 scallions, minced*
> *$\frac{1}{2}$ teaspoon sugar*
> *$\frac{1}{4}$ teaspoon freshly ground black pepper*
> *1 tablespoon plus 1 teaspoon bottled fish sauce* (nuoc mam)
> *1 small egg, lightly beaten*
> *1 tablespoon flour*
> *Vegetable oil for frying*

1. Preheat the oven to 400 degrees. Put the bread slices on a large baking sheet and toast the bread on the top shelf of the oven until golden brown on one side, about 3 minutes. Turn and toast the bread until golden brown on the other side, about 3 minutes. Set aside.

2. In a large bowl, combine the shrimp, pork, onion, scallions, sugar, pepper, and fish sauce and mix well. Stir in the egg and flour and blend well.

3. Put a heaping tablespoon of the shrimp and pork mixture on one side of each slice of the toasts and spread it thickly over the surface.

4. Heat about $\frac{1}{4}$ inch of oil in a large skillet over medium-high heat until hot. Add the first batch of toasts, filling sides down, without

overcrowding the skillet. Fry the toasts only on one side, until browned and cooked through about 4 minutes. Drain, filling side down, on paper towels and repeat with the remaining toasts. Serve hot or warm.

CLAMS WITH GINGER, GARLIC, AND BLACK BEANS
(Ngheu Xao Gung)

MAKES 4 TO 6 APPETIZER SERVINGS

If you like, you can make this with soft-shelled steamer clams, which have a superior sweet flavor, but require that the tough skin around the neck be peeled off before eating. Small razor clams are good, too.

2 tablespoons vegetable oil
3 cloves garlic, minced
1 2-inch piece ginger, peeled and finely chopped
½ teaspoon sesame oil
2 teaspoons Vietnamese bean sauce or Chinese bean paste
1 teaspoon sugar
1 small red chile, minced, or ¼ to ½ teaspoon dried chile flakes
4 pounds small littleneck clams
2 large scallions, chopped
½ teaspoon freshly ground black pepper

1. In a large skillet or wok over high heat, add the oil and garlic and cook for 5 seconds. Add the ginger and cook, stirring, for 1 minute. Stir in the sesame oil, bean sauce or paste, sugar, chile, and clams and boil, stirring occasionally, until all the clams open, about 3 minutes. With a slotted spoon, remove the clams to a platter and boil the sauce until thick, about 2 minutes. Add the scallions and black pepper, pour over the clams, and serve hot with rice or French bread.

CRAB FARCI *(Cua Farci)*

MAKES 6 APPETIZER SERVINGS

You will need the top shells from six whole cooked blue claw crabs for this dish. If you make a meal of boiled crabs or prepare Steamed Crabs with Chile, Black Pepper, Salt, and Lime (page 131), you may well have enough leftover crab *and* the shells to make this starter. If you don't have crab shells, use toasted bread as in the Shrimp Toasts (page 124).

Nuoc Cham Dipping Sauce (page 36)
2 tablespoons dried tree ears
½ ounce cellophane noodles, about half a 1.8-ounce package
1 small onion, minced
¾ pound cooked crab meat
1 teaspoon freshly ground black pepper
¼ teaspoon salt
1 egg
6 crab shells, about 6 inches across, scrubbed and dried
Peanut or vegetable oil for frying

1. Prepare the Nuoc Cham Dipping Sauce and set aside.

2. In a small bowl, cover the tree ears with hot water and soak until soft and inflated, about 3 minutes. Drain. Cut off any hard knobs, rinse, and chop coarse.

3. In a medium bowl, soak the cellophane noodles in cold water until pliable, about 3 minutes. Drain and cut into 2-inch lengths.

4. In a large bowl, combine the tree ears, cellophane noodles, onion, crab, pepper, salt, and egg. Mix well. Fill each crab shell with an equal amount of the filling, pressing *firmly* to pack the meat lightly in.

5. In a large skillet, heat $\frac{1}{3}$ inch of the oil over medium heat until very hot. Fry the crabs, filling side down, until deep brown and crisp, about 4 minutes. Turn and cook on the shell side to heat it through, about 1 minute. Drain, stuffing side down, on paper towels. Serve hot with the Nuoc Cham sauce.

MINI CRAB CAKES *(Cha Cua)*

MAKES 4 TO 5 APPETIZER SERVINGS

These are the best kind of crab cakes, made with the fewest number of other ingredients. Their small size makes for an elegant first course. Piquant Butter Sauce (page 50) should be served with the spicy pepper sauce below.

6 ounces cooked crab meat
1 medium onion, minced
$\frac{1}{2}$ teaspoon freshly ground black pepper
$\frac{1}{8}$ teaspoon salt
1 egg, beaten

RED PEPPER SAUCE
1 tablespoon plus 2 teaspoons vegetable oil
1 tablespoon butter
1 large red bell pepper, cut into small dice
1 small fresh hot green chile, seeds removed, chopped

1. In a large bowl, using a rubber spatula, gently combine the crab, onion, pepper, salt, and egg. Form the mixture into twenty-two 1-inch crab cakes. Put the crab cakes on a plate and chill in the refrigerator for about 20 minutes to firm up.

2. To make the sauce: In a medium saucepan, heat 2 teaspoons of the oil and all the butter over medium heat. Add the red bell pepper and green chile pepper and cook until tender, about 8 minutes. Season with salt and set aside.

3. In a large skillet, heat the butter with $\frac{1}{2}$ tablespoon of the oil over medium-high heat until hot. Add half the crab cakes and cook until deep brown, about 2 minutes. Turn and cook another 2 minutes or so until brown on the other side. Drain on paper towels and keep warm in a low oven. Repeat with the remaining crab cakes and oil. Pour the sauce onto a platter or divide among individual appetizer plates and arrange the crab cakes on top. Serve with Piquant Butter Sauce.

ARTICHOKES STUFFED WITH CRAB AND SHRIMP
(A-Ti-So Don Tom So)

MAKES 6 APPETIZER SERVINGS

Yes, artichokes do grow in Vietnam, but they are then usually dried and made into a sweet, pleasant tea. Here's one way a Vietnamese would honor (and eat) them. The sauce is refreshingly spicy.

Coriander-Chile Sauce (page 46)
6 large artichokes
$2\frac{1}{2}$ ounces cooked crab meat or $\frac{1}{2}$ pound sea scallops
$\frac{1}{4}$ pound medium shrimp, peeled, deveined, and finely chopped
1 small onion, finely chopped
1 scallion, finely chopped
$\frac{1}{2}$ teaspoon bottled fish sauce (nuoc mam)
$\frac{1}{2}$ teaspoon freshly ground black pepper

1. Prepare the Coriander-Chile Sauce and set aside.

2. In a large saucepan of boiling water, cook the artichokes over medium high heat until the bottoms are tender when pierced with a knife, about 25 minutes. Drain the artichokes and cool slightly. Pull off all the leaves and with a spoon scrape out the chokes.

3. In a small bowl, combine the crab, shrimp, onion, scallion, fish sauce, and pepper until just mixed. Fill the artichoke bottoms with the crab and shrimp mixture. Lightly oil a steamer basket and put the stuffed artichokes on it. Bring an inch of water to a boil in a large saucepan. Position the steamer in the saucepan and steam the stuffed artichokes, covered, over high heat until the stuffing is cooked through, about 8 minutes. Serve hot or warm with the Coriander-Chile Sauce.

STEAMED CRABS WITH CHILE, BLACK PEPPER, SALT, AND LIME *(Cua Hap)*

MAKES 2 TO 4 APPETIZER SERVINGS

With two kinds of heat from two different peppers, you'll find this a piquant, butterless way to enjoy steamed crabs. In Vietnam you are served a small saucer holding tiny mounds of salt, pepper, and chopped chile, brought to life with lime squeezed over all. You can divvy up these ingredients into individual saucers, if you like, or serve already combined.

When shopping for crabs, be sure they are more than just alive: They should be fighting mad. You'll need tongs to handle these beautiful bright blue creatures as they don't think twice about grabbing you.

1 dozen very large, very lively blue claw crabs
1 small red chile, minced
1 teaspoon freshly ground black pepper
½ teaspoon salt
1 large lime, cut into wedges or juiced

1. In a large pot or wok with a steamer rack or insert, bring 1 inch water to a boil over high heat. Put the live crabs in a large bowl, and when the water is at a rolling boil, lift the lid and dump the crabs onto the steamer rack, spreading them in an even layer as best you can. Quickly replace the lid and steam the crabs until they turn bright orange all over, about 10 minutes.

2. While the crabs are steaming, combine the remaining ingredients in a small bowl. Divide the mixture between individual dipping saucers. Or divide the chile, black pepper, and salt in separate little mounds between the saucers and serve with the lime wedges on the side.

SOUR AND SPICY BEAN THREADS
WITH CRAB AND SHRIMP *(Mien Xao Tom Cua)*

MAKES 6 APPETIZER SERVINGS

Though the Vietnamese are quite used to eating chiles—Binh likes to munch on a fresh red chile while having his dinner—there are some foods, he says, that have to be very spicy. It is the nature of particular dishes that they be delightfully hot and not be tamed. This appetizer is very simple, very spicy, but refreshing and nonfilling as bean threads are delicate and digestible. Practically all flavor is what we have here.

1 8.08-ounce package mung bean threads or cellophane noodles
2 tablespoons vegetable oil
8 medium shallots, thinly sliced
$\frac{1}{2}$ pound medium shrimp, peeled and deveined
$\frac{1}{4}$ teaspoon freshly ground black pepper
2 teaspoons dried chile flakes
$1\frac{1}{3}$ cups chicken stock
4 ounces cooked crab meat
1 tablespoon bottled fish sauce (nuoc mam)
3 tablespoons fresh lime juice
1 tablespoon chopped mint
1 tablespoon chopped coriander

1. Soak the bean threads in warm water until pliable, about 5 minutes. Drain. With scissors, cut the threads into 3 to 4-inch lengths and set aside in a colander.

2. In a large skillet or wok over high heat, heat 1 tablespoon of the oil. Add the shallots and stir-fry for about 1 minute. Add the shrimp and stir-fry another minute. Add the black pepper and chile flakes and cook 30 seconds. Pour in $\frac{1}{3}$ cup of the chicken stock and the fish sauce and remove the pan from the heat. Fold in the crab meat and transfer the mixture to a large bowl.

3. Put the skillet or wok back over high heat and add the remaining tablespoon oil. Add the bean threads and stir-fry for 1 minute. Add the remaining cup chicken stock and cook, tossing the bean threads often, until they are tender and the stock has been reduced to a thin sauce, about 1 minute. Dump the bean threads into the bowl with the shrimp mixture and season with the lime juice, mint, and coriander, blending well with two spoons. Serve hot or warm.

GARLIC FRIED CRABS *(Cua Rang Muoi)*

MAKES 4 TO 6 APPETIZER SERVINGS

This dish is often called "salt and pepper crab," but that hardly describes the great taste that the blending of sugar, garlic, salt, and pepper imparts to the shellfish—one of the best treatments of crab you're likely to have. You may want to heed some ancient advice and buy your crabs on certain days. The Vietnamese believe that during the new moon a crab's shell is at its hardest and most packed with meat. Don't be put off by these seemingly brutal directions—this is the best way to handle these creatures and the most authentic Vietnamese way.

1 dozen very lively large blue claw crabs
½ cup vegetable oil (take off 2 tablespoons for frying the crabs)
1 whole head garlic, peeled and minced
1 medium onion, thinly sliced
⅓ cup sugar
¼ cup bottled fish sauce (nuoc mam)
½ teaspoon freshly ground black pepper
½ teaspoon salt

1. Using tongs, grab a crab and flip it on its back. Take a chopstick and put it in the middle of its "stomach." Hold the crab in place with the chopstick and with a heavy knife in your other hand cut the crab all the way through behind the eyes. Pick up the stunned crab with the chopstick still in place and dump it in the sink. Repeat with the remaining crabs. Leave the crabs in the sink for about 10 minutes to die. Now, take each crab and first twist off the claws. Then loosen the top shell and pull it off in one piece. Remove the coral, the spongy lung tissue, and the head sac and discard. Break the body in half and scrub off any mud. With the back of the knife, very gently crack the claws in two or three places only without disturbing the meat. Repeat with the remaining crabs. (Scrub and dry the shells and reserve them, if you wish, for Crab Farci, page 126.)

2. In a small saucepan over high heat, heat all but 2 tablespoons of the oil. Reduce the heat to medium-high, add the garlic, and cook 1 minute. Reduce the heat to medium-low, add the onion, and cook until soft, about 10 minutes. Add the sugar, fish sauce, and pepper and cook until the sugar dissolves, about 2 minutes. Remove the sauce from the heat and set aside.

3. Heat the remaining oil in a wok over medium-high heat and fry the crabs with the salt stirring occasionally, until the crabs turn bright orange, about 5 minutes. Add the garlic sauce and bring to a boil. Cover and cook, stirring several times, until the sauce is syrupy, about 10 minutes. Pour the crabs and sauce onto a large platter and serve at once.

CURLY FRIED EGGPLANT *(Ca Tim Phet Bot)*

MAKES 6 TO 8 APPETIZER SERVINGS

These batter-dipped slices of eggplant are coated with cellophane noodles, which expand into puffy curls. The Preserved Prune Dipping Sauce, a good match for the eggplant, is unusual—tart but flowery.

> *Preserved Prune Dipping Sauce (page 55)*
> *$1\frac{1}{2}$ cups unbleached flour*
> *$\frac{1}{2}$ teaspoon salt*
> *$1\frac{1}{2}$ cups ice cold water*
> *2 teaspoons cider vinegar*
> *1 tablespoon vegetable oil plus oil for deep frying*
> *1 $1\frac{1}{8}$-ounce package cellophane noodles*
> *1 medium Italian eggplant or 4 small Japanese eggplants, cut in half lengthwise, then cut crosswise $\frac{1}{3}$ inch thick*
> *Leaves of fresh basil, perilla, or **shiso**, or coriander, optional*

1. Prepare the Preserved Prune Dipping Sauce and set aside.

2. In a large bowl, combine the flour and salt. Whisk in the water, vinegar, and oil and whisk just until smooth.

3. Pull the cellophane noodles apart and with scissors cut them into 2-inch lengths. Put the noodles on a large plate.

4. Heat $\frac{1}{3}$ inch of oil in a large skillet over high heat. When a drop of the batter sizzles, reduce the heat to medium-high. Take a slice of eggplant and, if you wish, adhere with a little batter an herb leaf to it. Dip the eggplant into the batter to coat on both sides and allow any excess batter to drip off. Put the eggplant on the cellophane noodles and coat it lightly on both sides with the noodle sticks. Drop in the hot oil and fry until the noodles are puffed and white and the eggplant is golden brown on one side, about $1\frac{1}{2}$ minutes. Turn and cook the other side another minute or so. Drain on paper towels. Hold in a warm oven. Repeat with the remaining eggplant, cooking it in batches without crowding the pan and adjusting the heat as necessary. Serve hot with the dipping sauce.

PORK AND CRAB SPRING ROLLS (Cha Gio)

MAKES 36 SPRING ROLLS

These spring rolls are considered a national dish of Vietnam and are sold in the marketplace and in every restaurant as snacks. They are made at home only on special occasions, as they require some handiwork. However, homemade is always best, and they are well worth the effort—just gather extra pairs of hands when it comes time to roll them. A real plus is that they can be filled, rolled, and lightly fried up to 2 days in advance. Let them cool, then cover and refrigerate. When ready to use, fry them again until golden brown and serve.

Nuoc Cham Dipping Sauce (page 36)
Table Salad for 6 to 8 (page 32)
2 tablespoons dried tree ears
1 1⅛-ounce package cellophane noodles
¾ pound ground pork
1 medium onion, minced
½ cup finely shredded carrot (about 1 small), rinsed and squeezed dry
3 eggs
3 ounces cooked crab meat
½ teaspoon salt
½ teaspoon freshly ground black pepper
36 triangle rice paper wrappers
Peanut or vegetable oil for frying

1. Prepare the Nuoc Cham Dipping Sauce and Table Salad and set aside.

2. In a small bowl, cover the tree ears with hot water and soak until they inflate, about 3 minutes. Drain, rinse well, and chop.

3. In a large bowl, cover the cellophane noodles with cold water and soak until pliable, about 3 minutes. Drain and with scissors cut them into 2-inch lengths.

4. In a medium bowl, combine the tree ears, cellophane noodles, pork, onion, carrot, 1 of the eggs, crab, salt, and pepper. Mix well, using your hands to combine thoroughly.

5. Put the remaining 2 eggs in a small bowl and beat them lightly. Lay the rice papers out on a work surface, 10 at a time, and using a pastry brush, coat both sides with the beaten egg. Allow to stand a few moments to soften. Peel each rice paper gently off the surface and place the point of the triangle away from you. Put a generous tablespoon of the filling mixture about $\frac{1}{2}$ inch from the bottom edge of each rice paper wrapper. Fold the bottom of the wrapper up over the filling, enclosing the filling in a 2-inch log. Fold the sides in and smooth the rice paper over the filling snugly. Roll the wrapper very tightly, ending with the tip of the triangle. Continue making rolls with the remaining rice paper wrappers and filling.

6. In a large skillet, heat $\frac{1}{3}$ inch of oil over medium-high heat to 350 degrees on a deep-fry thermometer. Be sure the oil stays at this temperature. If it gets too hot, the spring rolls might burst. Fry about 10 rolls at a time until golden brown, about 5 minutes per side, turning once. Drain on paper towels and repeat with the remaining rolls. Serve hot or at room temperature with the Nuoc Cham and the Table Salad.

HERBED SUMMER ROLLS *(Goi Cuon)*

MAKES ABOUT 12 ROLLS

Loosely translated, *goi cuon* means salad in a rice wrapper. The word summer was appended when Vietnamese restaurants in America wanted to emphasize their use of the many fresh herbs in this roll, and, thus, gave it this lyrical name. As an accompaniment the bean sauce gives a different twist from the usual *Nuoc Cham*. When composing the rolls, vary the ingredients, making each unique from the last. Use whatever mild fresh herbs you can obtain, even if they're not listed here.

Rich Bean Sauce (page 54)
½ pound piece pork, from the loin or lean shoulder
6 ounces medium shrimp, peeled and deveined
24 triangle rice paper wrappers
12 mint sprigs
24 blades garlic chives
12 perillo or shiso leaves
12 diec-ca leaves
12 coriander sprigs
½ cup chopped peanuts

1. Prepare the Rich Bean Sauce and set aside.

2. In a small saucepan of boiling water, simmer the pork over medium heat until cooked through, about 15 minutes. Drain and set aside. When cool enough to handle, cut the pork into 12 thin slices.

3. To a small saucepan of boiling water, add the shrimp. When the water comes back to a boil, remove from the heat, drain the shrimp, and set aside.

4. With a pastry brush dipped in water, brush the rice paper wrappers on both sides and moisten them well. Put 2 triangles together and lay them on a work surface to soften. Repeat with the remaining wrappers. To assemble, put a piece of pork and 1 shrimp about ½ inch from the bottom edge of each rice paper wrapper (the long side opposite the point of the triangle). Put 2 garlic chives and a sprig of the other herbs on top and hold the bottom of the wrapper up over the filling. Fold each side in and roll up the rice paper tightly, pressing as you go.

5. To serve, pour the sauce into individual dipping bowls and sprinkle each roll generously with some of the chopped peanuts.

SILVER DOLLAR CAKES (Banh Can)

MAKES ABOUT 66, ENOUGH FOR ABOUT 10 APPETIZER SERVINGS

The batter for these cakes is so simple it is often made in Vietnam when a rainy day disrupts plans to walk to the market. The cakes are wonderfully addictive: crunchy on the bottom and creamy in the center.

$1\frac{1}{2}$ cups long-grain rice
$\frac{1}{2}$ cup dried split yellow mung beans
2 ounces dried shrimp (about $\frac{1}{2}$ cup)
Light Nuoc Cham Dipping Sauce (page 36)
$\frac{1}{2}$ cup vegetable oil plus oil for frying
6 large scallions, sliced crosswise (about $1\frac{1}{2}$ cups)
1 pound medium shrimp, peeled, deveined, and cut in half crosswise

1. The night before, put the rice and beans in a large bowl and cover with water by 1 inch. Let sit at room temperature at least 5 hours or overnight. Put the dried shrimp in a small bowl, cover with hot water, and soak a few hours or overnight.

2. Make the Light Nuoc Cham Dipping Sauce and set aside.

3. Rinse the rice and beans 3 or 4 times, until the water runs clear, and drain well. Add 2 cups of water to the rice mixture. Process the mixture in a blender, in 2-cup batches, with water in each batch, and blend on high speed, until thick and smooth, about 1 minute. There should be just a trace of very tiny rice particles in the batter and it should have the consistency of heavy cream. Set aside.

4. Drain the dried shrimp and in a food processor process to a coarse paste. Or chop very fine with a knife. Pass the mixture through a coarse sieve; the shrimp paste should become fluffy and loose. Set aside.

5. In a small saucepan, heat the $\frac{1}{2}$ cup oil over high heat until almost smoking. Add the scallions, remove from the heat, and set aside.

6. Put the cast-iron Munk's or aebleskiver pan (page 3) on high heat for about 1 minute. As in making regular pancakes, make a trial batch first (without using the fresh shrimp) to practice the cooking method and get the heat right under the pan. Dip a paper towel into a small bowl of oil and generously grease each hole. Reduce the heat to medium high. Pour about 1 tablespoon of batter into each hole and cover with the lid. Wait about 3 minutes and remove the lid. Using a small spoon, remove each cake to paper towels to drain. Now begin to make the cakes using the fresh shrimp. Add about $\frac{1}{2}$ teaspoon oil to each hole again and pour a tablespoon of batter in. Put a half shrimp on each cake, cover, and cook until golden brown and crusty on the bottom, about 3 minutes. Remove the cakes and drain on paper towels. Adjust the heat if the cakes are burning on the bottom. Repeat until the batter and the shrimp are used up.

7. When all the cakes are cooked, spoon a generous amount, about $\frac{1}{8}$ inch, of the dipping sauce onto individual plates. Put 6 or so cakes on each plate. Add a teaspoon of the scallions with a little of the oil on each cake and sprinkle each with about $\frac{1}{2}$ teaspoon of the dried shrimp. Serve hot, with a spoon, so you can scoop up plenty of fish sauce with each cake.

ROLLED VIETNAMESE DUMPLINGS
WITH FRIED SHALLOTS AND CUCUMBER *(Banh Cuon)*

MAKES ABOUT 25 DUMPLINGS, ABOUT 5 APPETIZER SERVINGS

This very popular dish is often eaten for breakfast or lunch in Vietnam and is made to order at the marketplace or in neighborhood restaurants. The Vietnamese use a sieve-like disk with fine cheesecloth stretched over it to form the dumpling wrappers. Loose batter is spread thinly over the cheesecloth. It is cooked briefly covered, and lo, a sheet of dough forms and is pulled off the cheesecloth with a chopstick. The round is spread flat on a surface, a filling is spooned on it, and a dumpling is quickly rolled, the stickiness of the dough sealing it instantly. Traditionally these are served with slices of Vietnamese pâté, but they are very good by themselves, served hot with garnishes of blanched bean sprouts, fried shallots, cool cucumber, and Light Nuoc Cham Dipping Sauce: a delight of tastes, textures, and temperatures. Binh and I have adapted the recipe in order to use a nonstick skillet instead of the cheesecloth-disk set-up. As each sheet of dumpling dough is cooked, the skillet is over-turned and banged onto an oiled surface so the tender, white "crepe" falls out flat. After rolling, you can stack the dumplings on top of each other. When cool, the dumplings, which look like hand-rolled cigars, can be separated and arranged on plates. Eat hot or at room temperature.

Light Nuoc Cham Dipping Sauce (page 41)
3 tablespoons Fried Shallots (page 62)

THE FILLING

2 tablespoons dried tree ears
2 tablespoons vegetable oil
1 small onion, finely chopped
1 pound ground pork
½ teaspoon salt
½ teaspoon freshly ground black pepper

FOR THE DUMPLINGS
$1/2$ cup cornstarch
$1/2$ cup tapioca flour
$1/2$ cup rice flour
$1/2$ teaspoon salt
2 teaspoons vegetable oil plus more for rubbing the skillet

$1/2$ cup blanched mung bean sprouts
1 cup thinly sliced cucumber
2 tablespoons chopped mint

1. Prepare the Light Nuoc Cham Dipping Sauce and Fried Shallots. Set them aside.

2. Make the filling: In a small bowl cover the tree ears with very hot water and set aside until softened and inflated, about 3 minutes. Drain, cut off any hard knobs, and chop coarse.

3. In a large skillet, heat the oil over high heat. Add the onion and cook until wilted, 2 minutes. Add the pork and cook, stirring often, until cooked through, about 5 minutes. Stir in the tree ears and season with the salt and pepper. Set the filling aside.

4. Make the dumplings: In a medium bowl, combine the cornstarch, tapioca, and rice flours, and the salt. Whisk in 3 cups water and the oil. Combine well to thoroughly incorporate the flours.

5. Set an 8-inch skillet over medium-high heat and with an oil-soaked paper towel, rub its surface generously with the oil. When hot, pour in about 3 tablespoons of the dumpling batter and tilt the pan slowly to distribute it evenly. Let the batter cook a few seconds, then tilt the pan again to redistribute the batter and set it. Cover and cook about 30 seconds. Have ready a lightly oiled work surface, plastic cutting board, or counter. Uncover and bang out the "crepe." The first try, as with pancakes, may not be quite right, so try again. As soon as the sheet of dough comes out of the skillet, let it cool enough to handle. Then put 1 tablespoon of the pork filling in the center and pull one

(continued)

(continued)

side of the dough up and over it. Roll it up. Put the dumpling on a large plate. Continue to make dumplings with the remaining batter and filling.

6. To serve, put about 5 or 6 *banh cuon* on each plate (or arrange all of them on a large platter) and scatter the bean sprouts, cucumber slices, shallots, and fried mint over the top. Drizzle generously with the dipping sauce. Eat with a knife and fork.

SUGGESTIONS: You can make good but thinner-skinned dumplings using prepared won ton wrappers or *gyoza* skins, available in Asian markets usually in the freezer section. Fill as you would ravioli and boil gently in water until cooked through.

LEMON CHICKEN *(Ga Nuong Chanh)*

MAKES 4 APPETIZER SERVINGS

This is a popular appetizer at Truc Orient Express. Binh adds his own distinctive touch of lemon zest. Though not authentic, it is a perfectly good aromatic to use in any of the recipes calling for lime or lemongrass flavoring.

2 scallions, thinly sliced
Grated zest of 1 lemon (1 heaping teaspoon)
3 cloves garlic, minced
$\frac{1}{2}$ teaspoon freshly ground black pepper
1 tablespoon sugar
1 tablespoon plus 1 teaspoon bottled fish sauce (nuoc mam)
2 tablespoons vegetable oil
1 pound boneless skinless chicken breast, sliced crosswise on the diagonal into wide strips
$\frac{1}{2}$ recipe Nuoc Cham Dipping Sauce (page 36)
Table Salad for 4 (page 32)

1. In a medium bowl, combine all the ingredients and mix well. Marinate at room temperature for 2 hours or covered in the refrigerator overnight.

2. Prepare the Nuoc Cham Dipping Sauce and the Table Salad and set aside.

3. Preheat the broiler or grill. Thread the chicken onto 8 bamboo skewers. Broil the chicken 5 inches from the heat or over a hot fire until golden brown, about 4 minutes per side. Put the skewers on a platter and serve with the salad.

HUE DUMPLING FLOWERS *(Banh Bot Loc)*

MAKES ABOUT 28 DUMPLINGS

These translucent, white dumplings have a filling with a reddish hue signifying a flower. The Vietnamese use red food coloring. Here we've substituted annatto seeds, readily found in Asian and Latin markets. The dough is cooked first, then little pieces are pulled off and stretched into thin circles and filled. The dumplings can be wrapped in several different ways in the banana leaves that are called for. You will find they have a chewy, interesting texture.

THE FILLING
1 tablespoon vegetable oil
2 teaspoons annatto seeds
2 cloves garlic, minced
½ pound lean pork, cut into small cubes
½ pound shrimp, peeled, deveined, and cut crosswise into thirds
2 large scallions, white and green separately sliced
¾ teaspoon freshly ground black pepper
1½ tablespoons bottled fish sauce (nuoc nam)
1 tablespoon sugar

THE DOUGH
2 cups tapioca flour
1 teaspoon salt
2 cups water
1 tablespoon vegetable oil
1 package fresh or frozen banana leaves, thawed, torn into about 5-inch squares
Fish sauce for dipping
Small red chiles, chopped
Lime wedges

1. Make the filling: In a medium skillet heat the oil over high heat. Add the annatto seeds and cook, shaking the pan until the oil turns deep red, about 30 seconds. With a spoon, remove the seeds and discard. Still over high heat, add the garlic, pork, and shrimp and stir-fry for 1 minute. Stir in the white of the scallions, the pepper, fish sauce, and sugar and cook, stirring occasionally, until the liquid has been reduced to a thick glaze, about 3 minutes. Stir in the green of the scallions and set aside to cool.

2. Make the dough: In a large bowl, combine the tapioca flour and the salt. With a fork, stir in the water. In a large skillet, heat the oil over medium heat. Add the batter and cook, stirring with a whisk. The batter will start to form small lumps and as it cooks will form larger lumps. After about 2 minutes, it will start to mass together into a large ball. Now, with a chopstick in each hand, start stirring, cutting through the dough in opposite directions, to keep it flat. Turn it over a few times, until the white streaks disappear and it is translucent throughout, about 2 minutes. Put the dough in a bowl, cover with a damp paper towel, and set aside, until cool enough to handle.

3. With oiled hands, pull off about a tablespoon of the dough and flatten it into a small circle. Then, pull and stretch the dough into a 3-inch circle. Put about 2 teaspoons of the filling in the center and press the sides in to make a ball. Repeat with the remaining dough and filling.

4. Put 1 dumpling in the center of each banana leaf square and enclose it, making a package. Tie it with a cut-off ribbon of leaf. Or, fold the banana leaf into a triangle, then into a smaller triangle. Open the triangle where a pocket forms and drop the dumpling in. Fold in the bottom and sit it upright, it should look like a little pyramid. Repeat this procedure until all the leaves are filled. Steam the dumplings, folded side down, on a rack in a large steamer for 8 minutes.

5. Have ready on the table a small saucer for each diner. Pass the fish sauce, chiles, and lime wedges separately so that each person can create his own dipping sauce.

STUFFED CHICKEN WINGS *(Canh Ga Don Thit)*

MAKES 6 APPETIZER SERVINGS

If you have never deboned a chicken wing, don't feel daunted. It's easy to do and just takes three or four tries to get the feel of it. It is the middle section, or double-boned part of the wing, that is boned and stuffed. The single-boned drumstick is cut off and should be put to another use. Because the wing is covered with skin and stuffed with a very lean, pure breast-meat filling, the wings absorb very little oil when deep fried. You can debone chicken wings far in advance and freeze them to stuff and serve later, saving a great deal of preparation time. This is a mild but very crunchy and enjoyable appetizer that benefits from the Nuoc Cham Dipping Sauce. Or try Ginger Sauce (page 40) instead.

Nuoc Cham Dipping Sauce (page 36)
2 pounds chicken wings (about 12)
1 pound skinless boneless chicken breasts, thinly sliced crosswise
$1/2$ teaspoon freshly ground black pepper
2 teaspoons cornstarch
$1/2$ teaspoon baking powder
$1/4$ teaspoon sugar
1 tablespoon bottled fish sauce (nuoc mam)
$1 1/2$ teaspoons vegetable oil plus more for deep frying
1 large scallion, thinly sliced
$1/4$ pound white mushrooms, finely chopped

1. Prepare the Nuoc Cham Dipping Sauce and set aside.

2. Cut off the single bone "drumstick" joint of the wing and reserve for another use. On the double-boned section of the wing with a sharp, small knife, scrape around the exposed joint of the wing to loosen the meat. Holding the wing firmly with one hand, close your other hand around the joint of the wing where you have just loosened the meat.

With a squeeze, press and push the skin and meat down the double bone until you reach the small wing tip. Snap the double bones off at this joint. You should have a wing tip with a pocket of skin attached, ready to be filled.

3. In a medium bowl, combine the chicken breast slices, pepper, cornstarch, baking powder, sugar, fish sauce, and the 1½ teaspoons oil. Cover and chill in the freezer until very firm, about 20 minutes.

4. In a food processor, purée the chilled chicken breast mixture, scraping down the sides of the bowl a few times, until very smooth, about 1 minute. Return to the bowl and stir in the scallion and mushrooms.

5. With oiled hands, hold a boned wing in one hand and push the stuffing into the pocket, packing it in firmly and stuffing it generously. Repeat, using all the filling and wings. The wings should be slightly overstuffed.

6. Put half of the wings into a large saucepan set over high heat. Add enough oil to cover. Don't worry, the wings won't absorb oil. Cook, stirring occasionally, until golden brown and crisp, about 20 minutes. Remove the wings with tongs and drain on paper towels. Keep warm in a low oven, if you like, while frying the rest. Reduce the heat to medium, add the remaining wings, and cook until browned and crisp, about 15 minutes. Serve hot with the Nuoc Cham on the side.

NINH HOA GRILLED MEATBALLS *(Nem Nuong Ninh Hoa)*

MAKES 4 TO 6 APPETIZER SERVINGS

This is popular street food, prepared at home only on special occasions. Similar to Thu Duc, a meatball dish from Saigon, these meatballs originate from the town, Ninh Hoa, outside Binh's hometown of Nha Trang. The corn- and potato starches give the meat a puffy, crunchy texture, especially if the balls are cooked over charcoal. The sauce is meant to be served generously, in individual bowls; the meatballs are first wrapped using the Table Salad and dipped into the sauce, while any remaining sauce is eaten with a spoon.

1 pound ground pork
$\frac{1}{2}$ teaspoon freshly ground black pepper
5 cloves garlic, minced
$1\frac{1}{2}$ tablespoons sugar
1 teaspoon cornstarch
$1\frac{1}{2}$ teaspoons potato starch
1 tablespoon bottled fish sauce (nuoc mam)
Shrimp and Peanut Sauce (page 44)
Table Salad for 4 to 6 (page 32; try to include Chinese flat chives or garlic chives
    as they are the traditional accompaniment)

1. In a medium bowl, mix together the pork, pepper, garlic, sugar, starches, and fish sauce. Marinate, covered, in the refrigerator at least 2 hours or overnight.

2. Meanwhile, prepare the Shrimp and Peanut Sauce and the Table Salad and set aside.

3. Preheat a grill or the broiler. With oiled hands, make 21 meatballs, each about 1 inch in diameter. Form 3 of them around 7 bamboo skewers. (The mixture may be a bit loose.) Grill over a medium-high flame, turning the meatballs, until they are deep brown and crisp on all sides, about 3 minutes per side.

4. Gently reheat the Shrimp and Peanut Sauce and serve the meatballs hot with the Table Salad. Dip the rolls into the warm sauce and eat any remaining sauce with a spoon.

LEMONGRASS SPARERIBS *(Xuong Nuong Xa)*

MAKES 4 TO 6 APPETIZER SERVINGS

Cooking spareribs couldn't be simpler or faster than it is with this method. The ribs can also be grilled.

1 2½-pound rack of spareribs
8 cloves garlic, smashed
2 shallots, chopped
1 teaspoon freshly ground black pepper
1 teaspoon salt
3 tablespoons sugar
2 tablespoons fish sauce
1 tablespoon dry white wine or Spiced Wine (page 57)
1 teaspoon powdered dried lemongrass
1 tablespoon vegetable oil

1. Starting on one end, pull off the thin membrane that covers the bones and the flap of meat on the underside of the ribs. Use a knife to help loosen any stubborn spots. Then trim as much fat as you can from the ribs and cut down between the bones to separate them.

2. In a mortar, pound together the garlic, shallots, pepper, and salt. Stir in the sugar, fish sauce, wine, lemongrass, and oil.

3. Arrange the ribs in single layer in a large shallow dish. Pour the marinade over them and coat them well. Marinade at room temperature for at least 3 hours or, covered, in the refrigerator overnight.

4. Preheat the oven to 500 degrees. Put the ribs on a large baking pan and roast on the top shelf until crusty and dark, about 30 minutes. Serve hot or at room temperature.

TOMATO-GLAZED SPARERIBS *(Suon Nuong)*

MAKES 4 APPETIZER SERVINGS

Creating the sauce for these spareribs involves a Vietnamese technique of frying tomato paste in oil, which makes it very glossy and gives it a richer flavor that, in turn, makes for a better glaze.

1 2½-pound slab of spareribs
2 shallots, thinly sliced
2 tablespoons sugar
2 large cloves garlic, crushed
½ teaspoon freshly ground black pepper
2 tablespoons fish sauce
2 tablespoons vegetable oil
1½ tablespoons tomato paste

1. Remove the membrane and separate and trim the ribs as described on page 154.

2. In a mortar, combine the shallots and sugar and pound to a paste. Add the garlic and pound again to a paste. Add the pepper and fish sauce and pour the sauce over the ribs, mixing with your hands to distribute it.

3. In a small skillet over medium-high heat, heat the oil and add the tomato paste. Cook, stirring, for 1 minute. Remove from the heat and let cool slightly. Pour over the ribs, cover, and marinate at least 6 hours at room temperature or overnight in the refrigerator.

4. Preheat the grill or oven to 500 degrees. Grill the ribs over a medium flame until cooked through and crisp, turning occasionally, about 25 minutes. Or, put the ribs on a baking pan and bake until crispy, about 25 minutes. Serve hot or at room temperature.

SWEET AND SOUR BABY BACK RIBLETS *(Suon Chua Ngot)*

MAKES 4 TO 6 APPETIZER SERVINGS

These are small, battered, and fried pieces of spareribs. If you don't have a meat cleaver, have the butcher saw through the bones with an electric meat saw and when you get home you can then cut through the meat to make riblets. These are unusually good, particularly with the Sweet and Sour Sauce and its pieces of cauliflower. Binh re-created this appetizer after first trying it near the coast of Nha Trang.

Sweet and Sour Sauce (page 53)
2½ pounds baby back ribs
3 cloves garlic, minced
1 teaspoon freshly ground black pepper
1½ tablespoons fish sauce
1½ tablespoons vegetable oil plus more for deep frying
1 cup flour
Pinch salt
1⅓ cups beer

1. Prepare the Sweet and Sour Sauce and set aside.

2. Remove the membrane and separate and trim the ribs as described on page 154. With a meat cleaver or heavy knife, cut each rib in half crosswise.

3. In a large bowl, combine the garlic, pepper, and fish sauce. Add the riblets and toss to coat well. Marinate at least 1 hour at room temperature or overnight in the refrigerator.

4. In a wok over high heat, heat the oil until hot, add the riblets, and stir-fry until deep brown, about 5 minutes. Remove to paper towels to drain and let cool. Wipe the wok clean.

5. In a large bowl, combine the flour and salt. Whisk in the beer until well blended. Set the batter aside.

6. Add enough oil to the wok to reach 3 inches up the sides and heat over medium heat to 350 degrees on a deep-fry thermometer. Using tongs or chopsticks, dip a riblet into the batter and coat it evenly. Drop into the hot oil. Continue to batter enough ribs to fill the wok without crowding it. Fry the ribs until golden brown, about 6 minutes. Adjust the heat if they start to brown too quickly. Drain on paper towels and serve hot with the Sweet and Sour Sauce. The ribs can be prepared a day ahead and reheated in a moderate oven.

BEEF GRILLED IN LA-LOT LEAVES *(Bo Goi La-Lot)*

MAKES 4 TO 6 APPETIZER OR 2 TO 3 MAIN-COURSE SERVINGS

These are great served on a large platter with Ginger-Spiced Cucumber as a crunchy vegetable garnish for a grand first course. If you can't find *la-lot* leaves you can use *perilla* or *shiso* leaves or jarred grape leaves that have been rinsed and dried well. As a main course accompany this with rice.

$\frac{1}{2}$ *pound eye of beef round, cut against the grain into 30 very thin slices (see* NOTE*)*
1 teaspoon powdered lemongrass
4 cloves garlic, minced
2 tablespoons sugar
2 tablespoons soy sauce
2 teaspoons medium dry sherry
$\frac{1}{2}$ *teaspoon vegetable oil*
$\frac{1}{4}$ *teaspoon sesame oil*
$\frac{1}{4}$ *teaspoon freshly ground black pepper*
30 la-lot, *perilla, or grape leaves*
6 8-inch bamboo skewers

1. In a medium bowl, combine the beef with all the ingredients, except the leaves. Mix well, and marinate at room temperature for 2 hours or, covered, in the refrigerator overnight.

2. Wrap each piece of beef by placing it on 1 large leaf or 2 smaller ones and folding the top and bottom up to cover, leaving the sides open. Thread 5 beef bundles onto each bamboo skewer.

3. Preheat the broiler or light the grill. Broil or grill the skewers about 5 inches from the heat until the leaves are crisp and brown on one side, about 3 minutes. Turn and cook until lightly browned all over, another 3 minutes. Serve hot.

NOTE: You may want to ask your butcher to slice the beef for you for best results.

Salads

The farther south you go in Vietnam, the more tropical the scenery and the more numerous and varied are the salad-type dishes, or *goi*, you encounter. In this land of very fertile soil and a growing season that can yield two or three harvests, the Vietnamese waste not one foot of land. If a family has a small yard or just a few feet of land, you can be sure there will be a patch of scallions and herbs, some tomato plants, or perhaps chiles and cucumbers growing. On the outskirts of rice fields and on plantations grow many of the crops that will become part of *goi*. Extra large, green papayas bulge out precariously from the skinny trunks of their trees. The size of them makes it possible to cut long strands of their flesh for salad and in this form they are perfect for eating with chopsticks. The pink flower bud of the banana tree is appreciated as a vegetable and cut into tender shreds for salad. The *pumelo*, a type of grapefruit, but drier and denser in texture, with a flowery scent, is combined with sliced cabbage and chicken, making a very popular *goi*. And water spinach, soaked in cold water until it curls, then tossed with dressing, may be served with soup in the morning. *Goi* is a decidedly special preparation, made as a small meal in itself, during the lull between lunch and dinner and as part of a large banquet for weddings and holidays.

Vietnamese salads can be a challenge to make since they are a layered composition. Never contrived, but composed of various fruits, vegetables, meats, seafood, and other savory foods, which have been chosen for their different but compatible characters, the ingredients make a fascinating mesh of textures and flavors. The sauces that dress them (some are dipping sauces) are not meant to overwhelm, but to enliven. You may want an extra pair of hands on hand to help you the first time you make *goi*.

Cabbages, carrots, celery, and cucumber often are the staple salad vegetables. The cook may begin with one of them, then layer fruit, pork, shrimp, or strips of fried eggs, and tofu on top. A sprinkling of peanuts and chiles, a generous dose of chopped herbs, or some sesame seeds provide yet more enlivenment. Meats and seafood could also be the main ingredient, but would be expensive to buy, probably better reserved for a grand occasion.

The Vietnamese pay respectful attention to vegetables, whether it is the way they are cut, or whether they are marinated or fried. Though the Vietnamese consume many of their vegetables raw, they like to tenderize the tougher ones. Strips of cabbage, carrot, celery, and cucumber are first soaked in vinegar, salt, and sugar to soften and perk up and neutralize their natural bitterness, making them more digestible. To obtain these long strips that make the salads different and fun to eat, the Vietnamese use a grating sheet, often sold here attached to a plastic box in a set that includes an assortment of snap-in blades for slicing and grating (Graters, page 4).

When we visited Binh's mother and sisters in Nha Trang, they made a large feast for us and Binh prepared a salad just for me. Surprisingly, it was a lettuce and tomato salad with a creamy ranch-type dressing, very good, though not really Vietnamese. Perhaps it was a gesture from a gracious host to a weary Westerner who had made the long trip to his home. What follows are a variety of traditional *goi* and some of Binh's own ideas and inspirations for salads.

GREEN PAPAYA SALAD *(Goi Du Du)*

MAKES 8 SERVINGS

Of the many types of papaya grown, the Vietnamese like to use the very large green variety in its unripe state as a salad vegetable—it is mild tasting and has a wonderful crunch. This salad is especially good with Shrimp Chips (page 67).

Sour Lime Sauce (page 52)
$1\frac{1}{2}$ pounds green papaya, split, seeded, peeled, and cut into long, thin strips
$\frac{3}{4}$ pound lean shoulder or loin of pork
$\frac{1}{2}$ pound medium shrimp, peeled and deveined
2 tablespoons chopped coriander
2 tablespoons chopped peanuts
2 tablespoons chopped rau ram, *optional*
Sriracha chile sauce

1. Prepare the Sour Lime Sauce and set aside.

2. In a large bowl of ice water, soak the papaya to crisp it, about 10 minutes. Drain well.

3. In a medium saucepan of boiling water, simmer the pork over medium heat until cooked through, about 15 minutes. Drain and let cool slightly. Cut into long thin strips.

4. In a medium saucepan of boiling water, cook the shrimp over high heat for about a minute. Drain, cool, and cut in half lengthwise.

5. Put the papaya in a very large bowl. Add the pork, shrimp, and Sour Lime Sauce and toss. Put the salad on a large platter and sprinkle with the coriander and peanuts and optional *rau ram*. Pass the chile sauce separately at the table.

CORNISH HEN SALAD *(Ga Xe Phay)*

MAKES 4 FIRST-COURSE OR 2 LUNCH COURSES

This tart, fresh-tasting salad should be prepared, lightly chilled, and eaten the same day. The herb, *rau ram,* is a standard addition to chicken salad in Vietnam, but combined amounts of fresh coriander and mint are fine, too. The Vietnamese eat this with French bread.

1 1½-pound Rock Cornish hen
2½ teaspoons salt
1 small onion, thinly sliced
3 tablespoons fresh lime juice
½ teaspoon freshly ground black pepper
¼ cup chopped **rau ram** *or ¼ cup each chopped mint and coriander*

1. In a large saucepan, cover the hen with about 4 cups water, add 2 teaspoons of the salt, and bring to a boil over high heat. Reduce the heat to low, turn the hen breast side down, and simmer until cooked through, about 20 minutes. Remove the hen to a plate to cool. Strain and reserve the broth for another use.

2. Pull all the meat from the hen and cut into pieces. In a large bowl, combine the meat, onion, lime juice, remaining ½ teaspoon salt, pepper, and *rau ram.* Toss well. Chill, covered, in the refrigerator a few hours before serving.

SUGGESTIONS: Because there will be good chicken stock on hand, consider this salad as part of a meal that begins with a soup like Watercress-Shrimp Soup (page 90).

CLASSIC VIETNAMESE PORK AND SHRIMP SALAD
(Goi Tom Thit)

MAKES 6 TO 8 SERVINGS

This salad is found on nearly every restaurant menu in Vietnam. Here is a home-style version of it, generously layered with pork and shrimp, and served, as it should be, with shrimp chips.

1/2 cup Nuoc Cham Dipping Sauce (page 36)
Shrimp Chips as an accompaniment (page 67)
1/2 pound lean pork from the loin or shoulder, or fresh ham, trimmed of all fat
1/2 pound medium shrimp, peeled and deveined
1 large European (hothouse) cucumber, peeled, seeded, and cut into very thin 2-inch-long strips
2 teaspoons salt
6 tablespoons sugar
6 tablespoons white vinegar
3 celery ribs, peeled and cut into long thin strips
2 large carrots, peeled and cut into long thin strips
1 medium onion, halved and thinly sliced
1/3 cup chopped fresh coriander
3 tablespoons chopped fresh mint
1/2 cup chopped unsalted dry roasted peanuts

1. Prepare the Nuoc Cham Dipping Sauce and the Shrimp Chips and set aside.

2. Put the pork into a small saucepan with enough cold water to cover. Simmer over medium heat until cooked through, about 25 minutes. Drain, let cool slightly, and cut into thin 2-inch-long strips. Set aside.

3. In a medium saucepan of boiling water, cook the shrimp until just opaque throughout, 2 or 3 minutes. Drain, let cool slightly, and cut each shrimp in half lengthwise. Set aside.

4. Place the cucumber strips in a bowl and toss them with 1 teaspoon of the salt. Set aside for 5 minutes, then squeeze to remove excess moisture.

5. In a measuring cup, combine the remaining 1 teaspoon salt with the sugar and vinegar. Put the celery, carrots, and onion into 3 separate bowls and toss each vegetable with $\frac{1}{3}$ of the vinegar mixture. Let stand for 5 minutes. Remove the vegetables and squeeze dry. Put the vegetables in a large bowl and add the cucumber, pork, shrimp, $\frac{1}{4}$ cup of the coriander, and 2 tablespoons of the mint. Add the Nuoc Cham Dipping Sauce and toss well.

6. Spoon the salad onto a large platter. Sprinkle the top with the remaining coriander, mint, and the chopped peanuts. Scatter the Shrimp Chips around the salad and serve.

CHICKEN AND GRAPEFRUIT SALAD (Goi-Ga)

MAKES 6 TO 8 SERVINGS

Goi-ga is as well known in Vietnam as chicken salad is here in the United States. Most versions use poached chicken tossed with shredded cabbage, carrots, herbs and Nuoc Cham. Pink grapefruit blends exquisitely with the cabbage and tart dressing and is Binh's substitute for *pumelo*—the Vietnamese grapefruit equivalent. Toasted sesame seeds are scattered over the salad, providing yet another great taste and crunch.

Vegetarian Salad Dressing (page 296)
Nuoc Cham Dipping Sauce (page 36)
1 3-pound chicken
1 teaspoon salt
1/3 cup sesame seeds
1 large carrot, grated into thin, short strips, rinsed and squeezed dry
1/2 small head green cabbage, very finely shredded
1/4 head red cabbage, very finely shredded
1 medium onion, very thinly sliced
2 large pink grapefruits, skin and pith trimmed off, fruit sectioned
1/3 cup chopped mint
2 tablespoons chopped coriander or rau ram

1. Put the chicken in a large pot and cover with cold water. Bring to a boil over high heat. Reduce the heat to low, add the salt, and simmer until cooked through, about 50 minutes. Remove the chicken from the broth and let cool. Reserve the broth for another use. When the chicken is cool enough to handle, remove the skin and discard, then remove all the chicken meat and cut or tear into thin strips.

2. Meanwhile, prepare the Vegetarian Salad Dressing and the Nuoc Cham Dipping Sauce and set aside.

3. In a large skillet over medium heat, toast the sesame seeds, stirring often, until evenly golden brown, about 8 minutes. Empty onto a plate and set aside.

4. In a large bowl, combine the carrot, cabbages, and onion. Pour the Vegetarian Dressing over the salad and set aside to soften about 10 minutes. Drain off most of the dressing and add the Nuoc Cham Dipping Sauce. Add the chicken and grapefruit sections. Put the salad onto a large platter and scatter the sesame seeds over all. Sprinkle on the mint and coriander. The salad will stay fresh for a few hours, but should not be kept overnight.

SUGGESTIONS: Serve this as part of a meal that includes a chicken stock–based soup such as Watercress-Shrimp Soup (page 90), or La-Lot Beef Soup (page 100), or Garlic Chive and Tofu Soup (page 91). Poach the chicken and remove the meat, reserving the broth, the day before. Make the dressing and the Nuoc Cham that day as well. This also makes a perfect main-course salad for hot days.

VEGETABLE SALAD WITH PORK, SHRIMP, AND EGG STRIPS
(Goi Nam Trang)

MAKES 6 SERVINGS

This salad has a wide range of ingredients, each contributing its own unique texture and flavor. The result is fantastically good. The first time you make it get a friend to help.

$\frac{1}{2}$ *ounce dried white fungus (about $\frac{1}{4}$ cup)*
4 ounces lean shoulder or loin of pork
6 ounces medium shrimp, peeled and deveined
1 medium carrot, cut into long, thin strips
1$\frac{1}{2}$ teaspoons salt
$\frac{1}{2}$ *pound daikon, cut into long, thin strips*
1 hothouse cucumber, split, seeded, and cut into long, thin strips
2 stalks celery, peeled and cut into long, thin strips
1 tablespoon plus $\frac{1}{2}$ teaspoon sugar
3 cloves garlic, crushed
1 small red chile, chopped
$\frac{1}{2}$ *large lime*
1$\frac{1}{2}$ tablespoons bottled fish sauce (nuoc mam)
1 teaspoon vegetable oil
2 eggs
3 tablespoons chopped rau ram *and/or 3 tablespoons chopped coriander*
3 tablespoons chopped peanuts

1. In a small bowl, cover the dried white fungus with hot water and soak until softened and inflated, about 5 minutes. Drain and rinse well. Cut off any hard knobs and chop the fungus coarse. Put it in a large bowl.

2. In a medium saucepan of boiling, salted water, cook the pork over medium heat until cooked through, about 20 minutes. Remove the pork from the water and add the shrimp. Cook the shrimp about 1 minute, then drain. Cut the pork into long, thin strips and cut each shrimp into 3 pieces. Set aside to cool.

3. Put the carrot in a colander or strainer and sprinkle with $\frac{1}{2}$ teaspoon of the salt. With your hands, toss and squeeze the carrot for about 1 minute to exude moisture. Rinse with fresh water, squeeze dry, and put in a large bowl. Repeat this procedure with the daikon, cucumber, and celery together, using the $\frac{1}{2}$ teaspoon sugar instead of the salt.

4. In a mortar, pound the garlic and chile to a coarse paste. Add the remaining tablespoon of sugar and pound again. Squeeze the juice of the half lime and stir in with the fish sauce. Set aside to develop flavor about 5 minutes.

5. In a small well-seasoned or nonstick skillet, heat $\frac{1}{2}$ teaspoon of the oil over high heat. Beat 1 of the eggs lightly and pour it into the pan. Cook through, about 20 seconds to form a flat egg cake. Turn out onto a plate and repeat with the remaining egg and oil. Let cool, then cut the egg sheets into long, thin strips. Add the egg strips to the salad with the garlic-chile mixture and the *rau ram* and/or coriander and toss well. To serve, put the salad on a large platter and sprinkle the peanuts over the top.

SPAGHETTI SQUASH SALAD *(Goi Spaghetti Squash)*

MAKES 4 SERVINGS

Binh discovered this vegetable one day when he was out shopping for large green papaya. He decided to try preparing the squash Vietnamese style, and the dish he created—a salad—turned out wonderfully with a character all of its own. We decided to add the recipe to the book. By the way, the spaghetti squash is only partially cooked, which is why it remains crunchy and refreshing.

Nuoc Cham Dipping Sauce (page 36)
1 small spaghetti squash (about 2 pounds)
5 ounces pork loin
$1/4$ pound medium shrimp, shells on
$1/4$ teaspoon freshly ground black pepper
1 tablespoon sugar
$1^1/2$ tablespoons white vinegar
$1/4$ teaspoon salt
$1/2$ cup chopped rau ram *or $1/4$ cup each chopped coriander and mint*
2 tablespoons chopped peanuts
Sriracha Chile Sauce to serve on the side

1. Prepare the Nuoc Cham Dipping Sauce and set aside.

2. Trim both ends off the squash and with a large chef's knife, holding the squash upright, cut the skin off in a thin layer. Discard. Then cut the squash in half lengthwise.

3. In a large pot of boiling water, cook the squash until barely tender, about 6 minutes. Drain in a colander and run under cold water until cool enough to handle. With your hands, separate the squash into strands and set aside.

4. In a small saucepan of boiling water, cook the pork over high heat until cooked through, about 8 minutes. Remove the pork with a slotted spoon and add the shrimp. Bring the water back to a boil, then remove the shrimp. Shell, remove the vein, and cut the shrimp in half lengthwise. Cut the pork crosswise into thin slices. Stack the slices and cut crosswise again into thin sticks. Set aside.

5. In a small bowl, combine the pepper, sugar, vinegar, salt, and 2 tablespoons of water.

6. In a large bowl, mix together the squash and the vinegar mixture and set aside to soften for about 5 minutes. Drain well and add the pork, shrimp, *rau ram*, and the dipping sauce. Toss well. To serve, put equal amounts of the salad on 4 plates and top each with ½ tablespoon of the chopped peanuts. Pass the chile sauce at the table.

WATER SPINACH SALAD *(Rau Muong Tron)*

MAKES 6 TO 8 SIDE-DISH SERVINGS

Water spinach is commonly seen in Vietnam as a salad or raw vegetable addition to soups. It has a mild freshwater taste and can be quite stringy, which is why it is cut so fine. Water spinach is especially good as a side dish to something rich like Sweet and Sour Baby Back Riblets (page 156), or, on its own, with hot steamed rice.

1 large bunch water spinach (about 2 pounds)
1 teaspoon sugar
½ teaspoon salt
½ teaspoon freshly ground black pepper
2 teaspoons white vinegar
1 tablespoon vegetable oil
1 tablespoon water

1. Remove the leaves and small, tender stems from the water spinach and reserve for another use like Water Spinach Sauté (see page 000). Wash the stems well and with a swivel blade vegetable peeler cut the stems into thin strips. Begin at the base of the stem and push the peeler up the stem while you hold it firmly down on the work surface. Peel a long thin strip. Try making a few more strips from what's left of the stem, or just pull it apart lengthwise to make 2 more strips. Put the strips in a bowl of ice water and repeat with the remaining stems. Don't worry if they are not all very thin; the ice water will curl up even the thicker ones. Let the water spinach soak in the ice water for about 1 hour.

2. In a small bowl, make the salad dressing by combining the remaining ingredients. Drain the spinach well and dress it just before serving.

BANANA BLOSSOM SALAD (Goi Bap Chuoi)

MAKES 6 SERVINGS

Banana blossoms are pretty, pink, closed buds that look a bit like Belgian endive.

$1/4$ cup Nuoc Cham Dipping Sauce (page 36)
Shrimp Chips (page 67), optional
1 lime
1 banana blossom
1 whole boneless skinless chicken breast (about 6 ounces)
$1/4$ teaspoon salt
1 teaspoon sugar
2 tablespoons white vinegar
$1\,1/4$ cup chopped rau ram or coriander
$1/2$ cup chopped peanuts

1. Prepare the Nuoc Cham Dipping Sauce and Shrimp Chips and set aside.

2. In a large bowl of water, squeeze the juice from the lime. Slice the banana blossom crosswise very thinly until you reach the tough leaves and core at the end. Soak the slices about 5 minutes to avoid discoloration.

3. Meanwhile, in a small saucepan, cover the chicken breast with cold water and bring to a boil over high heat. Reduce the heat to medium, add the salt, and simmer until just cooked through, about 5 minutes. Drain and cool. Pull or cut the meat into thin shreds.

4. In a large bowl, combine the banana blossom and chicken with the sugar, vinegar, and $1/4$ cup water. Let stand to soften a bit, about 5 minutes.

5. Drain the salad and then toss it with the Nuoc Cham. Put the salad on a large platter and sprinkle the top with the rau ram and peanuts. Serve at once with the Shrimp Chips if you wish.

COOL AND SPICY BEAN SALAD *(Dau Tron)*

MAKES 4 SERVINGS

With thin slices of veal or pork, this tangy salad is best eaten the day it is made.

$1/2$ cup dried black beans
$2/3$ cup black-eyed peas, sometimes called white beans in Asian markets
6 cups chicken stock or water
1 $1/2$-pound piece lean veal or pork
1 small red chile, or to taste, minced
2 large shallots, thinly sliced
$1/4$ cup red wine vinegar
Pinch sugar
1 tablespoon vegetable oil or olive oil
Salt to taste
$1/4$ cup chopped coriander

1. Pick over the beans and remove any small pebbles. Rinse the beans and peas and put them in a large saucepan. Cover with the stock or water and bring to a boil over high heat. Boil for 3 minutes, cover, and remove the pan from the heat. Let stand for 1 hour. Uncover and simmer over medium-low heat until tender but still holding their shape, about $1/2$ hours. If necessary, put the pan over high heat and cook to evaporate any excess liquid, shaking the pan a few times. Remove from the heat and let stand to cool slightly.

2. In a small saucepan, bring lightly salted water to a boil over medium heat. Add the veal or pork and simmer until barely pink for the veal and cooked through for pork, 12 to 18 minutes. Remove the meat to a work surface and let cool for 10 minutes. Slice the meat crosswise into thin slices.

3. In a large bowl, combine the chile, shallots, vinegar, sugar, and oil. Stir in the cooked beans and sliced meat. Season with salt and let stand at room temperature for at least 1 hour before serving to develop the flavors. Just before serving, fold in the coriander. Eat at room temperature or slightly chilled.

SQUID SALAD WITH TAMARIND *(Goi Muc)*

MAKES 4 TO 6 SALAD SERVINGS

Light, cool, and gutsy, this salad is best if served lightly chilled the day it is made. You can also grill the squid, then toss it with the remaining ingredients making this a superior summer dish.

1 tablespoon tamarind pulp
3 tablespoons bottled fish sauce (nuoc mam)
3 tablespoons fresh lime juice
1 tablespoon sugar
6 cloves garlic, minced
1 medium onion, thinly sliced
3 to 4 fresh small chiles, minced
3 stalks lemongrass, smashed
$\frac{1}{2}$ teaspoon salt
$2\frac{1}{2}$ pounds cleaned squid, cut into 2-inch pieces
$\frac{1}{4}$ cup chopped mint
$\frac{1}{4}$ cup chopped coriander
$\frac{1}{2}$ cup chopped peanuts

1. In a small bowl, soak the tamarind pulp in 2 tablespoons hot water to dissolve for about 5 minutes. Push the tamarind through a small strainer to remove the seeds.

2. In a large bowl, combine the tamarind paste, fish sauce, lime juice, sugar, garlic, onion, and chiles. Set the dressing aside.

3. In a large saucepan of boiling water, cook the lemongrass with the salt for 3 minutes. Over high heat, add the squid and cook, stirring a few times until the squid just starts to curl and turn opaque, about 1 minute. Drain.

4. Add the hot squid to the dressing and toss well. Let cool to room temperature, stirring often. Add the mint and coriander and toss to combine. Let cool if desired. Divide the salad among plates and sprinkle the chopped peanuts over the servings.

GLAZED BEEF SALAD WITH ROASTED RICE POWDER *(Goi Bo)*

MAKES 6 SERVINGS

The meat in this beef salad will be very rare in the center, but when tossed with the tart dressing it will "cook" a bit more. The salad could also be served slightly chilled, or at room temperature with Shrimp Chips (page 67).

1 tablespoon Roasted Rice Powder (see page 60)
1 1¼-pound piece of lean beef, such as eye of round, cut in half lengthwise
10 small cloves garlic, minced
3 tablespoons oyster sauce
3 tablespoons vegetable oil
1 small fresh chile, minced
¼ cup chopped mint
3 tablespoons chopped coriander
1 small onion, thinly sliced
2½ tablespoons fresh lime juice
3 tablespoons chopped peanuts

1. Prepare the Roasted Rice Powder and set aside.

2. In a medium bowl, coat the beef with the garlic and oyster sauce and marinate at room temperature for 1 hour.

3. In a large skillet over medium-high heat, heat the oil until hot. Add the beef and cook until crusty on all sides, about 5 minutes. Remove to a plate to rest for about 10 minutes.

4. In a large bowl, combine the chile, mint, coriander, onion, and lime juice. Cut the beef crosswise into very thin slices. Add the beef to the lime dressing and toss to coat well.

5. To serve, arrange the beef on plates and sprinkle with equal amounts of the Roasted Rice Powder and peanuts.

Seafood

The people of Vietnam depend on seafood as a major source of protein. *Nuoc mam*, their fish sauce, a seasoning staple, is equally nutritious. Fortunately, Vietnam's entire eastern border, 1,400 miles of coastline, fronts the sea, providing an abundant source of its treasures. This tropical, monsoon country also has generous access to the Gulf of Tonkin to the north and the South China Sea to the south.

Its beaches are some of the most beautiful in the world. There are striking contrasts: the sea and mountains; the farmland and rice paddies and cactus-filled deserts. Rivers and lakes, like veins and arteries, form vital, intricate networks throughout the country. Two prominent rivers, the Red River in the north and the Mekong in the south, frame Vietnam, top and bottom. Surrounded on three sides by large bodies of water, the country has always had a strategic location and offers passage to much of the lower continent.

Although Vietnam is a coastal country, freshwater fish is an important part of the diet and an easily raised crop for inland communities as well as those near the coast. The Vietnamese learned the art of aquaculture from the Chinese but as with everything else they do, they have their own highly practical way of farming that utilizes the land to its utmost. They can cultivate their own small food chain even on the smallest piece of land. In the case of fish farming, ponds are dug, or in some instances, fashioned from bomb craters (permanent scars from the war), for raising carp, catfish, perch, frogs, and some species of crab and shrimp. Often, these ponds are in the form of canals that border rice paddies or other field crops and serve as irrigation ditches as well.

Preparations of freshwater fish are quite similar to saltwater fish dishes—steamed whole with vegetables, cut up for hot and sour fish soup, steamed crab, and stir-fried shrimp. Freshwater, or mud, crabs are best cracked and sizzled in hot oil with garlic, salt, and sugar; a sublime treatment for one of Vietnam's most delectable native foods.

The ocean's harvest is an open market and one will see children gathering their catch from seaworthy baskets alongside large wooden skows that can venture farther off shore. Outside of Ho Chi Minh City, in the seaside town of Vung Tau, under colorful umbrellas, one is attended by a group of women who carry burning charcoal cookers to steam and roast clams for you. Cold beer, peanuts, and banana fritters are also offered, making it hard to leave such a delicious, impromptu picnic. Binh and I watched women gather tiny, bean clams, sifting them by the handfuls from soft, wet sand. The clams looked like glossy, flat, pink-and-gray marbles, their size making them suitable for pickling and for use in a preparation similar to oyster sauce. Larger Venus-type clams as well as mild, soft-fleshed sea crabs, are steamed and dipped in salt, pepper, and lime juice. Small crabs, shrimp, and langoustines, all plentifully available, will be eaten whole, usually fried until crisp and crunchy.

Squid, as in other parts of Asia, is also abundant, relatively cheap, and therefore a staple, either fresh or in its longer-keeping state, dried. At the beaches, dried squid are strung across vendor's carts like little banners and are sold along with carved pineapples. Cut into strips, the meat is salty and chewy and much more flavorful than fresh squid. Lobsters are common: both the beautifully marked spiny type and the flat, wide slipper lobsters. There are fat saltwater eels and slender orange-bellied eels, sweet-tasting mantis shrimp that look like water bugs, stingrays, sharks, jellyfish, and seaweeds, enough to fill many books and a world in themselves.

Certain herbs and spices are commonly used in fish cookery. Powdered turmeric, for one is thought to keep fish fresh and prevent deterioration in the hot climate of Vietnam. In the market you'll see displays of cut fish coated with this bright yellow but mildly flavored spice. Ginger is considered to be a purifier and its spicy flavor is meant to enhance fish while freshening it. The Vietnamese herb, *ngo om*, has a sour bite to it and is always included in Hot and Sour Soup. One thing more, if ever you are presented with a whole fish, consider yourself honored. Whole fish steamed or fried, warrants a special occasion and the more ingredients it is cooked with the more expensive and special it becomes.

CARAMELIZED SHRIMP *(Tom Rim)*

MAKES 3 OR 4 SERVINGS

This garlicky stir-fry is generously seasoned with black pepper and chile oil or flakes; and the pan juices are enriched with caramel syrup, giving the sauce an appealing golden color.

1 teaspoon Caramel Syrup (page 42) or 1½ teaspoons sugar
1 teaspoon Sate-Chile Oil (page 58) or dried chile flakes
Half rice recipe (page 34)
1½ tablespoons vegetable oil
8 small cloves garlic, minced, or pounded to paste in a mortar
1 pound medium shrimp, peeled and deveined
½ teaspoon freshly ground black pepper
½ teaspoon salt
1 large scallion, finely chopped

1. Prepare the Caramel Syrup, Sate-Chile Oil, and rice and set aside.

2. In a wok or large skillet, heat the oil over medium-high heat. Add the garlic and stir-fry until golden, about 30 seconds. Add the shrimp and black pepper and stir-fry 1 minute. Add the salt and Caramel Syrup and cook 1 minute. Add the chile oil and cook 30 seconds. Sprinkle with the scallion and mix well. Serve hot with the rice.

CURRIED GRILLED JUMBO SHRIMP *(Tom Nuong Vi)*

MAKES 4 SERVINGS

Extra-large shrimp are gently loosened from their shells and a fiery curry-coriander paste is tucked in between. The shrimp are grilled, then pulled out of the roasted shells with their aromatics and eaten with lots of rice.

Half rice recipe (page 34)
1½ pounds jumbo shrimp
4 cloves garlic
2 small red chiles, chopped
2 teaspoons sugar
¾ teaspoon salt
½ cup finely chopped coriander
1 teaspoon curry paste or powder
1 tablespoon vegetable oil

1. Prepare the rice and set aside.

2. With scissors, snip the legs off the shrimp. Turn over and cut down the back where the vein is and remove it. Gently loosen the shell around the shrimp but keep it in place. Set aside.

3. In a mortar, pound the garlic and chiles to a coarse paste. Add the sugar and salt and pound to a finer paste. Stir in the coriander and curry and the oil.

4. Gently pull open the shell of each shrimp and, dividing the coriander paste evenly, push some of it down the back of the shrimp where the vein was and under the shell a bit. Close up the shell around the shrimp. Fill the remaining shrimp in the same manner. Marinate at room temperature at least 2 hours or, covered, in the refrigerator up to 4 hours.

5. Preheat a grill or broiler. Grill the shrimp over a medium-hot fire, until the shells are charred on one side and the shrimp is cooked halfway through, about 3 minutes. Turn and grill the other side. Serve at once.

SUGGESTIONS: As an accompaniment, pare stalks of broccoli into strips and cook them with the shrimp over the cooler areas of the grill.

SUMMER SEAFOOD SAUTÉ WITH VEGETABLES AND BASIL *(Hai San Bien Xao Rau)*

MAKES 4 SERVINGS

This fresh and lively sauté is known as a summer, or southern, dish—meaning that it is from the south of Vietnam. The combination is representative of the area, abundant with a variety of seafood and vegetables, all sparked with herbs and chiles.

Half rice recipe (page 34)
1 1½-pound lobster
2 teaspoons bottled fish sauce (nuoc mam)
2 cloves garlic, minced
½ teaspoon freshly ground black pepper
½ pound medium shrimp, peeled and deveined
½ pound sea scallops
6 dried shiitake mushrooms, soaked in hot water, covered, for 20 minutes
1 tablespoon vegetable oil
1 small red chile, thinly sliced
1 red bell pepper, sliced ¼ inch thick
½ pound asparagus, trimmed and cut on the diagonal into 2-inch pieces
5 baby corn or ½ cup fresh scraped corn
2 teaspoons oyster sauce
½ teaspoon cornstarch mixed with ½ teaspoon water, optional
½ cup chopped or sliced basil leaves

1. Prepare the rice and set aside.

2. Into a large pot of boiling water over high heat, plunge the lobster, head first, and boil for 8 minutes. With tongs, remove the lobster and set aside to cool slightly. Over a large bowl, crack off the shell of the lobster and remove the meat. Cut the tail in half lengthwise. Reserve the green tomalley if you wish. Strain ½ cup of the lobster cooking water and set aside.

3. In a medium bowl, combine the fish sauce, garlic, and black pepper. Add the shrimp and scallops and toss to coat well. Marinate about 10 minutes.

4. Drain and rinse the mushrooms and trim off the stems. Cut the mushrooms into quarters.

5. In a wok or large skillet over high heat, heat the oil until smoking. Add the shrimp and scallop mixture. Stir-fry until almost cooked through, about 2 minutes. Then remove them. Add the chile and cook about 10 seconds. Add the mushrooms and all the vegetables and stir-fry about 3 minutes. Stir in the reserved lobster cooking liquid, tomalley, if using, and the oyster sauce, and simmer until slightly reduced, about 3 minutes. And the cornstarch mixture, if using, and bring to a boil. Add all the seafood and cook just to heat through. Remove from the heat and turn out onto a large platter. Sprinkle with the basil and serve with the rice.

CRISPY RED SNAPPER
WITH SPICY TOMATO SAUCE *(Ca Chien)*

MAKES 2 SERVINGS

The skin on this snapper becomes hard and crusty by letting it sizzle, undisturbed, in hot oil for a good long time. A simple method, it's important to note that if you fiddle and poke the fish around in the pan, the skin curls up and you've disrupted the process of creating an even thick crust. The sauce is delectably tangy and hot, the perfect counterpoint to the snapper. Try cooking small sea or striped bass and porgy this way as well.

1 tablespoon vegetable oil plus more for frying
2 cloves garlic, minced
1 medium tomato. peeled, seeded, and chopped
1 to 2 small red chiles, minced, or ½ teaspoon dried chile flakes, or to taste
2 tablespoons sugar
2 tablespoons bottled fish sauce (nuoc mam)
2 tablespoons water
2 tablespoons chopped coriander
2 tablespoons chopped scallion green
1 whole red snapper (about 1 pound), cleaned, scaled, and gills removed

1. In a medium skillet over high heat, heat the oil until hot. Reduce the heat to medium-high and add the garlic. Cook, stirring, for 30 seconds. Add the tomato and chiles and cook for 1 minute. Add the sugar, fish sauce, and water and simmer, stirring occasionally, until thickened, about 3 minutes. Remove the sauce from the heat and set aside.

2. In a large skillet, heat about ½ inch of oil. Lay the snapper in carefully and cook over moderately high heat, without moving, until very brown and crusty, about 14 minutes. (You may want to use a screen to cover the skillet.) Turn the fish and cook the other side, about 10 minutes longer. Drain the snapper on paper towels. To serve, put the fish on a platter, pour the sauce over it, and using a large fork lift the meat with the skin from the bones. Turn the fish over and do the same. Serve with the steamed rice.

SUGGESTIONS: A simple dinner for two could begin with Vegetarian Summer Rolls (page 275) or Ninh Hoa Grilled Meatballs (page 152), both served with Table Salad (page 32). Or, start with Classic Vietnamese Pork and Shrimp Salad (page 164).

SEAFOOD WITH GINGER, TOMATO, AND CHILES (Cau Da)

MAKES 4 SERVINGS

Simple and elegant, the fresh-tasting tomato sauce that accompanies the seafood is made in a matter of minutes and is zesty with garlic, ginger, and chile. Reminiscent of the vibrant cooking of South Vietnam, this makes a striking presentation for a dinner party.

Half rice recipe (page 34)
2 tablespoons vegetable oil
6 cloves garlic, pounded in a mortar to a paste
1 1-inch piece ginger, peeled and very finely chopped
½ pound medium shrimp, peeled and deveined
½ pound sea scallops
8 ounces flounder or sole fillets, cut into 2-inch pieces
1 tablespoon sugar
¼ cup bottled fish sauce (nuoc mam)
½ to 1 teaspoon dried chile flakes, or to taste
1 large, ripe tomato, halved, seeded, and diced
2 large scallions, thinly sliced
¼ cup chopped coriander

1. Prepare the rice and set aside.

2. In a large skillet or wok over high heat, heat the oil. Add the garlic and ginger and stir-fry for 30 seconds. Add the shrimp, scallops, and flounder in an even layer and cook, turning once, until just done, about 2 minutes. Remove the seafood to a plate. Return the skillet or wok to the fire. Add the sugar, fish sauce, and chile flakes and boil until slightly thickened, about 2 minutes. Stir in the tomato and scallions and cook 1 minute. Gently return the seafood with any accumulated juices to the pan and cook until heated through, about 30 seconds. Transfer to a platter, sprinkle with the coriander, and serve with the rice.

TROUT STUFFED WITH
SHRIMP AND SCALLOPS *(Ca Hap Voi Tom So)*

MAKES 2 SERVINGS

Freshwater fish, such as perch and bass, are just as prominent in the Vietnamese diet as saltwater fish. Our own trout makes a fine substitute for the milder species found there. This dish is eye pleasing as well as delectable.

Creamy Coriander Sauce (page 47)
Half rice recipe (page 34)
$1/4$ pound medium shrimp, peeled and deveined
$1/4$ pound sea or bay scallops
2 scallions, finely chopped
$1/2$ teaspoon freshly ground black pepper
2 teaspoons bottled fish sauce (nuoc mam)
2 8-ounce whole trout, boned
Salt to taste
Sriracha Chile Sauce

1. Prepare the Creamy Coriander Sauce and the rice and set aside.

2. In a mortar, pound the shrimp and scallops to a coarse paste. Or chop them fine. Blend in the scallions, pepper, and fish sauce.

3. Season the inside of the trout with salt. Divide the filling in half and stuff each trout generously.

4. Put the trout on a large plate that fits on the rack of a steamer or in a large saucepan with 2 inches of water. Bring the water to a boil and add the trout. Cover and steam for 10 minutes.

5. Remove the trout to dinner plates and drizzle a small amount of the chile sauce over them. Serve with the Creamy Coriander Sauce and the rice.

STUFFED SQUID *(Muc Don)*

MAKES 4 TO 6 SERVINGS

This dish is delicious just by itself, with rice to soak up the sauce. For more impact, serve it with Coriander-Chile Sauce.

Coriander-Chile Sauce (page 46), optional
1 ounce cellophane noodles
1½ tablespoons dried tree ears
6 medium whole squid with tentacles (about 2 pounds)
1 small onion, finely chopped
1½ teaspoons freshly ground black pepper
2 tablespoons bottled fish sauce (nuoc mam)
¼ cup vegetable oil
2 small tomatoes, cut into thin wedges
3 large scallions, green only, cut into 2-inch lengths

1. If desired, prepare the Coriander-Chile Sauce and set aside.

2. In a small bowl, soak the noodles in cold water until pliable, about 5 minutes. Drain and cut into 2-inch lengths. Set aside.

3. In a small bowl, soak the tree ears in hot water until softened, about 2 minutes. Drain, rinse, cut off the hard knobs, and chop coarse. Set aside.

4. Remove the tentacles and little side "wings" from the squid. Finely chop the tentacles and wings and set aside in a large bowl. Remove and discard the long piece of cartilage and the ink sacs if still there. Rinse the squid well under cold running water. Make a small incision just below the closed end of the squid (This prevents the stuffed squid from inflating during cooking.)

5. To the bowl of chopped tentacles and wings, add the cellophane noodles, tree ears, onion, pepper, and 1 tablespoon plus 1 teaspoon of the fish sauce. Mix well. Stuff each squid with an equal amount of filling. Be sure to leave a small space at the point and don't overstuff.

6. In a large skillet over medium-high heat, heat the oil until hot. Add the squid. Put a spatter screen over the skillet or partially cover with a lid and fry until golden brown, about 5 minutes per side. Don't worry if some of the filling spills out; it will become part of the sauce.

7. Pour off as much of the oil as possible from the skillet. Add the tomatoes and remaining 2 teaspoons of fish sauce and simmer, stirring a few times, for about 2 minutes. Remove from the heat and add the scallion greens. Serve hot with rice and the Coriander-Chile Sauce, if you like.

CORAL LOBSTER *(Tom Hum Vung Tau)*

MAKES 4 SERVINGS

Many kinds of lobsters are found in the waters off the coast of Vietnam except, of course, the North American cold water lobster. Here is Binh's favorite way of preparing it, cracked and simmered in a hot, tomato sauce. This delectable dish uses the tomalley found in the upper body of the lobster. An optional ingredient, the sauce will taste good, just not as rich, without it.

Half rice recipe (page 34)
4 1½-pound lobsters
¼ cup vegetable oil
6 cloves garlic, minced
1 medium onion, chopped
⅓ cup tomato paste
1½ teaspoons dried chile flakes
1 teaspoon freshly ground black pepper
2 tablespoons sugar
2½ tablespoons bottled fish sauce (nuoc mam)
½ cup chicken stock or water

1. Prepare the rice and set aside.

2. Using a large chef's knife, insert the point just behind the eyes of the lobster and cut all the way down between them. Now take the knife and facing the other direction, down the rest of the body, split the lobster in two through the tail. Remove the tomalley from the lobster and reserve. Remove the claws with the knuckles attached and with the back of the chef's knife, crack them lightly all over on both sides. Pull the tail halves from the body section. Discard the body.

3. In a wok over high heat, heat the oil until it starts to smoke. Add the lobster pieces and stir-fry until bright red and almost cooked through, about 5 minutes. Remove the lobster to a plate.

4. Add the garlic to the wok and stir-fry for about 10 seconds. Add the onion and stir-fry about 1 minute. Add the reserved tomalley, tomato paste, chile flakes, black pepper, sugar, fish sauce, and stock. Reduce the heat to medium-high and cook, stirring, until the sauce is fragrant and thickened, about 5 minutes. Add the lobster pieces and simmer another minute to let the sauce penetrate the lobster meat. Serve with the rice.

LOBSTER, SCALLOPS, AND SHRIMP WITH ORANGE AND CHILE *(Hai San Nau Cam)*

MAKES 4 SERVINGS

Having trained with French chefs, Binh admires the style and elegance of classical French cooking. He found the cuisine too heavy for his stomach, however, which is not accustomed to the rich ingredients. But when he wants to create a special dish, he will prepare it with that French sophistication in mind. For this fancy dish, he lightened the cream sauce with a smart touch of chile and orange. You can season the dish at the end with salt and pepper if you wish, but you will notice that Binh marinates the shrimp and scallops first so that by the time the dish is finished, this seasoning should be well dispersed and properly balanced. Serve this with steamed asparagus if you wish.

Half rice recipe (page 34)
1 orange
10 ounces large shrimp, peeled and deveined
10 sea scallops
2 cloves garlic, minced
1 teaspoon bottled fish sauce (nuoc mam)
$1/4$ teaspoon freshly ground black pepper
2 $1^1/2$-pound lobsters
1 tablespoon vegetable oil
1 small red chile, minced
1 teaspoon honey
$1/2$ cup heavy cream
2 teaspoons butter

1. Prepare the rice and set aside.

2. With a vegetable peeler, remove a number of strips of peel from the orange, but do not include any white pith. Cut the strips into very thin, long strands. You'll need a large, sharp knife. Measure out $1\frac{1}{2}$ tablespoons and set aside. Squeeze $\frac{1}{2}$ cup of juice from the orange and set aside.

3. In a large bowl, combine the shrimp and scallops with 1 clove of the garlic, the fish sauce, and black pepper. Mix well and set aside to marinate at least 10 minutes.

4. Into a large pot of rapidly boiling water, plunge the lobsters, heads first. Boil over high heat for 8 minutes. With tongs, remove the lobsters to a bowl to cool. Remove the claw and tail meat and any other meat you wish to save. Cut the tails in half lengthwise and set the meat aside.

5. In a small saucepan, heat the oil over high heat until very hot. Add the remaining garlic, the orange strips, and chile and cook, stirring, until fragrant, about 30 seconds. Add the orange juice and honey and bring to a boil. Add the heavy cream and reduce the heat to medium. Simmer until slightly thickened, about 3 minutes. Remove the sauce from the heat and keep warm.

6. In a large skillet over medium-high heat, melt the butter. When the sizzling stops, add the shrimp and scallops and cook, stirring a few times, until opaque but still juicy, about 2 minutes. Add the lobster meat and orange sauce and cook until the lobster heats through, about 1 minute. Serve at once with the rice and steamed asparagus, if you wish.

LIGHT LOBSTER CURRY *(Tom Hum Sai-Gon)*

MAKES 2 SERVINGS

The gentle touch of curry here enlivens a mild coconut sauce, a great match with meaty lobster.

Half rice recipe (page 34)
2 1½-pound lobsters
1 medium carrot, cut into thin sticks
8 asparagus spears, trimmed and cut into 2-inch pieces
1 tablespoon butter
½ small onion, thinly sliced
5 medium white mushrooms, thinly sliced
½ teaspoon curry paste or powder
Pinch cayenne
1 small tomato, cut into small dice
½ cup canned coconut milk or heavy cream
1 teaspoon bottled fish sauce (nuoc mam)

1. Prepare the rice and set aside.

2. Into a large pot of boiling water over high heat, plunge the lobsters, heads first, and boil until bright red all over, about 8 minutes. With tongs, remove the lobsters to a large bowl to cool. When cool enough to handle, crack the lobsters over the bowl and remove the tail, claw, knuckle meat, and any other meat you can. Cut the tails in half lengthwise. Strain ½ cup of the liquid from the bowl and set aside. Reserve the green tomalley, if you wish, as well.

3. To a medium saucepan, add an inch of water and a steamer basket. Over high heat, steam the carrot, covered, until almost tender, about 8 minutes. Scatter the asparagus over the carrot and steam until tender, about 3 minutes. Remove the basket and set aside.

4. In a large skillet over medium heat, melt the butter. Add the onion and mushrooms and cook, stirring, until wilted, about 5 minutes. Add the curry and cayenne and cook for 1 minute. Add the tomato, reserved lobster water, coconut milk, and fish sauce, increase the heat to medium-high, and simmer until slightly thickened, about 5 minutes. Stir in the lobster meat and steamed vegetables and cook until all is heated through, about 4 minutes. Serve with the rice.

STEAMED WHOLE BASS WITH TIGER LILIES *(Ca Hap)*

MAKES 2 SERVINGS

This steamed fish is elaborately garnished with many different flavorings and vegetables and is made sometimes with two or three different fish as a special dish for family gatherings when the cook wishes to impress with a beautiful presentation. The small amount of cellophane noodles here serves to add texture and to absorb the flavors of the abundant cooking juices. The only trick is to find a steamer with a wide enough base and a plate that is large enough to hold all the vegetables and aromatics and still fit into the steamer.

Half rice recipe (page 34)
1 ounce tiger lily buds
8 dried shiitake mushrooms
Half a 1.8-ounce package cellophane noodles
1 2-pound sea bass, scaled, cleaned, and tail and fins trimmed
1½ tablespoons bottled fish sauce
½ teaspoon freshly ground black pepper
½ teaspoon fermented black beans, finely chopped
1 2-inch piece ginger, peeled, thinly sliced, stacked, and cut into thin sticks
1 small onion, thinly sliced
1 medium tomato, halved and thickly sliced
2 small fresh chiles, red and green, thinly sliced
½ tablespoon preserved cabbage
1 large scallion, thinly sliced
1 tablespoon vegetable oil
Coriander sprigs for garnish

1. Prepare the rice and set aside.

2. In a medium bowl, cover the lily buds and *shiitake* mushrooms with hot water and soak until soft, about 20 minutes. Rinse well and squeeze dry. Cut the hard knobs off the ends of the buds and tie the buds in single knots. Remove the stems and cut the mushrooms in half.

3. In a small bowl, soak the cellophane noodles in cold water until pliable, about 3 minutes. Drain and set aside.

4. Rub the fish inside and out with the fish sauce and black pepper. Put the fish on a large, round plate that will fit onto the rack of a steamer or wok. Be sure there is plenty of room for all the vegetables. Refrigerate the fish for about 20 minutes.

5. Prepare the steamer, adding at least 2 inches of hot water to the bottom and at least 3 inches of space between the water and the rack. Sprinkle the fish inside and out with the black beans. Cover and surround the fish with the lily buds, mushrooms, ginger, onion, tomato, chiles, and the preserved cabbage. Sprinkle with the scallion and oil. Put the plate into the steamer and cover. Bring the water in the steamer to a boil over high heat and steam the fish for 25 minutes, until just cooked through. Remove the vegetables and cellophane noodles to serving plates. Remove the fish to a platter and top with the coriander sprigs. With a fork, lift the meat from the bones, discarding any bones. Spoon the juices over the fish and eat with the rice.

TUNA WITH DILL AND TOASTED ALMONDS *(Ca Nuong Vi)*

MAKES 4 SERVINGS

In Hanoi, pairing fresh dill with fish is a favorite combination. Tuna and mackerel are abundant off the coast of Vietnam as are other rich-fleshed fish. You can use swordfish or salmon here, as well.

5 cloves garlic, crushed
3 small shallots or 3 whites of scallion
$1/2$ teaspoon freshly ground black pepper
1 teaspoon sugar
2 tablespoons bottled fish sauce (nuoc mam)
2 heaping teaspoons vegetable oil
$1/4$ teaspoon ground turmeric
4 8-ounce tuna steaks
Scallion Oil (page 59)
Salt to taste
2 tablespoons sliced almonds, toasted
$1/4$ cup chopped dill

1. In a mortar, pound the garlic, shallots, pepper, and sugar to a paste. Blend in the fish sauce, vegetable oil, and turmeric. Put the tuna in a large, shallow dish and pour the sauce over it. Marinate in the refrigerator for 1 hour. Meanwhile, prepare the Scallion Oil.

2. Preheat the grill or broiler. Season the tuna with salt and grill until browned on both sides but still pink in the center, about 3 minutes per side. For swordfish or salmon, you may wish to cook it a little longer.

3. To serve, put the tuna on plates and spoon about 1 tablespoon of the scallion with a little of the oil over it. Top with the almonds and dill. Serve with rice or French bread.

CURRIED FROG LEGS *(Ech Xao Lan)*

MAKES 4 APPETIZER OR 2 MAIN-COURSE SERVINGS

Here is an elegant and subtly aromatic curry that doesn't overwhelm the mild and sweet flavor of frog legs.

Half rice recipe (page 34)
1 small onion, half finely chopped, half thinly sliced
2 cloves garlic, minced
1 teaspoon curry paste or powder
1 small red chile, minced
1 stalk lemongrass, very thinly sliced
$\frac{1}{2}$ teaspoon freshly ground black pepper
2 tablespoons bottled fish sauce (nuoc mam)
1 pound frog legs, split apart
$1\frac{1}{2}$ tablespoons vegetable oil
$\frac{1}{3}$ cup chicken stock
$\frac{1}{4}$ cup coconut milk
2 tablespoons chopped peanuts
2 tablespoons chopped ngo om *or coriander*

1. Prepare rice and set aside.

2. In a large bowl, combine the chopped onion, garlic, curry paste, chile, lemongrass, black pepper, and fish sauce. Add the frog legs and coat them well. Marinate at room temperature for about 20 minutes.

3. In a large skillet or wok over high heat, heat the oil, add the sliced onion, and cook for 1 minute. Add the frog legs and the marinade and cook, stirring, for about 2 minutes. Stir in the chicken stock and coconut milk. Reduce the heat to medium, cover, and cook until the legs are cooked through, about 5 minutes. Spoon onto plates, sprinkle with the chopped peanuts and *ngo om* or coriander, and serve with rice.

KEY INGREDIENTS. CLOCKWISE: chiles; la-lot leaves; sugarcane; banana leaves; lemongrass; water spinach; bitter melon; green papaya; purple perilla (or red shiso); lime leaves; *ngo om; ngo gai;* Asian basil. MIDDLE: Rau ram and jicama

GARLIC
FRIED
CRABS
(Cua Rang Muoi)

SIMPLE
SHRIMP ROLLS
(Cha Ram)

CRISPY
RED SNAPPER
WITH
SPICY TOMATO SAUCE (Ca Chien)

HOT AND SOUR
LEMONGRASS
SOUP
(Canh Chua Ca)

SHRIMP
ON
SUGAR CANE
(Chao Tom)

ARTICHOKES
STUFFED WITH
CRAB AND SHRIMP
(a-Ti-So-Don Tom So)

HAPPY
PANCAKE
(Banh Xeo)

SILVER
DOLLAR
CAKES
(Banh Cang)

BEEF
GRILLED
IN
LA-LOT LEAVES
(Bo Goi La-Lot)
AND
GINGER-SPICED
CUCUMBER
(Dua Leo Dau Dam Gung)

CHICKEN AND GRAPEFRUIT SALAD
(Goi-Ga)

A VEGETARIAN FEAST. Top to bottom: Fried Tofu Salad (Goi Dau Khuon); Curly Fried Eggplant (Ca Tim Phot Bot); and Vegetarian Summer Rolls (Goi Cuon)

CHICKEN
CURRY
(Ca-Ri Ga)

FAMOUS
HANOI
SOUP
(Pho Ga)

DUCK
WITH
SPICY EGGPLANT
(Vit Nuong Vi)

CRUNCHY
SWEET POTATO
NESTS
WITH SHRIMP
(Khoai Lan
Chien Voi Tom)

CORAL LOBSTER (Tom Hum Vung Tau Rim)

COCONUT RICE CAKES FILLED WITH BANANA (Chuoi Nuong)

Poultry, Game, and Meat

CHICKEN

The Vietnamese are in the habit of eating only freshly killed poultry, whether it be backyard birds or chickens from the market dressed to order. With refrigeration very limited, it is the most sanitary and sensible procedure. The birds are raised lean, and while their meat is a bit tough, it is especially tasty. Though the Vietnamese eat pork and beef well done, they prefer chicken cooked pink, underdone by our standards. Of course, all the chicken in these recipes is completely cooked through.

WILD GAME

Vietnam's unique geography has long supplied its people with abundant and varied meats. The great Truong Son Mountain range that runs through the center of the country and the Central Highlands, are home to both rare and common species of pheasant, quail, thrushes, and fowl. Wild oxen, cattle, and buffalo, as well as deer and elk, live in these mountains, woods, and jungle. Hence, the Vietnamese have developed a taste for wild and unusual meats that has led them to raise and domesticate a large variety of animals. Their preparations of game remain versatile and interesting. At a roadside stand outside Ho Chi Minh City, we tried a dried-meat speciality, a kind of jerky, made with deer meat. Candied with sugar and coated with sesame seeds, it was a deliciously sweet and salty snack.

PORK

The pig yields more by-products than any other animal in Vietnam. In the country and on small farms, pigs are kept under the house where it is cool, wet, and shady. There pigs can wallow, and no farmland is wasted. Pigs are more practical to raise than beef cattle because they do not need pasture for grazing, and, being omnivores, require no special feed. Though for most Vietnamese all meat is still a luxury, pork is the most available and affordable. Though the less-fat cuts are more desirable, the fresh ham serves as a multipurpose cut with lean meat enclosed, as it is, in a thick layer of fat and skin. The bone is used for soups and stews that often contain fat and gristle, which some Vietnamese treasure.

BEEF

Though cattle are raised in many parts of the country, beef is a rare and expensive treat for most Vietnamese. Up north, near Hanoi, there are wide plains and grazing pastures; there beef is more available, and two national dishes—*pho bo* (beef noodle soup) and *vien bo* (beef ball soup)— were invented. Most beef and meat entrées are grilled and stretched to feed large families by serving them with Table Salad. Meats are poached, stewed, stir-fried, or sautéed, depending on whether the local influence is Chinese or French. Lesser cuts and scrapings of pork and beef are made into a forcemeat called pâté, similar to a kind of bologna, which has specks of fat evident.

SINGING CHICKEN *(Ga Kho)*

MAKES 4 SERVINGS

Here is another of those stinging hot dishes that Binh insists must be that way. Use whatever amount of chile suits you, for no matter how much heat is in this preparation, the rest of the ingredients are well balanced and the resulting sauce is smooth and flavorful. The process from start to finish is done in a flash. Serve with rice and steamed broccoli.

Half rice recipe (page 34)
1½ tablespoons vegetable oil
1 2-inch piece ginger, peeled, thinly sliced, stacked, and cut into thin sticks
2 cloves garlic, minced
1 pound boneless skinless chicken, cut crosswise into many 2- to 3-inch-long pieces
2 tablespoons sugar
¼ cup soy sauce
1 teaspoon bottled fish sauce (nuoc mam)
¾ cup dry white wine
2 or 3 small red chiles, minced, or 1 teaspoon dried chile flakes, or to taste
1 teaspoon freshly ground black pepper

1. Prepare the rice and set aside.

2. In a wok or large skillet over medium-high heat, heat the oil. When smoking, add the ginger and garlic and stir-fry 1 minute. Add the chicken and stir-fry 1 minute. Add the remaining ingredients and cook, stirring often, until the chicken is cooked and the sauce is slightly thickened, about 8 minutes.

CHICKEN LEMONGRASS CURRY *(Ga Xao Lan)*

MAKES 4 SERVINGS

This is a simpler, quicker-cooking version of Chicken Curry, more like a stir-fry, using boneless chicken breast. Serve with fried cellophane noodles, steamed rice, or warm French bread.

2 tablespoons vegetable oil
1 small onion, thinly sliced
1 clove garlic, minced
1½ pounds boneless skinless chicken breast, cut crosswise into wide strips
½ teaspoon freshly ground black pepper
2 stalks lemongrass, smashed with the side of a knife and cut into 1-inch pieces
2 tablespoons bottled fish sauce (nuoc mam)
Pinch sugar
1 teaspoon curry paste or powder
1 small red chile, minced
2 tablespoons chicken stock or water
½ cup canned coconut milk or heavy cream
2 tablespoons chopped peanuts
¼ cup chopped ngo om *or coriander*

1. In a wok or large skillet, heat the oil. When hot, add the onion and garlic and stir-fry for about 1 minute. Add the chicken, black pepper, lemongrass, fish sauce, sugar, curry, and chile and stir-fry until fragrant, about 3 minutes. Add the stock and simmer about 5 minutes. Add the coconut milk and simmer until slightly thickened and creamy, about 3 minutes. Serve sprinkled with the peanuts and *ngo om* or coriander.

CHICKEN CURRY (Ca-Ri Ga)

MAKES 4 TO 6 SERVINGS

This classic, colorful Vietnamese stew is simple and, therefore, in its finest form when very fresh coconut is used to make the milk that is called for and a fine curry mixture, such as Indian curry paste, is employed (page 14). In case you're assuming the flavors here are heavy and overly curried, they aren't. Chunks of fried taro root or potatoes add taste and an interesting texture. French bread, which has become a favorite staple for the Vietnamese, is preferred with this dish for dunking the marvelous sauce. Probably the strongest testament to the French influence in their food, French bread is everywhere in Vietnam—fat, crusty loaves displayed on open market shelves along city streets and even in the smallest wayside towns.

1 small onion, chopped

1 1-inch piece ginger, peeled and chopped

6 stalks fresh lemongrass, 3 stalks very thinly sliced, 3 stalks crushed with the side of a knife

3 cloves garlic, chopped

$1\frac{1}{2}$ teaspoons salt

$\frac{1}{2}$ teaspoon freshly ground black pepper

1 teaspoon dried chile flakes, or to taste

1 3-pound chicken, split and cut into 8 pieces, or quartered

2 teaspoons curry paste or powder

2 cups fresh grated coconut (page 13 and see NOTE) to make coconut cream and milk, or 2 14-ounce cans unsweetened coconut milk, $\frac{2}{3}$ cup for the "cream" and the remaining diluted with 2 cups water for the "milk"

$\frac{1}{2}$ cup vegetable oil

2 pounds taro root or potatoes, peeled and cut into 2-inch chunks

2 bay leaves

1 teaspoon sugar

2 red chiles, finely chopped

2 teaspoons salt

Lime wedges

Coriander sprigs

Chopped scallions

1. In a mortar, pound the onion, ginger, sliced lemongrass, garlic, salt, and pepper to a coarse paste and stir in the chile flakes and curry paste. Put the chicken pieces in a bowl and pour the marinade over them. Toss to coat thoroughly. Marinate at room temperature for 1 hour.

2. Put the fresh grated coconut in a large bowl and pour in 1 cup hot water. Let sit for about 10 minutes, then strain into another bowl, pressing to extract as much "cream" as possible. Put the grated coconut back in the large bowl and cover with 3 cups hot water. Let sit for about 20 minutes and strain the "milk" into a separate bowl. Set aside.

3. In a large heavy casserole, heat $\frac{1}{4}$ cup of the oil over medium-high heat until very hot. Add the taro or potatoes and cook until brown all over, about 2 minutes per side. Drain on paper towels and pour off the oil.

4. Add the remaining oil to the casserole. Heat over medium-high heat until hot, add the chicken pieces, skin side down, and cook until brown on one side, about 5 minutes. Add the 3 stalks crushed lemongrass, bay leaves, coconut "milk," and the taro root or potatoes. Bring to a boil, reduce the heat to low, and simmer, stirring occasionally, until the chicken is cooked through, about 30 minutes.

5. Add the coconut "cream" and sugar to the curry and simmer another 10 minutes. Meanwhile, in a mortar pound together the chile and salt to combine thoroughly. Serve the curry with cooked rice noodles or French bread. On the side, mound the chile salt in saucers for dipping at the table along with the lime. Top with coriander and scallions.

NOTE: If you can't find fresh coconut, use two 14-ounce cans unsweetened coconut milk; take $\frac{2}{3}$ cup off the top of one can for the "cream" and dilute the remaining $1\frac{1}{3}$ cans with 2 cups water for the "milk."

GINGER RICE WITH CHICKEN *(Com Ga)*

MAKES 4 TO 6 SERVINGS

The simple goodness of Vietnamese cooking is this plain poached chicken paired with fragrant, chewy rice. After the chicken is poached, the broth is used to cook the rice. A very flavorful ginger sauce is served. Run the chicken briefly under the broiler to crisp the skin if you like.

Ginger Sauce (page 40)
4 cups long-grain rice, preferably jasmine
1 3½-pound chicken, quartered, or 4 whole chicken legs, halved at the joint;
    reserve any fat that clings to the chicken
1 2 × 3-inch piece ginger, peeled and finely chopped
4 cloves garlic, finely chopped
1 teaspoon salt
1 teaspoon sugar
1 small onion, very thinly sliced
½ cup chopped rau ram *or ¼ cup each chopped mint and coriander*

1. Prepare the Ginger Sauce and set aside.

2. Put the rice in a large bowl and rinse it several times in cold water until the water runs clear. Drain the rice in a colander and set it aside, preferably in the sun, tossing it occasionally until it is quite dry, about 2 hours.

3. In a large saucepan or pot, cover the chicken with 6 cups water. Bring to a boil over high heat, reduce to low, and simmer, skimming occasionally, until the chicken is just cooked through, about 30 minutes. Skim the surface again and pour off 4 cups of the broth and set aside. Cover the pot and set aside until ready to serve. Then cut the chicken into serving pieces.

4. About 30 minutes before serving, heat a large heavy flameproof casserole over medium heat, add the chicken fat, and cook to melt it until you have about 3 tablespoons rendered fat. Discard any extra fat. (You can use 3 tablespoons vegetable oil if you wish.)

5. Increase the heat to high and add the rice, ginger, garlic, salt, and sugar and stir well to distribute the seasonings. Cook the rice, stirring constantly to coat and harden it, about 3 minutes. Reduce the heat to medium and continue to cook the rice another 2 minutes. Stir in the 4 cups broth, bring to a simmer, cover, and cook over low heat, stirring a few times, until the rice is tender but still a little firm, about 25 minutes.

6. When the rice is done, remove from the heat and serve with the chicken. Pass the Ginger Sauce separately at the table. Serve with the thinly sliced onion and chopped *rau ram*.

SUGGESTIONS: This is a sensational party dish; it looks like plain chicken and rice, but the ginger sauce dazzles. Start the party with Crunchy Sweet Potato Nests with Shrimp (page 114) or Shrimp on Sugar Cane (page 112).

FIVE SPICE HENS (Ga Xoi Mo)

MAKES 2 TO 4 SERVINGS

This is "fried chicken" Vietnamese style, subtly spiced and beautifully matched with a quick-cooking tamarind sauce. Portions will vary depending on the appetites of your guests and the menu. Incidentally, Cornish hens have tastier and more succulent meat than most chickens and cook more evenly when left whole.

$1/4$ teaspoon five spice powder
$1/2$ teaspoon salt
2 Rock Cornish game hens, about $1 1/2$ pounds each
$1/3$ cup tamarind pulp (about 3 ounces)
$1/3$ cup sugar
$1/3$ cup bottled fish sauce (nuoc mam)
1 small red chile, minced
3 cloves garlic, minced
Vegetable oil for deep frying

1. In a small bowl, combine five spice powder with the salt. Season the hens all over with the spice mixture. Set aside to marinate at room temperature for at least $1/2$ hour or covered in the refrigerator overnight.

2. In a small bowl, cover the tamarind pulp with 1 cup hot water. Set aside to soften about 5 minutes. Mash the tamarind with a fork and pick out the seeds or pass the pulp through a strainer. Put the pulp in a small saucepan with the sugar and fish sauce. Bring to a boil over high heat and remove from the burner. Stir in the chile and garlic and set aside until ready to use.

3. Use a heavy deep, high-sided pot, Dutch oven, or flameproof casserole just wide enough to hold the hens in one layer. Add enough oil to cover the hens, about 3 cups. Heat the oil over high heat until very hot, about 325 degrees on a deep-fry thermometer. Carefully put the hens in the hot oil and reduce the heat to medium. The oil may boil up a bit at first but will soon regain a steady simmer. Fry the hens until deep brown and crisp and cooked through, about 25 minutes. Halfway through cooking, turn the hens with tongs. Drain on paper towels and cut the hens into serving pieces. To serve, pour some of the tamarind sauce onto a large platter or dinner plates and put the fried hens on top. Or serve the tamarind sauce on the side in small bowls for dipping.

ROAST CHICKEN WITH FIVE SPICE GLAZE *(Ga Quay)*

MAKES 2 TO 4 SERVINGS

This recipe has been adapted from the traditional deep-fried version of it for an oven is not a standard part of the Vietnamese kitchen. As it roasts, the chicken is glazed and richly flavored by the marinade.

2 shallots, chopped
4 cloves garlic, chopped
$1/2$ teaspoon freshly ground black pepper
2 tablespoons dark brown sugar
$1/4$ teaspoon five spice powder
$1/2$ teaspoon sesame oil
1 tablespoon vegetable oil
2 tablespoons bottled fish sauce (nuoc mam)
1 3-pound chicken

1. In a mortar, pound together the shallots, garlic, and pepper. Add the brown sugar and pound to a coarse paste. Stir in the five spice powder, sesame and vegetable oils, and fish sauce.

2. Put the chicken in a large bowl. Add the marinade and rub it all over the chicken, inside and out. Cover and refrigerate, turning a few times, overnight.

3. Preheat the oven to 400 degrees. Put the chicken in a roasting pan and pour any excess marinade into the cavity. Roast about 30 minutes, then begin basting the bird, using the juices that have collected in the cavity. When the juices run clear when a thigh is pierced with a knife, after about 45 minutes, the chicken is done. The skin will be brown and crisp. Let the chicken stand for 5 minutes before carving.

SUGGESTIONS: Try Water Spinach Sauté (page 291) and Fried Vegetables with Noodles (page 286) as accompaniments.

ORANGE HONEY CHICKEN *(Ga Nuong Cam)*

MAKES 4 SERVINGS

These oven-roasted chicken legs come out as crusty and good as the traditional grilled version.

1 shallot, thinly sliced
6 large cloves garlic, sliced
1 1-inch piece ginger, peeled and sliced
2 tablespoons honey
$\frac{1}{2}$ teaspoon freshly ground black pepper
2 teaspoons soy sauce
$2\frac{1}{2}$ tablespoons bottled fish sauce (nuoc mam)
2 teaspoons sesame oil
1 tablespoon sherry
1 teaspoon grated orange zest
Juice of 1 orange (about $\frac{2}{3}$ cup)
1 tablespoon vegetable oil
4 pounds whole chicken legs, halved at the joint

1. In a mortar, pound the shallot, garlic, and ginger to a paste. Add the honey and pepper and blend well. Stir in the soy sauce, fish sauce, sesame oil, sherry, orange zest, orange juice, and vegetable oil.

2. Put the chicken in a large bowl and pour the marinade over it. Toss to coat well and marinate, covered, in the refrigerator overnight, turning occasionally.

3. Preheat the oven to 450 degrees. Put the chicken on a baking sheet, skin side up, and bake, without turning, until brown and crisp, about 35 minutes. Serve hot or cold.

LAQUE DUCK *(Vit Quay)*

MAKES 2 TO 4 SERVINGS

Similar to Peking duck, Laque Duck is much more aromatic and darkly glazed. Its execution is simpler than the many steps involved in making the authentically prepared Chinese version. To obtain a thoroughly crisp skin, the duck sits, uncovered in the refrigerator, to dry before roasting. Serve with Orange Brandy Sauce (page 56) if desired.

1 tablespoon Spiced Wine (page 57)
5 cloves garlic, smashed
$\frac{1}{2}$ teaspoon freshly ground black pepper
3 tablespoons soy sauce
$\frac{1}{4}$ teaspoons five spice powder
1 tablespoon sesame oil
$\frac{1}{2}$ teaspoon salt
1 $5\frac{1}{2}$-pound duck, trimmed of excess fat, wing tips removed

1. Have ready the Spiced Wine.

2. In a mortar, pound the garlic and pepper to a paste. Stir in the soy sauce, five spice powder, sesame oil, wine, and salt. Put the duck in a large, shallow baking dish and pour the marinade into the cavity and all over it. Rub the marinade well into the flesh. Refrigerate, uncovered, basting occasionally, overnight.

3. Preheat the oven to 425 degrees. Pour any excess marinade into the duck cavity and put the duck in a shallow roasting pan. Roast the duck until deep brown and crisp, about 1 hour. If during cooking the pan fills up with fat, very carefully pour it off and continue roasting.

4. To serve, using a cleaver, cut the duck through the backbone, then make crosswise chops, cutting the breast into 5 or 6 slices. Remove the legs and halve them at the joints. Serve hot or at room temperature; be sure to include a crisp piece of skin with each piece of meat.

DUCK WITH SPICY EGGPLANT *(Vit Nuong Vi)*

MAKES 4 SERVINGS

This is another of Binh's creations: a wonderful combination of crisp duck served over roasted eggplant pureé that has been enlivened with Nuoc Cham. The fermented, or red, bean curd gives the duck skin a lovely bronze hue. Broiled tomatoes go beautifully with the eggplant and make a complete meal.

$1/4$ cup plus 2 tablespoons Nuoc Cham Dipping Sauce (page 36)
1 whole duck (about $4^{1}/_{2}$ pounds)
6 cloves garlic, minced
1 tablespoon sugar
$1/4$ teaspoon freshly ground black pepper
2 1-inch pieces red bean curd (page 11)
2 teaspoons medium dry sherry
$1/4$ cup vegetable oil
2 large eggplants (about 3 pounds each)
2 large scallions, thinly sliced
2 whole tomatoes, halved, for garnish

1. Prepare the Nuoc Cham Dipping Sauce and set aside.

2. Carve the breast meat from the bone of the duck, leaving the skin intact. Remove the legs and thighs. Set the legs, skin side down, onto a cutting board or work surface and with a small sharp knife, cut down the center of the leg to the bone. Scrape against the bone and pull the meat away to remove it in one piece, severing the connections around the knuckle. Remove as many tendons as possible from the leg meat. Put the duck pieces in a shallow dish large enough to hold them in a single layer.

3. In a small bowl or mortar, pound 4 of the garlic cloves with the sugar and pepper to make a paste. Stir in the bean curd, sherry, and 2 tablespoons of the oil, mashing the bean curd and making a coarse paste. Rub the mixture evenly over the duck pieces and let stand, covered, at room temperature for 2 hours or in the refrigerator overnight.

4. Preheat the oven to 450 degrees. Place the eggplants on a baking sheet and pierce them in a few places with a knife. Roast in the oven, turning once, until very soft and charred all over, about 45 minutes. Let cool slightly, then cut off the stem end and peel off the skin; it should come off easily in large pieces. Leave the eggplant as whole as possible. Preheat the broiler.

5. In a large skillet, heat the remaining 2 tablespoons oil over high heat. Add the remaining 2 cloves garlic and the scallions and cook, stirring, until fragrant, about 1 minute. Add the eggplants and cook, stirring with chopsticks. Some of the cooked eggplant will turn to purée and some, with the help of the chopsticks pulling it in opposite directions, will separate into long, thin strands. This should take about 5 minutes. Add the Nuoc Cham and bring to a boil. Remove from the heat and set aside while you broil the duck.

6. Put the duck pieces, skin side down, on a baking sheet and broil at least 5 inches from the heat until deep brown, about 5 minutes. Turn the duck and cook until the skin is deep brown and the meat is tender and still pink, about 5 minutes more. Remove the duck to a plate. Put the tomatoes halves on the baking sheet and run them under the broiler until browned, about 2 minutes.

7. To serve, heat the eggplant purée, if necessary, and put it on a large platter. Top with the duck pieces and serve with the tomatoes, if you wish.

BROILED QUAIL WITH PRESERVED PRUNES *(Chim Cut Nuong)*

MAKES 6 APPETIZER OR 2 MAIN-COURSE SERVINGS

Preserved prunes have a sugary coating that when bitten into impart a salty, sweet, and intensely tart sensation. To eat them on their own is an acquired taste. They produce, however, a fascinating sauce when simmered with cinnamon, sherry, and hoisin, which is especially good with grilled fowl, such as the garlicky marinated quail we have here.

3 cloves garlic, minced
3 shallots, minced
$1/4$ teaspoon freshly ground black pepper
2 teaspoons sugar
$3^1/2$ teaspoons medium dry sherry
1 tablespoon bottled fish sauce (nuoc mam)
1 tablespoon vegetable oil
6 quail, boned and butterflied
6 whole candied sour plums
1 stick cinnamon
1 tablespoon hoisin sauce
Pinch dried chile flakes
1 teaspoon cornstarch
1 medium zucchini, thickly sliced on the diagonal
1 medium yellow squash, thickly sliced on the diagonal
1 small onion, quartered
6 medium mushrooms
6 8-inch-long bamboo skewers

1. In a small bowl, combine the garlic, shallots, pepper, sugar, $1^1/2$ teaspoons of the sherry, fish sauce, and oil. Put the quail in a single layer in a large shallow baking dish and pour the marinade over them. Coat each quail thoroughly and marinate at room temperature for 2 hours or covered in the refrigerator overnight.

2. In a small saucepan, cover the prunes with 1½ cups water and add the cinnamon stick. Bring to a boil over high heat. Reduce to medium and simmer until the prunes are soft, about 12 minutes. Remove the prunes from the water and take out the pits. Chop the prunes fine and return them to the water. Stir in the hoisin, the remaining 2 teaspoons of sherry, and chile flakes and simmer a few minutes. Mix the cornstarch with 1 teaspoon water and add to the sauce. Bring to a boil, stirring, and cook until thickened, about 2 minutes. Remove from the heat and set aside the prune sauce until ready to use.

3. Preheat the broiler. Thread the vegetables, alternating them, onto the skewers. Put them on a baking sheet and brush them lightly on both sides with the prune sauce.

4. Arrange the quail, skin side down, on a baking sheet in a single layer. Broil, 5 inches from the heat, for 1 minute. Turn the quail over and broil, rotating the pan as needed, until the skin is deep brown and crisp and the meat is cooked but still juicy, about 3 minutes. Remove from the oven and keep warm.

5. Broil the skewers until the vegetables are softened and deep brown, about 3 minutes per side. Pour about 1 tablespoon of the warm sauce over each quail just before serving with the vegetable skewers.

SUGGESTIONS: The vegetable skewers that accompany the quail make this a good entrée choice, but these tiny birds, with or without the vegetables, can begin an elaborate meal that would be followed perhaps with Steamed Whole Bass with Tiger Lilies (page 200) or Stuffed Squid (page 192).

NOTE: Whole boned quail can be purchased in butcher shops and in the freezer section of many supermarkets.

QUAIL ROTI *(Chim Cut Roti)*

MAKES 6 APPETIZER OR 2 MAIN-COURSE SERVINGS

Quail thrive in the mountain highlands of Vietnam near Hue, which is where Binh's parents are from and it's the country's cultural center. Binh created this delightful dish in honor of his heritage. The juice from green or immature coconuts is clear and sweet, much different from that of mature, white coconuts. Since it is not available here, Binh uses coconut soda from Puerto Rico.

Half rice recipe (page 34)
1 shallot, sliced
4 cloves garlic, smashed
$1/4$ teaspoon freshly ground black pepper
2 teaspoons brown sugar
$1/8$ teaspoon five spice powder
1 tablespoon soy sauce
$1/2$ teaspoon sesame oil
2 teaspoons bottled fish sauce (nuoc mam)
6 quail, halved first through the backbone, then split through the breastbone
$1/4$ cup plus 1 tablespoon vegetable oil
1 tablespoon butter
1 small onion, thinly sliced
$1/2$ pound small white mushrooms, stems cut off
$1/4$ cup dry white wine
1 cup coconut soda

1. Prepare the rice and set aside.

2. In a mortar, pound the shallot, 3 of the garlic cloves, pepper, and brown sugar. Stir in the five spice powder, soy sauce, sesame oil, and 1 teaspoon of the fish sauce. Put the quail, skin side up, in one layer in a large shallow dish. Pour the marinade over them, rubbing it all over the birds. Marinate the quail at least 2 hours or covered overnight in the refrigerator.

3. In a large skillet over medium heat, heat ¼ cup of the oil until it starts to smoke. Add three of the quail, skin side down, and cook until brown and crisp, about 3 minutes. Turn and cook on the other side about 3 minutes. Remove them to a plate and repeat with the remaining quail.

4. Pour off the oil in the skillet and add the remaining tablespoon of oil and the butter over medium-high heat. Add the onion, the remaining clove of garlic, and the mushrooms and cook, stirring occasionally, until the onions start to soften, about 3 minutes. Add the wine and cook for 1 minute. Add the coconut soda and cook for 2 minutes. Arrange the quail on top and add any accumulated juices. Cover and cook until the sauce is slightly reduced and the quail is heated through, about 7 minutes. Stir in the remaining teaspoon fish sauce and serve with the rice or French bread.

GRILLED RABBIT *(Tho Nuong Vi)*

MAKES 2 SERVINGS

Rabbit is a lean, mild, and versatile meat with more character than chicken and is relatively inexpensive. In Vietnam, you can select your rabbit with the chickens in the market and it will be cleaned for you on the spot. One of the best ways to prepare rabbit is as follows, marinated and grilled.

2 tablespoons Spiced Wine (page 57)
5 cloves garlic, chopped
2 large shallots, chopped
1 teaspoon freshly ground black pepper
2 tablespoons sugar
2 tablespoons bottled fish sauce (nuoc mam)
2 tablespoons vegetable oil
2 teaspoons dried powdered lemongrass
1 3-pound young rabbit, separated into 2 loin pieces, 2 hind legs, and 2 front legs

1. Have ready the Spiced Wine. In a mortar, pound the garlic, shallots, pepper, and sugar to a coarse paste. Stir in the fish sauce, wine, oil, and lemongrass powder. Put the rabbit pieces in a large bowl and pour the marinade over them. Toss to coat well. Marinate at least 3 hours or, covered, in the refrigerator overnight.

2. Light a grill or preheat the oven to 475 degrees. Remove the rabbit from the marinade and grill slowly over a medium-low fire, turning once. The smaller pieces should be done after 5 minutes on each side. The hind legs will take at least 10 minutes per side. Grill the rabbit to a deep toasty brown without charring it too much. Or, put the rabbit pieces on a baking sheet and roast in the upper third of the oven, without turning, checking the smaller pieces after about 12 minutes. The juices should run clear when pricked with a fork. The larger pieces may take up to 20 minutes.

SUGGESTIONS: Serve this with Chayote (Su Hao, page 238) and French bread or rice.

RED RABBIT STEW *(Tho Ham Ruou Chat)*

MAKES 2 TO 4 SERVINGS

Gentle stewing is another great way to prepare rabbit. The red wine and bay leaves here are a Western innovation.

1 3-pound rabbit, sectioned, loin cut crosswise into 2 1/2-inch pieces, hind and fore legs cut at the joint
3 cloves garlic, minced
1/2 teaspoon freshly ground black pepper
2 tablespoons vegetable oil
2 medium carrots, split and cut into 2-inch sticks
12 shallots, peeled and left whole
2 Idaho potatoes, peeled and cut into 1-inch cubes
2 tablespoons tomato paste
1 cup dry red wine
4 cups chicken stock
2 bay leaves
Salt to taste

1. In a large bowl, combine the rabbit with the garlic and pepper. Set aside at room temperature for 30 minutes.

2. In a large Dutch oven or flameproof casserole, heat the oil over high heat. Add the rabbit and brown well, about 3 minutes per side. Remove the rabbit and reduce the heat to medium-high. Add the carrots, shallots, and potatoes and cook, stirring, for 3 minutes. Add the tomato paste and cook for another minute. Add the red wine, stock, bay leaves, and rabbit. Bring to a simmer, reduce the heat to low, and cook, partially covered, until the meat is tender, about 1 1/2 hours. Season with salt. Serve with rice, noodles, or French bread.

SUGGESTIONS: To begin this cool-weather meal, try something mild and light like Vegetarian Tofu Soup (page 274).

VIETNAMESE CINNAMON PÂTÉ *(Cha Que)*

MAKES ABOUT 1 POUND

This tightly textured firm pâté is different from the soft fatty French pâtés we are accustomed to. In fact, there is no fat at all here and the cinnamon is a Vietnamese touch that is particularly good with the rich flavor of the pork. Serve this pâté as you would meat loaf or cooked ham, in sandwiches, salads, or alongside Banh Cuon (page 144).

1 pound lean shoulder or leg of pork, trimmed of all fat and sinew, cut into 1-inch pieces
3 tablespoons bottled fish sauce (nuoc mam)
1 teaspoon sugar
1½ teaspoons baking powder
1 teaspoon potato starch or cornstarch
1½ teaspoons vegetable oil
½ teaspoon freshly ground black pepper
⅛ teaspoon ground cinnamon

1. In a large bowl, combine all the ingredients and 3 tablespoons water. Mix well and chill in the freezer until very firm, about 40 minutes.

2. Preheat the oven to 350 degrees. Put the meat mixture in a food processor and grind to a fine consistency, scraping the bowl a few times, about 2 minutes. Oil a 9 × 13-inch baking dish and spread the mixture evenly into the pan. Bake until cooked through and very firm, about 45 minutes. Cool in the pan. Serve warm or cold, thinly sliced or cut into sticks. Keeps well, wrapped, in the refrigerator for up to 1 week.

BREAKFAST PORK AND CHINESE SAUSAGE *(Thit Xiu Mai)*

MAKES 6 SERVINGS.

Popular morning food, these pork meatballs are topped with slices of sweet Chinese sausage, placed in individual ceramic bowls, and cooked in a bamboo steamer. The cooking juices collect in the bowls and the dishes are then served with slices of chile, coriander leaves, and sometimes with sliced onion. Binh, like many Vietnamese, also likes this breakfast dish served with dark, strong Maggi sauce for spreading on the bread, but that's definitely optional.

1 pound ground pork
1 medium onion, finely chopped
3/4 teaspoon freshly ground black pepper
3/4 teaspoon salt
1/2 teaspoon sugar
2 Chinese sausages, cut into 24 thin slices
1 fresh red chile, thinly sliced
1/4 cup coriander leaves

1. In a medium bowl, mix together the pork, onion, pepper, salt, and sugar. Form into 24 meatballs. Put the meatballs into a large shallow heatproof bowl.

2. Put a slice of sausage on top of each meatball and place on the rack of a large steamer or wok. Cover and steam about 15 minutes, or until the pork is cooked through. Alternately, you can divide the meatballs among 6 individual bowls if the bowls will fit in your steamer. Then you can serve breakfast directly from the steamer. Otherwise, when the pork is cooked, put 4 meatballs with their sausage slices into small serving bowls and spoon some of the cooking liquid over them. Sprinkle with some of the chile and coriander leaves and serve with French bread for dipping.

NOTE: This dish can be cooked a day ahead and kept in the bowl. Reheat in a steamer.

GRILLED PORK CHOPS WITH LEMONGRASS
(Thit Heo Nuong Vi)

MAKES 6 SERVINGS

The Vietnamese have a way with grilling and with pork; this is an excellent example of their creativity with both.

1 tablespoon Spiced Wine (page 57)
8 small cloves garlic
2 tablespoons dark brown sugar
1 teaspoon whole peppercorns
1 stalk lemongrass, chopped, or 1½ teaspoons powdered lemongrass
2½ tablespoons bottled fish sauce (nuoc mam)
1 teaspoon sesame oil
2 tablespoons vegetable oil
6 6- to 8-ounce loin pork chops with bone

1. Have ready the Spiced Wine.

2. In a mortar, pound the garlic, brown sugar, and peppercorns to a paste. Add the lemongrass and pound to blend. Stir in the fish sauce, sesame oil, wine, and vegetable oil.

3. Put the pork chops in a large shallow baking dish in one layer. Pour the marinade over them and spread to coat evenly. Allow to marinate, covered, in the refrigerator overnight. Let the pork chops come to room temperature before cooking.

4. Preheat the grill or broiler. Grill the chops over a medium flame or about 7 inches from the broiler, turning once, until dark but not burned and crispy on both sides, about 9 minutes per side. Serve at once.

PORK WITH FRESH TOMATO SAUCE *(Thit Heo Sot Ca)*

MAKES 6 SERVINGS

The marinade for these pan-fried pork chops contributes a caramelized enrichment to the sauce, which consists of just briefly cooked tomatoes.

Full rice recipe (page 34)
5 cloves garlic, minced
1½ tablespoons dark brown sugar
1 tablespoon bottled fish sauce (nuoc mam)
6 5-ounce, boneless loin pork chops, cut about ½ inch thick
1½ tablespoons vegetable oil
3 tablespoons dry white wine
½ teaspoon dried chile flakes
2 large ripe tomatoes, peeled, seeded, and chopped

1. Prepare the rice and set aside.

2. In a large shallow baking dish, mix together the garlic, brown sugar, and fish sauce. Add the pork chops and coat well. Marinate at least 2 hours or covered overnight in the refrigerator.

3. In a large skillet, heat the oil over medium heat until hot. Add the pork chops and cook until brown on one side, about 5 minutes. Turn and cook until cooked through and browned on the other side, about 5 minutes. Remove to a plate.

4. Discard the oil and to the skillet over medium-high heat, add the wine and the chile flakes. Cook for 1 minute, scraping up the browned bits. Add the tomatoes and cook rapidly for about 2 minutes. Nestle the pork chops evenly in the sauce and simmer to heat the pork through and to thicken the sauce slightly, about 3 minutes. Serve hot with the rice.

ROASTED RICE POWDER PORK *(Bi Cuon)*

MAKES 6 TO 8 SERVINGS

This meat salad is first wrapped in rice paper, then dipped in Nuoc Cham. The pork skin threads in it, which reconstitute in water, are mild in flavor, but chewy, and add an unusual dimension. When served as a casual dinner that is assembled by each guest to order, this dish makes great party food.

> *Nuoc Cham Dipping Sauce (page 36)*
> *3 tablespoons Roasted Rice Powder (page 60)*
> *5 cloves garlic, smashed*
> *1 tablespoon sugar*
> *$\frac{1}{2}$ teaspoon freshly ground black pepper*
> *$1\frac{1}{4}$ tablespoons bottled fish sauce (nuoc mam)*
> *$\frac{1}{2}$ teaspoon sesame oil*
> *1 tablespoon plus 2 teaspoons vegetable oil*
> *1 $1\frac{1}{2}$-pound piece pork butt or fresh ham with a thin layer of fat, cut into 4 pieces*
> *$\frac{1}{2}$ cup dried pork skin threads*
> *$\frac{1}{4}$ teaspoon salt*
> *15 to 18 8-inch round rice paper wrappers*
> *Coriander sprigs*
> *Mint sprigs*

1. Prepare the Nuoc Cham Dipping Sauce and the Roasted Rice Powder and set aside.

2. In a mortar, pound the smashed garlic, sugar, and pepper to a coarse paste. Stir in the fish sauce and sesame oil and 2 teaspoons of the vegetable oil. Put the pork pieces in a large bowl and pour the marinade over, coating on all sides. Marinate for 1 hour.

3. In a medium bowl, cover the pork skin threads with cold water and let soften for about 1 hour. Drain and cut the strands into 2-inch lengths.

4. In a large skillet over medium heat, add the remaining tablespoon of oil and when hot add the marinated pork. Panfry until cooked through, crusty and brown all over, about 5 minutes per side. Remove the pork to a plate to cool for about 20 minutes. Slice the pork across the grain thinly. Stack the slices and cut the pork into thin sticks. Put the pork in a large bowl and stir in the pork skin threads.

5. With your hands, mix in the garlic, rice powder, and salt. To serve, dampen the rice paper wrappers and arrange them on a platter with the other accompaniments. Each guest makes his or her own packages. Have bowls of Nuoc Cham for dipping.

STIR-FRY OF NOODLES, PORK, AND SHRIMP
(Hu Tieu Hap Chao)

MAKES 4 TO 6 SERVINGS

Rice noodles don't appear in many Vietnamese sautés as they can be tricky to stir-fry. As they are only soaked, not cooked, before incorporating, it takes some experience with them to know just how long to soak them so they will hold up properly to the rigors of being tossed repeatedly in a wok. Wheat noodles, on the other hand, are easier to deal with, especially for Americans. Here they are simply boiled, rinsed, and cooled, and remain reliably resilient.

½ pound lean pork, sliced very thin into wide strips
½ pound medium shrimp, peeled and deveined
4 scallions, green and white sliced separately
¼ teaspoon salt
½ teaspoon freshly ground black pepper
3 tablespoons vegetable oil plus additional for the noodles
¾ pound dried wide Chinese wheat noodles
3 cloves garlic, minced
1 small onion, thinly sliced
3½ tablespoons bottled fish sauce (nuoc mam)
1 teaspoon dried chile flakes, or to taste
1 tablespoon lime juice
2 cups mung bean sprouts
3 tablespoons chopped peanuts

1. In a large bowl, combine the pork and shrimp with the white of the scallions, the salt, and pepper. Set aside.

2. In a large pot of boiling, salted water with a little oil added cook the noodles, stirring frequently with chopsticks, until tender but firm, about 6 minutes. Drain the water out of the pot and run cold water into it to rinse the noodles. Pour off and repeat two more times. Drain the noodles in a colander and toss with the chopsticks to dry and separate.

3. In a wok or large skillet, heat the 3 tablespoons oil over high heat. Add the garlic and stir-fry for 5 seconds. Add the onion and stir-fry about 1 minute. Add the pork and shrimp mixture and stir-fry until cooked, about 3 minutes. Add the fish sauce, 2 tablespoons of water, and the chile flakes. Cook for about 1 minute. Toss in the noodles, by the handful, and add the lime juice. Turn off the heat and stir in the bean sprouts and scallion greens. Arrange on a large platter and sprinkle with the peanuts.

CHAYOTE *(Su Hao)*

MAKES 2 TO 4 SERVINGS

Chayote squash, commonly associated with Cajun cooking, is also a popular Asian vegetable. This delightful recipe contains small amounts of pork and shrimp, which flavor rather than dominate the dish. The chayote is the main ingredient and when it is simmered briefly becomes tender but still remains slightly crisp.

Half rice recipe (page 34)
6 ounces lean shoulder or loin of pork, very thinly sliced
¼ pound medium shrimp, peeled and deveined
1 large scallion, finely chopped
1 teaspoon bottled fish sauce (nuoc mam)
½ teaspoon freshly ground black pepper
1 tablespoon vegetable oil
1 large clove garlic, minced
2 teaspoons oyster sauce
2 chayotes, peeled, split, pitted, and sliced thin crosswise
1 tablespoon chopped coriander

1. Prepare the rice and set aside.

2. In a large bowl, combine the pork and shrimp with the white of the scallion, fish sauce, and pepper. Marinate for about 10 minutes.

3. In a wok or large skillet, heat the oil over medium-high heat. When hot, add the garlic and stir-fry for about 10 seconds. Add the pork and shrimp mixture and stir-fry for about 2 minutes. Add the oyster sauce and cook another minute. Add the chayote and cook until the vegetable gives up its moisture. Increase the heat to high, cover, and cook until the chayote is translucent but still crunchy, about 2 minutes, then stir in the green scallion. Serve with the rice.

SUGGESTIONS: This could stand as a light main-course meal with the rice, or it could serve as a vegetable side dish with Grilled Rabbit (page 226), Tuna with Dill and Toasted Almonds (page 202), or Beef Grilled in La-Lot Leaves (page 158).

FRIED NOODLE CAKES WITH PORK, SHRIMP, AND VEGETABLES *(Mi Xao Don)*

MAKES 4 SERVINGS

This is Binh's version of a Chinese dish that uses fresh thin pan-fried wheat noodles in the form of round disks that serve as the base for the pork, shrimp, and vegetable stir-fry.

Vegetable oil for frying
½ pound very thin, fresh Chinese egg noodles or mein, 2 bunches from a bag of 4
½ pound lean pork, very thinly sliced
½ pound medium shrimp, peeled and deveined
½ teaspoon freshly ground black pepper
2 cloves garlic, minced
1 tablespoon bottled fish sauce (nuoc mam)
2 tablespoons vegetable oil
1 small carrot, cut into short thin sticks
2 medium stalks celery, peeled and sliced on the diagonal, ¼ inch thick
1 medium onion, thinly sliced
½ head broccoli, cut into small florettes
1 small tomato, cut into thin wedges
1 tablespoon oyster sauce
1 cup Chicken Stock (page 86) or Vegetable Stock (page 272)
8 canned baby corn, optional
1 teaspoon cornstarch

1. In a large skillet, heat ¼ inch of oil over high heat. When almost smoking, add half the noodles, pressing them down in the skillet to form an even, thin layer. Cook until brown and crisp on the bottom, about 1 minute. Turn and cook until crisp on the other side, another minute. Drain on paper towels. Repeat with the remaining noodles.

2. In a medium bowl, combine the pork and shrimp. Add the pepper, garlic, and fish sauce and toss well. Set aside.

3. In a wok or large skillet over high heat, heat 1 tablespoon of the oil until smoking. Add the pork and shrimp mixture and stir-fry until almost cooked through, about 2 minutes. Remove to a plate. Add the remaining tablespoon of oil and the carrot, celery, and onion and stir-fry until the vegetables start to wilt, about 2 minutes. Add the broccoli and tomato and stir-fry for 1 minute. Add the oyster sauce and stock and cook for 30 seconds. Return the pork and shrimp to the wok with the baby corn, if using, let simmer 2 minutes.

4. In a small bowl, combine the cornstarch with 1 teaspoon water and add to the wok. Cook, stirring until slightly thickened, about 2 minutes. To serve, put the noodle cakes on a wide platter and pour the pork, shrimp, and vegetables over them. With a sharp knife, cut the noodle cakes in half and serve one half to each person.

FRIED TOFU STUFFED WITH PORK AND MUSHROOMS
(Dau Khuon Don Thit)

MAKES 4 TO 6 SERVINGS

Bean curd cubes can be bought ready fried. With a mild toasty flavor they are excellent when stuffed and simmered briefly in tomato sauce.

Full rice recipe (page 34)
1/2 pound ground pork
2 small onions; 1 finely chopped, 1 thinly sliced
3/4 teaspoon freshly ground black pepper
2 1/2 teaspoons sugar
3 tablespoons plus 2 teaspoons fish sauce
2 2-ounce packages fried bean curd
1 tablespoon vegetable oil
2 cloves garlic, minced
3 medium tomatoes, cut into thin wedges
10 large dried shiitake mushrooms, soaked in hot water 20 minutes, stemmed, rinsed, and quartered
1 cup chicken stock or water
1 teaspoon dried chile flakes or Sate-Chile Oil (page 58)
2 large scallions, greens only, cut into 2-inch lengths
2 tablespoons chopped coriander

1. Prepare the rice and set aside.

2. In a medium bowl, combine the pork with the chopped onion, pepper, $\frac{1}{2}$ teaspoon of the sugar, and 2 teaspoons of the fish sauce. Make a cut almost all the way to the center of each bean curd cube. Stuff each cube with a heaping teaspoon of the pork filling.

3. In a large skillet, heat the oil over high heat. Add the garlic and sliced onion and stir-fry for about 30 seconds. Add the tomatoes and mushrooms and cook for 1 minute. Add the stuffed bean curd cubes, fish sauce, and remaining 2 teaspoons sugar and cook, stirring, for 1 minute. Add the chicken stock and chile flakes, reduce the heat to medium, and cook, stirring occasionally, for 15 minutes. Stir in the scallion greens and sprinkle with the coriander just before serving with the rice.

GRILLED PORK WITH NOODLE CAKES *(Banh Hoi Thit Nuong)*

MAKES 4 MAIN-COURSE SERVINGS

You will find this classic dish in just about every Vietnamese restaurant, here and in Vietnam.

3 large shallots, chopped
3 cloves garlic, chopped
1 tablespoon sugar
2 tablespoons bottled fish sauce (nuoc mam)
½ teaspoon freshly ground black pepper
1 tablespoon Spiced Wine (page 57)
2 tablespoons vegetable oil
1 pound pork loin, thinly sliced crosswise
Noodle Cakes (page 66)
Half recipe Scallion Oil (page 59)
Half recipe Light Nuoc Cham Dipping Sauce (page 41)
8 8-inch-long bamboo skewers
3 tablespoons chopped peanuts

1. In a mortar, pound together the shallots, garlic, and sugar to make a coarse paste. Stir in the fish sauce, pepper, wine, and oil. Put the pork in a medium bowl and pour the marinade over it. Toss well to coat the meat. Set aside to marinate at room temperature for at least 2 hours or cover and refrigerate overnight.

2. Prepare the Noodle Cakes, Scallion Oil, and Light Nuoc Cham Dipping Sauce, up to 2 hours before serving.

3. Light the grill or preheat the broiler. Thread the pork slices snugly onto the bamboo skewers. Grill over a medium hot fire or broil 5 inches from the heat, turning once, until deep brown and crisp around the edges, about 3 minutes per side. Arrange the noodle cakes on a large platter and drizzle them with scallion oil. Using the tines of a fork, push the pork off the skewers and onto the noodle cakes. Sprinkle with peanuts and drizzle evenly with some of the dipping sauce, passing extra sauce at the table. Serve at once.

RICE NOODLES TOSSED WITH GRILLED PORK AND PEANUTS *(Bun Thit Nuong)*

MAKES 4 SERVINGS

This main-course pork and noodle salad is elaborately garnished with an assortment of distinct flavors: herbs, fried crisps of shallots and pork rinds, and peanuts.

$1/4$ cup Fried Shallots (page 62)
$1/4$ cup Crispy Pork Rinds (page 68)
$1/2$ cup Nuoc Cham Dipping Sauce (page 36)
3 shallots, chopped
3 cloves garlic, chopped
1 tablespoon sugar
2 tablespoons bottled fish sauce (nuoc mam)
$1/2$ teaspoon freshly ground black pepper
1 tablespoon Spiced Wine (page 57), optional
2 tablespoons vegetable oil
1 teaspoon sesame oil
1 pound lean shoulder or loin of pork, very thinly sliced crosswise
8 8-inch-long bamboo skewers
$1/2$ pound rice vermicelli
1 cup mung bean sprouts
2 tablespoons chopped mint
2 tablespoons chopped coriander
$1/4$ cup thinly sliced perilla leaf or basil
$1/3$ cup chopped peanuts

1. Prepare the Nuoc Cham Dipping Sauce, Fried Shallots, and Crispy Pork Rinds and set aside.

2. In a mortar, pound the shallots, garlic, and sugar to a coarse paste. Stir in the fish sauce, pepper, wine, and oils. Put the pork in a medium bowl and pour the marinade over it. Toss well to coat. Marinate at room temperature for at least 2 hours or cover and refrigerate overnight.

3. Light the grill or preheat the broiler. Thread the pork snugly onto bamboo skewers. Grill over a medium-hot flame or broil 5 inches from the heat, turning once, until deep brown and crisp around the edges, about 3 minutes per side. Set aside.

4. In a large pan of boiling water, cook the rice vermicelli, stirring often, until firm but tender, about 4 minutes. Pour the water off and fill the pot with hot water. Drain and repeat. Drain well, tossing the noodles often to dry them and keep them separate.

5. In a large bowl, using tongs, combine the noodles with the bean sprouts, mint, coriander, perilla, Fried Shallots, pork rinds, and the grilled pork. Add the Nuoc Cham and mix well. Arrange on a large platter and sprinkle with the peanuts. Serve warm or slightly chilled.

STAR ANISE BEEF STEW WITH LEMONGRASS *(Bo Kho)*

MAKES 4 TO 6 SERVINGS

Cinnamon trees, peppercorn vines, and the evergreen that produces star anise thrive in Vietnam and are of the highest quality. This is a luxurious beef stew, due in part to the good cut of brisket used and to the combination of flavors: star anise, lemongrass, tomato, and the last-minute garnish of fresh basil, which has its own pleasant anise taste.

> 3 pounds trimmed beef brisket or chuck, cut into 1-inch cubes
> 2 stalks lemongrass, finely chopped
> $1/8$ teaspoon five spice powder
> $3/4$ teaspoon freshly ground black pepper
> 4 cloves garlic, minced
> 1 teaspoon salt
> 1 tablespoon soy sauce
> 2 teaspoons sugar
> 2 tablespoons vegetable oil
> 1 small onion, chopped
> 2 tablespoons tomato paste
> 3 carrots, split and cut into 2-inch pieces
> 3 whole star anise
> $1/4$ teaspoon dried chile flakes
> $1/4$ cup chopped basil, for garnish
> 1 small red chile, thinly sliced, optional

1. In a large saucepan of boiling water, add the beef and when the water comes back to a boil drain it.

2. In a medium bowl, combine the beef with half the lemongrass, the five spice powder, black pepper, 2 cloves of the garlic, salt, soy sauce, and sugar. Set aside to marinate for about 10 minutes.

3. In a large saucepan over high heat, heat the oil until hot, add the onion and the remaining garlic and lemongrass. Cook, stirring for about 1 minute, then add the tomato paste and cook another minute. Add the beef and coat it well. Add $4\frac{1}{2}$ cups water, the carrots, star anise, and chile flakes. Bring to a boil, reduce the heat to low, and simmer about $1\frac{1}{2}$ hours, or until the beef is very tender. When ready to serve, top with the chopped basil and sliced chile, if desired. Serve with French bread or cooked rice noodles.

SHAKING BEEF *(Bo Luc Lac)*

MAKES 4 TO 6 SERVINGS

The Vietnamese named this dish to describe the shaking action of the pan used in stir-frying the beef for this garlicky sauté. It is served hot over cool, dressed watercress.

1/2 cup Soy Vinaigrette (page 51)
1 1/2 pounds beef sirloin or tenderloin, cut into 1-inch cubes
5 cloves garlic, minced
3 tablespoons soy sauce
2 tablespoons sugar
1 1/2 tablespoons dry sherry
2 whites of scallion, cut into 1/4-inch pieces
1 teaspoon freshly ground black pepper
1/4 cup vegetable oil
2 large bunches watercress, torn into small sprigs
1 small red onion, thinly sliced

1. Prepare the Soy Vinaigrette and set aside.

2. In a large bowl, combine the beef with the garlic, soy sauce, sugar, sherry, scallion, pepper, and 2 tablespoons of the oil. Cover and refrigerate 3 hours or overnight.

3. When ready to serve, put the watercress and onion on a large platter and toss with the vinaigrette.

4. In a large skillet over high heat, add the remaining 2 tablespoons of oil and when smoking, add the beef mixture in an even layer. Let it sit in the pan undisturbed, until it forms a brown crust on the bottom, about 1 minute. Now, shake the pan to release the beef, using chopsticks if needed. Cook, shaking the pan occasionally, to desired doneness, about 4 minutes for medium-rare. Spoon the hot beef over the watercress and serve.

LEMONGRASS BEEF *(Bo Nuong Vi)*

MAKES 4 APPETIZER SERVINGS

In Vietnam, this grilled beef is traditionally quickly seared at the table in a light cast-iron pan over a small charcoal pot. The diners have already helped themselves to the Table Salad and will roll up the hot beef with the other cool components to dip in the Pineapple Chile Sauce.

Table Salad for 4 (page 32) with Noodle Cakes (page 66), optional
Pineapple Chile Sauce (page 43)
1 stalk fresh lemongrass, finely chopped, or 2 teaspoons powdered lemongrass
8 cloves garlic, minced
2½ tablespoons soy sauce
2 tablespoons sugar
1 teaspoon sesame oil
1 tablespoon dry sherry
1 teaspoon freshly ground black pepper
3 tablespoons vegetable oil
1 pound lean beef from the top, bottom, or eye of round, cut into very thin slices
about 3 inches wide

1. Prepare the Table Salad, Noodle Cakes if using, and Pineapple Chile Sauce and set aside.

2. In a medium bowl, combine the lemongrass, garlic, soy sauce, sugar, sesame oil, sherry, pepper, and 2 tablespoons of the oil. Add the beef and mix well to coat evenly. Cover and marinate at room temperature at least 4 hours or in the refrigerator overnight.

3. In a large skillet over high heat, heat about ½ tablespoon of the oil. When it starts to smoke, add some of the beef slices in an even layer. Brown quickly on one side, about 30 seconds, then turn and brown the other side. Remove the beef to a warm plate and repeat with the remaining slices, adding more oil as necessary. Pass the beef at the table, inviting the diners to compose their own rolls as they please.

BEEF ROLLS FILLED WITH GINGER *(Bo Cuon Gung)*

MAKES 4 TO 6 SERVINGS

Binh created this dish when a famous French chef was coming to his restaurant for dinner. If you can find it, young or spring ginger is preferred. Skewering the small rolls seals them as they brown.

½ teaspoon Sate-Chile Oil (page 58) or dried chile flakes
1 2-inch piece ginger, peeled
4 cloves garlic, minced
½ teaspoon salt
½ teaspoon freshly ground black pepper
1 teaspoon sesame oil
2 tablespoons vegetable oil
1 pound lean beef round, very thinly sliced, about 3 inches wide and pounded
*   flat*
1 carrot, split and thinly sliced
6 8-inch-long bamboo skewers
2 bay leaves
¼ cup dry red wine
2 teaspoons rinsed chopped fermented black beans, optional
1 tablespoon butter

1. Prepare the Sate-Chile Oil and set aside.

2. Slice the ginger lengthwise very thin. Stack the slices and cut into long thin sticks.

3. In a medium bowl, combine the garlic, salt, pepper, sesame oil, and 1 tablespoon of the vegetable oil and combine with the beef to coat evenly. Set aside to marinate for about 20 minutes.

4. In a small saucepan of boiling water, cook the carrot slices over high heat until just tender, about 4 minutes. Reserve ¼ cup of the cooking liquid and drain the carrots.

5. Lay each piece of beef out flat and put about 3 sticks of ginger in the center, or more if you prefer. Bring the sides together to enclose the ginger and roll up. Thread the beef rolls snugly, onto each 8 inch bamboo skewer.

6. In a large skillet over high heat, heat a ½ tablespoon of the remaining oil. When the oil starts to smoke, add half the beef skewers and brown well, about 1 minute per side. Remove to a plate and repeat with the remaining oil and skewers. Pour off the oil, add the bay leaves, Chile Oil, and carrots and cook, stirring, for about 30 seconds. Add the red wine, black beans, and reserved carrot water and boil until reduced slightly, about 3 minutes. Remove the beef rolls from the skewers, reduce the heat to low, and put the rolls back in the skillet with any accumulated juices from the plate. Simmer until heated through, about 3 minutes. Off the heat stir in the butter until blended.

SUGGESTIONS: Serve the Spaghetti Squash Salad (page 170) as a first course or the Green Papaya Salad (page 162), and rice with the beef.

BEEF AND JICAMA CREPINETTES *(Bo Cuon Mo Chai)*

MAKES 4 TO 6 APPETIZER SERVINGS

These small sausage patties, spiked with jicama sticks and coarse black pepper, use flavorful caul fat as a wrapping to contain and glaze the meat as it cooks. If you can't find caul fat, grill the beef as is for a little less time.

Pineapple Chile Sauce (page 43)
Table Salad for 6 (page 32)
1 teaspoon whole black peppercorns
4 cloves garlic, chopped
2 teaspoons sugar
$1/4$ teaspoon five spice powder
2 teaspoons dry sherry
1 tablespoon bottled fish sauce (nuoc mam)
2 teaspoons sesame oil
1 teaspoon vegetable oil
1 pound lean ground beef
$1/2$ small onion, finely chopped
$1/2$ cup short thin jicama sticks
$1/2$ pound caul fat, cut into 20 3×2-inch pieces, optional

1. Prepare the Pineapple Chile Sauce and Table Salad and set aside.

2. In a mortar, pound the peppercorns coarse. Add the garlic and pound to a paste. Add the sugar and five spice powder and pound to combine. Stir in the sherry, fish sauce, and sesame and vegetable oils.

3. In a large bowl, use a wooden spoon to mix the beef and onion together, lifting the mixture up as you stir to incorporate air. Add the flavorings from the mortar and the jicama and mix well. Set aside to marinate at least 30 minutes or covered overnight in the refrigerator.

4. If you're using caul fat, lay a number of pieces out flat and put a heaping tablespoon of the filling in the center. Flatten the beef slightly into an oval shape. Fold in the sides of the caul fat and roll up like a spring roll. Repeat with the remaining fat and beef; you should have about 20 rolls. Otherwise, just form the beef into 20 oval shapes.

5. Preheat a grill or broiler. Grill the crepinettes over a medium-to-low fire, turning frequently, as the caul fat tends to flare up. Cook slowly and evenly until crispy, lightly charred, but still pink in the center, about 7 minutes per side. Serve hot with the salad and the sauce in bowls on the side.

BEEF FONDUE *(Bo Nhung Dam)*

MAKES 4 TO 6 APPETIZER SERVINGS

Similar to Mongolian hot pot, from which this dish probably originated, beef fondue Vietnamese style, is served as part of the traditional beef banquet called Beef in Seven Courses. Beef is an expensive and rare treat for most Vietnamese, and so is given special honor in a meal that consists of all beef dishes. The number of courses can range from four to eight, but seven being a lucky number is favored. Many Asian cuisines use ceramic cookers made expressly for the table that can hold the heat element—be it white hot charcoal chunks from the kitchen brazier, a candle, or small alcohol or Sterno burners—with a platform to hold the vessel of simmering hot broth. You'll find these cookers in Chinese, Korean, Japanese, and Thai specialty stores. The beef slices are held with chopsticks, then dipped into a lemony broth to delicately poach and infuse them. Table Salad accompanies the fondue and Pineapple Chile sauce is a tantalizing enhancer, though Nuoc Cham is fine, too.

Pineapple Chile Sauce (page 43)
Table Salad for 6 (page 32)
2 cups club soda
2 teaspoons sugar
3 tablespoons white vinegar
2 stalks lemongrass, flattened with the side of a knife and cut into 2-inch lengths
1 pound lean beef, from the round, cut into very thin, wide slices
1 medium onion, thinly sliced
1 3-inch piece ginger, peeled and cut into very thin sticks

1. Prepare the Pineapple Chile Sauce and set aside. Arrange the Table Salad components on a platter.

2. In a medium saucepan, combine the club soda, sugar, vinegar, and lemongrass. Simmer over medium heat until the sugar dissolves and the flavors blend, about 5 minutes.

3. Pour the liquid into a fondue pot or chafing dish. Bring to the table and place over a heat source, like a Sterno burner.

4. Put the beef, onion, and ginger on a platter and bring to the table with the Table Salad and small bowls of dipping sauce. Using chopsticks, each person dips a slice of beef into the fondue pot to cook until just rare, about 10 seconds. Then swirl the onion slices in the broth to soften for a few seconds. Put the beef on a lettuce leaf and roll up with onion, ginger, and other accompaniments. Dip into the sauce.

SUGGESTIONS: Fried Vegetables with Noodles (page 286) as a starter and rice with the beef would complete this menu.

BEEF WITH SNOW PEAS AND MUSHROOMS
(Bo Xao Dau Hoa-Lan)

MAKES 2 TO 4 SERVINGS

This is an uncomplicated but textural, satisfying, and spicy dish adapted from the Chinese. For two people it constitutes a one-course meal; for four, it could be part of a large dinner.

Half rice recipe (page 34)
4 cloves garlic, minced
2 teaspoons sugar
1 tablespoon soy sauce
2 teaspoons dry sherry
$\frac{1}{2}$ teaspoon sesame oil
$\frac{1}{2}$ teaspoon freshly ground black pepper
2 teaspoons plus $1\frac{1}{2}$ tablespoons vegetable oil
$\frac{1}{2}$ pound lean beef such as round, cut into very thin slices about 3 inches wide
10 dried shiitake mushrooms
1 medium onion, cut into thin wedges
1 teaspoon dried chile flakes or Sate-Chile Oil (page 58)
1 carrot, cut into very thin rounds
1 tablespoon oyster sauce
$\frac{1}{2}$ cup chicken stock
$\frac{1}{2}$ pound snow peas

1. Prepare the rice and set aside.

2. In a large bowl, combine the garlic, sugar, soy sauce, sherry, sesame oil, pepper, and 2 teaspoons of the vegetable oil. Add the beef and mix to coat evenly. Set aside to marinate at room temperature 1 hour or cover and refrigerate overnight.

3. In a medium bowl, cover the mushrooms with hot water and soak until soft, about 20 minutes. Drain, rinse well, remove the stems, and cut into quarters.

4. In a wok over high heat, add ½ tablespoon of the oil and when smoking, add the onion. Stir-fry for 1 minute, then add the beef and chile flakes. Stir-fry until the beef is just cooked, about 2 minutes. Remove to a plate.

5. Return the wok to high heat and add the remaining 1 tablespoon oil. When smoking, add the mushrooms and carrot rounds and stir-fry for 1 minute. Add the oyster sauce and chicken stock and cook until reduced by half, about 2 minutes. Add the snow peas and cook for 1 minute. Return the beef mixture to the wok and cook just to heat through. Serve with the rice.

SUGGESTIONS: Serve Shrimp on Sugar Cane (page 112) or Crunchy Sweet Potato Nests with Shrimp (page 114), as a first course.

GOLDEN PEPPER STEAK *(Bo Xao Ot)*

MAKES 4 SERVINGS

Though pepper steak is associated with Chinese cuisine, it is a standard Vietnamese dish as well. Many cultures, in fact, combine beef and bell peppers, but the Vietnamese have a light touch with their version. We favor sweet yellow and red bell peppers to the underripe green peppers often used. They make all the difference.

Half rice recipe (page 34)
1 pound eye of beef round, cut crosswise into $\frac{1}{8}$-inch-thick slices
1 teaspoon freshly ground black pepper
4 cloves garlic, minced
$\frac{1}{2}$ teaspoon sesame oil
2 tablespoons soy sauce
$1\frac{1}{2}$ tablespoons sugar
$\frac{1}{2}$ tablespoon sherry or dry white wine
$3\frac{1}{2}$ tablespoons vegetable oil
2 large yellow bell peppers, cut into 1 × 3-inch pieces
1 red bell pepper, cut into 1 × 3-inch pieces
1 medium onion, cut into 1 × 3-inch pieces
$\frac{1}{2}$ teaspoon salt
1 teaspoon oyster sauce
$\frac{2}{3}$ cup chicken stock
1 teaspoon cornstarch

1. Prepare the rice and set aside.

2. In a large bowl, combine the beef, black pepper, garlic, sesame oil, soy sauce, sugar, and sherry. Set aside and marinate at least 1 hour but no more than 3 hours.

3. In a wok over high heat, heat 2 tablespoons of the vegetable oil. Add the peppers, onion, salt, and oyster sauce and cook, stirring, for 1 minute. Add the chicken stock, cover, and cook for about 10 minutes, until the peppers are tender.

4. Meanwhile, in a large skillet over high heat, heat the remaining $1\frac{1}{2}$ tablespoons oil until almost smoking. Add the beef and brown on both sides, about 1 minute per side.

5. Add the peppers to the beef. Dissolve the cornstarch in 1 teaspoon water and stir it into the mixture. Boil once. Serve with the rice.

GRILLED CURRIED STEAK
WITH ROASTED PEPPERS *(Bo Nuong Ca-Ri)*

MAKES 4 SERVINGS

Here is Binh's unorthodox version of pepper steak, using a popular American cut of beef and fulfilling our modern taste for roasted peppers. While preheating the grill, you can char the peppers directly over the flames instead of in the oven. The oven method, however, softens and sweetens the peppers more effectively than does the grill.

FOR THE STEAK

4 cloves garlic, crushed
1 small red chile, chopped
1 teaspoon freshly ground black pepper
1 tablespoon sugar
1 teaspoon curry paste or powder (page 15)
2 tablespoons soy sauce
1 tablespoon dry white wine
1 tablespoon vegetable oil
*1 1½-pound flank steak, trimmed of excess fat, cut crosswise on the diagonal into
    ¼-inch-thick slices*

FOR THE PEPPERS

3 large red bell peppers
2 tablespoons vegetable oil or olive oil
2 cloves garlic, minced
½ teaspoon salt
½ teaspoon freshly ground black pepper

1. To prepare the steak: In a mortar, pound the garlic, chile, and black pepper to a coarse paste. Add the sugar, curry paste, soy sauce, wine, and oil and stir to blend. Put the beef in a large shallow dish and pour the marinade over it. Toss the meat with the marinade to coat it all over. Marinate at least 2 hours at room temperature or covered overnight in the refrigerator.

2. Meanwhile, prepare the peppers: Preheat the oven to 400 degrees. Put the peppers on a baking sheet and roast in the oven until charred on one side, about 20 minutes. Turn and roast for 20 minutes more. Cool slightly and remove the blackened skin, seeds, and core. Cut the peppers into thick strips and put them in a medium bowl. Toss the peppers with the oil, garlic, salt, and pepper. Let the peppers sit at room temperature for at least 2 hours. They should be eaten the day they are made.

3. Preheat the grill and grill the beef slices over a very hot fire until lightly charred and crisp, about 2 minutes per side. Arrange the beef on a platter with the roasted peppers surrounding it.

BEEF MEDALLIONS WITH WATER SPINACH
(Thit Bo Xao Rau Muong)

MAKES 4 SERVINGS

Garlic has a great affinity for beef and for spinach. Here is a Vietnamese garlicky beef dish that uses water spinach, which is easier to prepare than regular spinach as it requires no special cleaning.

Half rice recipe (page 34)
3 cloves garlic, minced, and 4 cloves garlic, very thinly sliced
1 tablespoon sugar
1½ tablespoons soy sauce
1 teaspoon sesame oil
¾ teaspoon freshly ground black pepper
2 tablespoons plus 2 teaspoons vegetable oil
½ teaspoon dried chile flakes
1 pound beef tenderloin, cut crosswise into slices ¼ inch thick
1 pound water spinach, tough lower stems removed
2 teaspoons bottled fish sauce (nuoc mam)

1. Prepare the rice and set aside.

2. In a large bowl, mix the minced garlic with the sugar to form a syrup. Stir in the soy sauce, sesame oil, ½ teaspoon of the black pepper, 2 teaspoons of the oil, and the chile flakes. Add the beef slices and coat well. Set aside to marinate at room temperature for 2 hours or cover and refrigerate overnight.

3. In a large skillet, combine 1 tablespoon of the remaining oil and the sliced garlic. Cook slowly over low heat until the garlic softens and becomes golden, about 4 minutes. Increase the heat to high and add the water spinach. With chopsticks, stir the spinach to wilt it. Add 2 tablespoons water, the fish sauce, and the remaining $\frac{1}{4}$ teaspoon black pepper. Cook, stirring, until most of the liquid evaporates, about 1 minute. Put the water spinach on a warm platter and cover with foil.

4. Put the skillet back on the fire and over high heat add the remaining 1 tablespoon oil. When almost smoking, add half of the beef slices in an even layer and cook about $1\frac{1}{2}$ minutes per side for medium-rare. Remove to a plate. Repeat with the remaining beef. To serve, arrange the beef over the water spinach. Serve with the rice.

ANISE BEEF BUNDLES *(Bo Cach-Vach)*

MAKES 5 TO 6 APPETIZER OR 3 TO 4 MAIN-COURSE SERVINGS

Star anise–scented beef slices are wrapped around cooked pork, then grilled. Use any unsmoked streaky bacon for this if you wish. Because Binh doesn't like any fat on his meat, including spareribs, he adapted this recipe to suit his tastes, using lean boiled pork to replace fresh belly bacon that is favored by the Vietnamese.

Pineapple Chile Sauce (page 43)
Table Salad for 4 to 6 (page 32)
1 whole star anise, broken into pieces
3 cloves garlic, crushed in a mortar or minced
$1\frac{1}{2}$ tablespoons sugar
$1\frac{1}{2}$ tablespoons soy sauce
2 tablespoons dry white wine
1 tablespoon vegetable oil
$\frac{1}{4}$ teaspoon freshly ground black pepper
$\frac{1}{4}$ teaspoon paprika
$\frac{1}{4}$ teaspoon dried chile flakes
$\frac{3}{4}$ pound lean beef, such as eye of round, cut crosswise into 16 very thin slices
$\frac{1}{4}$ pound piece lean shoulder or loin of pork
4 8-inch-long bamboo skewers

1. Prepare the Pineapple Chile Sauce and the Table Salad and set aside.

2. In a small skillet over high heat, toast the star anise pieces until fragrant, shaking the pan often, about 2 minutes. Put them in a mortar or a spice grinder and pound to a coarse powder. Measure out $\frac{1}{4}$ teaspoon and save the rest in a small jar for another use.

3. In a medium bowl, combine the pulverized star anise, garlic, sugar, soy sauce, wine, vegetable oil, black pepper, paprika, chile flakes, and 1 tablespoon water. Add the beef slices and marinate at room temperature for about 30 minutes.

4. In a medium saucepan, cover the pork with water and boil over medium-high heat until cooked through, about 15 minutes. Remove from the water, let cool slightly, and cut crosswise into 8 slices. Cut those slices in half and set aside.

5. Preheat the broiler or grill. Take the beef slices from the marinade and lay them out flat. Put a piece of pork in the center and fold the beef around the pork like an envelope. Repeat using all the meat. Thread 4 beef rolls onto each skewer. Grill or broil 4 to 5 inches from the heat until crusty, about 4 minutes per side. Serve hot with salad and sauce.

Vegetarian Cooking of the Vietnamese Buddhists

All creatures of ten classes, are you there?
Women and men, the young and old, all come!
All enter Buddha's house and hark his word!
This life is just a bubble or a flash-
"the sum of myriad shapes amount to naught."
O friends, make room for Buddha in your hearts,
and you'll escape the cycle of rebirths!
At his behest, we set a bowl of gruel
and incense candles on the hallowed board;
we offer paper gold and paper clothes
to help you speed your heavenward ascent.
All who have come, be seated and partake.
Spurn not these trifles, gifts of our good will:
by Buddha's grace they'll grow a millionfold,
and all of you shall get your even shares.
—FROM "CALLING ALL WONDERING SOULS"
A POEM BY NGUYEN DU

270

Buddhism began in India when Gautama, a member of the royal family, experienced a revelation. In a series of visions, he saw much pain and suffering, and then, beyond, he saw a place of peace and serenity, Nirvana. He spread his word through kind actions to the many who became his followers. He was called Buddha, or the Enlightened. Buddhism teaches that birth and existence is founded in pain and until one can redeem himself by doing good for others, he will suffer through rebirth, or reincarnation. By following what Buddha developed as the Noble Eightfold Path, living to help and serve others, one will be strenghtened and enlightened, and will not be reborn, but die in supreme peace, finding everlasting happiness in eternal life.

When Buddhism came to Vietnam from China, the religion had already divided into two major sects: Mahayana and a lesser, simpler form, Hinayana. When tribes from India wandered long ago to southern parts of Vietnam, they helped spread Mahayana Buddhism throughout the area around the Mekong Delta and up the Annamite (Truong Son) mountain range and out to the sea, an area known then as Annam, the peaceful South. Based on complete equality and individual good deed, Buddhism has no supreme power, or leader, but is guided by groups of monks. Buddhist monks are pure vegetarians who believe that all living creatures have souls and feast mainly on fruits, vegetables, and rice.

Many Vietnamese are Buddhists, yet are not strict vegetarians, though they will prepare authentic vegetarian dishes, especially during certain times of the month that have spiritual significance. This means that even by-products, such as fish sauce, are forbidden during these times. Soy sauce is the staple liquid seasoning. Soybean curd is a most perfect food for vegetarians because it is rich in protein and vitamins and can be made into other bean curd products—from dried bean curd sheets to red fermented bean curd—for variations in texture and gains in flavor. The yin and yang of vegetarian cooking combines the young textures and flavors of fresh vegetables and tofu with the aged flavors of preserved and dried tofu and other ingredients.

Though there are dietary laws in Buddhism, the Vietnamese vegetarian cooks dishes that are well balanced, varied, and extremely nutritious. An important technique in vegetarian cooking is to use two or three different cooking methods for one ingredient and combine those into one dish.

Scallions and garlic are excluded from the diet of the Vietnamese Buddhists because of legend. Leeks provide an onion flavor. The legend entails a story about a Buddhist temple that was invaded. The enemy killed the monks' dogs and tried but failed to make the monks eat them. When the monks later buried the dogs, garlic and scallions grew over the graves, a sign that these were forbidden vegetables.

The authentic and adapted vegetarian recipes that follow are faithful to the recipes of the Buddhist monks who take their food very seriously. As you will see, with such a high regard for nourishment and so much talent for deftly incorporating both yin and yang into a restricted diet, the monks eat very well indeed.

VEGETABLE STOCK

MAKES ABOUT 5 CUPS

1 large onion, quartered
2 large carrots, cut into small pieces
$\frac{1}{2}$ small head of cabbage, cut into thin wedges
5 stalks celery, cut into small pieces
1 leek, split and rinsed
1 bay leaf
$\frac{1}{4}$ teaspoon dried thyme
$\frac{1}{2}$ teaspoon whole white peppercorns
1 teaspoon sugar
2 teaspoons salt

1. In a large saucepan or stockpot, combine all the ingredients, except the salt, and cover with 8 cups water. Bring to a boil over high heat, reduce the heat to medium low, and add the salt. Simmer about 1 hour. Strain. The stock will keep, covered, in the refrigerator for up to 1 week.

MUSHROOM AND LEEK SOUP
WITH DRIED WHITE FUNGUS *(Sup Nam Trang)*

MAKES 4 TO 6 SERVINGS

Made with a trio of earthy, delicate ingredients, this soup gets its special quality from dried white fungus, which turns frilly and translucent when reconstituted. With a mild taste and indestructible crunchiness, the dried mushrooms are supposed to have medicinal properties as well. Just a drop of chile sauce at the end is all that's needed.

3 cups Vegetable Stock (page 272)
$1/3$ cup dried white fungus (about $3/4$ ounce), soaked in hot water for 20 minutes
1 tablespoon vegetable oil
1 large white of leek, split, rinsed thoroughly, and thinly sliced
$1/2$ teaspoon freshly ground black pepper
$1/4$ teaspoon salt
5 large white mushrooms, caps and stems separated and thinly sliced
2 teaspoons cornstarch mixed with 1 tablespoon water
10 snow peas, sliced crosswise $1/4$ inch thick
2 tablespoons coriander leaves
Chile sauce

1. Prepare the Vegetable Stock and set aside.

2. Drain the fungus and rise well. Cut off the hard knobs. Chop coarse.

3. In a medium saucepan over high heat, heat the oil until hot. Add the leek and stir-fry 1 minute. Add the pepper, salt, and mushrooms and stir-fry for 1 minute. Add the stock and white fungus and simmer over medium-high heat until the leek is tender, about 4 minutes. Turn the heat down to medium and stir in the cornstarch mixture. Cook, stirring until thickened, about 1 minute. Remove from the heat and stir in the snow peas. Serve hot in small bowls and top with the coriander leaves. Pass the chile sauce separately.

VEGETARIAN TOFU SOUP *(Canh Chua Chay)*

MAKES 4 TO 6 SERVINGS

Deceptively mild-looking, this soup is not only fragrant but sour and spicy as well. As a first course serve as is; if you'd like to serve it as a main course, however, prepare rice.

3 cups Vegetable Stock (page 272) or water
$1/4$ cup tamarind pulp
1 teaspoon salt
1 teaspoon sugar
3 3-ounce tofu cakes, cut into 2-inch pieces
1 medium tomato, cut into thin wedges
$1^1/2$ cups mung bean sprouts
2 tablespoons chopped gno gai, *the saw-leaf herb, or coriander*
1 teaspoon dried chile flakes, or to taste

1. Prepare the Vegetable Stock and set aside.

2. In a small bowl, cover the tamarind pulp with $1/2$ cup hot water. Let stand for about 5 minutes. Mash with a fork and pick out the seeds or pass the pulp through a strainer.

3. In a large saucepan over high heat, combine the tamarind pulp, stock, salt, and sugar and bring to a boil. Add the tofu and tomato and bring to a boil. Turn off the heat and stir in the bean sprouts, herb, and chile flakes. Serve hot.

VEGETARIAN SUMMER ROLLS *(Goi Cuon Chay)*

MAKES 4 TO 6 SERVINGS

These summer rolls are filled with cooked sweet potato, egg sheets, and fried tofu—an unusual and winning combination.

Hoisin Dipping Sauce (page 294)
Table Salad for 6 (page 32, be sure to include rice vermicelli and garlic chives)
1 large sweet potato (about 12 ounces)
Vegetable oil for frying
3 3-ounce tofu cakes, each cut into 4 lengthwise slices
2 eggs, beaten
Pinch salt and freshly ground black pepper

1. Prepare the Hoisin Dipping Sauce and Table Salad and set aside.

2. In a small saucepan over medium heat, cover the sweet potato with water and simmer until tender when pierced with a fork, about 20 minutes. Drain and peel. Halve lengthwise and cut into wide sticks.

3. In a medium skillet over medium-high heat heat $\frac{1}{4}$ inch of oil. Pat the tofu dry with paper towels and add the slices. Cook until crisp, about 5 minutes per side. Drain on paper towels. Cut into thin strips.

4. In a small well-seasoned pan or nonstick skillet, heat about a teaspoon of the oil over medium-high heat until it starts to smoke. Add $\frac{1}{3}$ of the beaten eggs and swirl the pan to distribute the egg evenly. Cook, without stirring, until set on the bottom, about 30 seconds. Turn and cook about 10 seconds. Remove to a plate and repeat the procedure, making 2 more egg sheets. Cut the egg sheets into wide strips.

5. To serve, arrange the cooked items on the platter with the Table Salad and have small bowls of the dipping sauce on the side.

VEGETARIAN SPRING ROLLS *(Cha Gio Chay)*

MAKES 36 ROLLS

Cabbage adds crunch and good flavor and with tofu becomes the meaty ingredient of these spring rolls. Feel free to use other vegetables in the filling—*shittake* mushrooms or fresh water chestnuts—if you have them.

Soy Dipping Sauce (page 295)
Table Salad for 6 (page 32)
2 tablespoons dried tree ears
Half a 1.8-ounce package cellophane noodles
1 carrot, finely shredded and rinsed
1½ cups finely shredded cabbage
1 medium onion, minced
3 3-ounce, firm tofu cakes
1 teaspoon freshly ground black pepper
1 teaspoon salt
1 egg, optional
54 triangle rice papers
2 beaten eggs, or ⅓ cup water mixed with 2 tablespoons white vinegar
Oil for deep frying

1. Prepare the Soy Dipping Sauce and Table Salad and set aside.

2. In a small bowl, cover the tree ears with hot water and soak until softened and inflated, about 10 minutes. Rinse, cut off any hard knobs, and chop fine.

3. In a small bowl, soak the cellophane noodles in cold water until pliable, about 3 minutes. Drain and with scissors cut into 2-inch lenghts.

4. In a large bowl, combine the tree ears, cellophane noodles, carrot, cabbage, onion, tofu, pepper, salt, and egg, if using. Mix the filling well.

5. Take 18 of the rice paper triangles and with scissors cut them in half, lengthwise. Put a half triangle in the center of a regular triangle, points and wide bottom facing similarly. Working with about 6 at a time, brush both sides with the beaten eggs or vinegar-water mixture and lay flat on a work surface to soften. Place about 1 tablespoon of the filling on the wide bottom of the rice paper about ½ inch from the edge. Bring the bottom flap up and over the filling, pressing around the edges to eliminate air. Fold in the sides and press again to keep the bundle tight. Now roll up tightly. Continue making rolls with the remaining wrappers and filling.

6. In a large skillet, add about ½ inch oil to the pan. Turn the heat to medium-high and add enough spring rolls to fill the skillet without overcrowding. Cook the rolls until brown on one side, about 7 minutes. Turn and fry until golden brown on all sides. If the oil gets too hot, adjust the heat to maintain a steady simmer without smoking, no more than 350 degrees on a deep-fry thermometer. Remove the skillet from the burner and let it cool slightly before adding the next batch. (If the oil is too hot, the spring rolls may burst.) Drain the rolls on paper towels. Serve hot or at room temperature with the dipping sauce and salad.

FRIED TOFU SALAD *(Goi Dau Khuon)*

MAKES 6 SALAD SERVINGS

Like many Vietnamese salads, each vegetable here is treated separately, with either vinegar, salt, or sugar, and is then tossed together with fried tofu pieces.

> *4 3-ounce, firm tofu cakes, sliced in half lengthwise, then cut into 4 long pieces*
> *Vegetable oil for frying*
> *1 large carrot, peeled and cut on a grating box into 2- to 3-inch-long thin strips*
> *$\frac{1}{2}$ cup plus 1 tablespoon white wine vinegar*
> *2 stalks celery, peeled and cut into 2-inch-long thin strips*
> *3 tablespoons sugar*
> *1 European (hothouse) cucumber, cut into 2-inch-long thin strips*
> *$2\frac{1}{8}$ teaspoons salt*
> *1 medium onion, thinly sliced*
> *2 small red chiles, seeded and finely chopped, or to taste*
> *$\frac{1}{2}$ teaspoon freshly ground black pepper*
> *$\frac{1}{4}$ cup plus 2 tablespoons chopped peanuts*

1. Pat the tofu dry with paper towels. In a large skillet over medium-high heat, heat $\frac{1}{4}$ inch oil until hot. Add half the tofu and fry until golden brown and crisp on both sides, about 3 minutes per side. Drain on paper towels and repeat with the remaining tofu.

2. Put the carrot in a bowl and rinse with water. Drain and add the $\frac{1}{2}$ cup vinegar. Let sit a few minutes, then squeeze dry and put in a large bowl.

3. Put the celery in a colander and sprinkle it with 2 tablespoons of the sugar. Toss the celery with the sugar and mix well for about 2 minutes. (The celery will release a lot of juice.) Squeeze the celery dry with your hands and put in the bowl with the carrot.

4. Put the cucumber in a colander, sprinkle with 2 teaspoons of the salt, and mix well for about 1 minute. Squeeze the cucumber dry and add to the other vegetables. Add the onion, chiles, fried tofu and toss gently.

5. In a small bowl, combine the remaining vinegar, sugar, and salt with 3 tablespoons water and the pepper. Pour over the salad and mix well.

6. To serve, arrange equal amounts of the salad on 6 plates and sprinkle each salad with 1 tablespoon of the peanuts.

CARROT, JICAMA, AND TOFU SALAD *(Goi Chay)*

MAKES 6 SERVINGS

This savory salad, layered with fried and raw vegetables, features the yin and yang of tofu—fresh tofu cakes and dried tofu sheets—both fried, but with different effects.

> 1 cup Vegetarian Salad Dressing (page 296)
> Vegetable oil for frying
> 3 3-ounce tofu cakes, each cut into 4 slices lengthwise
> 1 large sheet dried bean curd, broken in half crosswise
> 1 large carrot, peeled, grated into thin strips, rinsed, and squeezed dry
> 1 pound jicama, peeled and grated into thin strips
> 2 tablespoons chopped mint
> 2 tablespoons chopped rau ram or coriander
> $1/4$ cup chopped peanuts
> Sriracha chile sauce

1. Prepare the Vegetarian Salad Dressing and set aside.

2. In a large skillet over medium-high heat, heat $1/3$ inch oil until hot. Pat the tofu slices dry with paper towels, then fry, in batches until crisp, about 5 minutes per side. Drain on paper towels. Cut the tofu into thin strips. In the hot oil, fry the bean curd sheet until puffed and crisp, about 5 seconds per side. Drain on paper towels.

3. In a large bowl, combine the carrot and jicama and toss with the dressing. Let sit and tenderize about 5 minutes. Add the fried tofu, mint, *rau ram*, and peanuts and toss gently. Put the salad on a platter and crumble the fried bean curd sheets over the top. Pass the chile sauce on the side.

FRIED TOFU WITH GREEN BEANS *(Dau Khuon Xao Dau)*

MAKES 4 MAIN-COURSE SERVINGS

These are quite simply braised green beans embellished with fried tofu. A good sauce here deserves plenty of rice.

Full rice recipe (page 34)
4 3-ounce firm tofu cakes, cut into 1-inch cubes
1 tablespoon vegetable oil plus more for deep frying
1 medium onion, thinly sliced
2 medium tomatoes, cut into thin wedges
2 tablespoons sugar
2 tablespoons soy sauce
1 1/4 cup dry white wine
1 1/2 cups thinly sliced bamboo shoots
1/2 pound green beans, trimmed
1 small red chile, thinly sliced
1/2 teaspoon freshly ground black pepper

1. Prepare the rice and set aside.

2. In a large skillet, heat 1/3 inch oil over medium-high heat until hot. Add the tofu cubes and cook until crisp on all sides, about 10 minutes. Drain on paper towels.

3. In a large skillet, heat the 1 tablespoon oil over high heat until hot. Cook the onion for 1 minute. Add the tomatoes and cook 1 minute. Stir in the sugar, soy sauce, wine, and 1/4 cup water. Bring to a boil and add the bamboo shoots, green beans, chile, black pepper, and fried tofu. Reduce the heat to medium, cover, and simmer until the green beans are tender, about 5 minutes. Serve with the rice.

GRILLED TOFU AND VEGETABLES
(Dau Khuon Va La Ghiem Nuong Vi)

MAKES 2 TO 4 SERVINGS

The tofu and vegetables here are first marinated and then grilled to form a nicely caramelized coating. When grilling the skewers, cook undisturbed allowing the crust to develop before grilling the other side.

Half rice recipe (page 34)
3 3-ounce tofu cakes, cut into 1½-inch cubes
Vegetable oil for frying plus 1 tablespoon oil
1 large white of leek, halved lengthwise and rinsed well
1½ tablespoons sugar
½ teaspoon freshly ground black pepper
2 tablespoons soy sauce
1 tablespoon dry sherry
½ teaspoon sesame oil
About 12 8-inch-long bamboo skewers
1 medium zucchini, cut into slices ½ inch thick
1 medium yellow squash, cut into slices ½ inch thick
12 large mushrooms

1. Prepare the rice and set aside.

2. In a large skillet, heat ¼ inch oil over medium-high heat until hot. Pat the tofu dry with paper towels. Add the tofu cubes and cook until crisp, about 5 minutes per side. Drain on paper towels.

3. Finely chop enough leek to make 2 tablespoons. Cut the rest of the leek into 6 two-inch pieces.

4. In a small bowl, combine the chopped leek, sugar, pepper, soy sauce, sherry, sesame oil, the 1 tablespoon vegetable oil, and 2 tablespoons water. Put the fried tofu in a medium bowl and cover with ⅓ of the marinade. Coat well and set aside to marinate at least 15 minutes.

5. Thread the leek pieces, zucchini and yellow squash slices, and mushrooms onto 2 skewers, crosswise through the middle. Put the vegetable skewers on a large baking pan. Brush all sides of the skewers with ⅓ of the marinade, saving the rest for basting. Set aside to marinate at least 15 minutes or up to 3 hours. When ready to grill, thread the tofu cubes onto 2 skewers.

6. Over a medium-high flame, grill the skewers, basting occasionally, until deep brown and crusty, about 4 minutes per side. Serve hot with the rice.

NOTE: The tofu browns more quickly than the vegetables, about 1 minute per side. The leeks cook more slowly than the other vegetables, and should be cooked, cut side down, on a slower part of the grill until tender, about 10 minutes.

CURRIED TOFU SAUTÉ (Dau Khuon Xao Lan)

MAKES 4 SERVINGS

Long ago, when southern Vietnam was called Annam, meaning "the peaceful south," many tribes from India, making their way through Southeast Asia, settled there. While practicing the Buddhist religion, they helped spread their beliefs in the region and introduced as well their unique blend of native spices we now know of as curry.

$1/2$ cup Vegetable Stock (page 272) or water
Half rice recipe (page 34)
4 3-ounce, firm tofu cakes, cut crosswise into $1/2$-inch-thick slices
Vegetable oil for frying plus $1 1/2$ tablespoons oil
1 green bell pepper, sliced $1/4$ inch thick
1 small onion, cut into thin wedges
$1/2$ teaspoon curry paste or powder
$1/4$ cup coconut milk
$1/2$ teaspoon dried chile flakes, or to taste
1 tablespoon ngo om or coriander
$1/4$ cup chopped peanuts

1. Prepare the Vegetable Stock and the rice and set aside.

2. In a large skillet, heat about $1/3$ inch oil over medium-high heat until hot. Pat the tofu dry with paper towels and add enough of the tofu slices to fill the pan without overcrowding it. Cook until brown and crisp on both sides, about 3 minutes per side. Drain on paper towels. Repeat with the remaining tofu slices.

3. In the large skillet or wok over high heat, heat the $1 1/2$ tablespoons oil and cook the pepper and onion, stirring, for 1 minute. Add the curry paste and cook, stirring, for 1 minute. Add the stock, coconut milk, chile flakes, and tofu and simmer, stirring occasionally, to heat through and thicken slightly, about 3 minutes. Sprinkle with the ngo om and chopped peanuts and serve with the rice.

LEMONGRASS-SCENTED VEGETABLE SAUTÉ *(Rau Xeo Chay)*

MAKES 4 SERVINGS

Substantial enough as a main course, this sauté also makes a great side dish.

1 cup Vegetable Stock (page 272)
Half rice recipe (page 34)
Vegetable oil for frying
3 3-ounce tofu cakes, cut into 1½-inch cubes
1 stalk lemongrass, very finely chopped
1 large white of leek, split, washed, and thinly sliced, plus some of the tender
*   green, cut into wide strips*
1 long mild green chile, such as Anaheim, thinly sliced
1 green bell pepper, sliced ¼ inch thick
4 leaves of green cabbage, center rib removed, cut into wide strips
5 large white mushrooms, quartered
6 canned baby corns
2 tablespoons soy sauce
½ teaspoon sugar

1. Prepare the Vegetable Stock and the rice and set aside.

2. In a large skillet, heat ⅓ inch oil over medium-high heat until hot. Cook the tofu until crisp, about 5 minutes per side. Drain on paper towels.

3. In a wok or large skillet over high heat, heat 1 tablespoon oil until it starts to smoke. Add the lemongrass and white of leek and stir-fry for 1 minute. Add the remaining vegetables, handfuls at a time, to keep the wok hot. Stir-fry, tossing together, for about 1 minute. Add the stock, fried tofu, soy sauce, and sugar, cover, and cook, stirring occasionally, until the vegetables are tender, about 7 minutes. Serve with the rice.

FRIED VEGETABLES WITH NOODLES *(Bi Chay)*

MAKES 4 TO 6 SERVINGS

This noodle dish is chock full of many different fried vegetables, all in long strands and perfect to eat with chopsticks. But this recipe can easily be transformed into finger food. Take small handfuls and roll in dampened rice paper wrappers, then cut in half and serve with the Soy Dipping Sauce.

Soy Dipping Sauce (page 295)
3 tablespoons Roasted Rice Powder (page 60)
Vegetable oil for frying
2 3-ounce tofu cakes, each cut into 4 slices lengthwise
$1/2$ pound jicama, peeled and cut into $1/4$-inch-thick whole slices
2 medium Idaho potatoes, peeled and cut into julienne strips, or grated, rinsed, drained, and dried
1 large sweet potato, peeled and cut into julienne strips or grated, rinsed, drained, and dried
1 large white of leek, split, washed, and thinly sliced
1 large sheet dried bean curd, broken in half
$1/2$ pound rice vermicelli
$1/4$ teaspoon salt
3 tablespoons chopped peanuts
2 tablespoons chopped mint
2 tablespoons chopped coriander

1. Prepare the Soy Dipping Sauce and Roasted Rice Powder and set aside.

2. In a large skillet, heat $1/4$ inch oil over medium-high heat. Add the tofu slices and fry until brown, about 5 minutes per side. Drain on paper towels and cut into thin strips. Add the jicama and fry until brown but still crunchy, 1 minute per side. Drain on paper towels. Fry the Idaho

potatoes in 2 batches, stirring often, until crisp, about 5 minutes. Drain on paper towels. Fry the sweet potatoes the same way, about 3 minutes. Drain on paper towels. Fry the leek about 10 seconds. Drain. Quickly fry the 2 pieces of bean curd sheets, until puffed and crisp, about 3 seconds per side. Drain on paper towels.

3. In a large saucepan of boiling water, cook the noodles, stirring frequently, until tender, about 4 minutes. Drain and rinse well and with tongs or chopsticks, toss the noodles to cool and separate them.

4. In a large bowl, toss the noodles with the Roasted Rice Powder to combine thoroughly. Add the salt, all the fried vegetables, crumbling in the bean curd sheets, the peanuts, mint, and the coriander. Pour the dipping sauce over all and toss well. Serve as is or at room temperature.

SQUASH AND SWEET POTATO STEW
WITH COCONUT AND PEANUTS *(Kiem)*

MAKES 6 SERVINGS

Kiem is a soothing vegetable stew full of slightly sweet flavors. The tapioca shreds in it can be found in Chinese and Asian markets. They have little flavor but contribute a pleasing chewy quality.

Full rice recipe (page 34)
$1^1/_2$ dried bean curd sheets
$^1/_2$ cup tapioca shreds
Vegetable oil for frying
3 3-ounce tofu cakes, cut into 1-inch cubes
$^1/_2$ coconut, grated (about $1^1/_3$ cups) or about 3 cups canned unsweetened coconut milk
$^1/_2$ pound winter squash such as butternut, acorn, or hubbard, split, peeled, and cut into large chunks
$^1/_2$ pound sweet potato, peeled and cut into large chunks
$^1/_2$ pound zucchini, cut into large chunks
$^1/_2$ pound taro root, peeled and cut into large chunks, optional
$^1/_3$ cup unsalted dry roasted peanuts, or raw, skinned peanuts (see NOTE)
2 tablespoons sugar
1 small red chile, thinly sliced, optional

1. Prepare the rice and set aside.

2. Soak the dried bean curd sheets in cold water to cover and the tapioca shreds in hot water to cover for 20 minutes.

3. In a large skillet, heat about $^1/_4$ inch oil over medium-high heat. Pat the tofu dry with paper towels. Add the tofu and fry until brown and crisp, about 5 minutes per side. Drain on paper towels.

4. Drain the softened bean curd sheets and dry well on paper towels. Fry in the hot oil to stiffen, about 30 seconds per side. Drain on paper towels and cut into 2-inch pieces.

5. Put the grated coconut in a large bowl and cover with ½ cup hot water. With your hands, squeeze the coconut to extract the "cream." Let stand about 3 minutes and pour the mixture through a coarse strainer into a bowl, pressing to extract as much liquid as possible. You should have about ⅓ cup coconut "cream." Set aside. Return the coconut meat to the bowl and cover with 3 cups hot water. Repeat the procedure to extract about 2½ cups coconut "milk." Pour the milk into a large, heavy saucepan or Dutch oven.

   If using canned coconut milk, skim off approximately ⅓ cup of the thickened coconut milk that rises to the top of the can and set aside for the "cream." Stir the remaining 2½ cups liquid and use.

6. Drain the tapioca shreds and in a large saucepan combine with the coconut milk, winter squash, and raw peanuts, if using. Bring to a boil over high heat. Reduce the heat to low, partially cover, and cook for 10 minutes. Add the rest of the vegetables and the fried fresh tofu. Simmer, partially covered, stirring occasionally, until all the vegetables are tender, about 12 minutes.

7. Uncover, add the fried bean curd sheets, the roasted peanuts, sugar, and the chile, if using. Cover and cook 5 minutes more. Off the heat, stir in the reserved coconut cream. Serve with the rice.

NOTE: If you prefer to use the raw peanuts found in Asian markets soak them the day before in cold water.

FRIED TOFU WITH TOMATO AND VEGETABLES
(Dau Khuon Xao Thap Cam)

MAKES 4 SERVINGS

This dish is lovely in its simplicity, yet varied in the number of vegetables used. Vegetarians have clever ways with a limited number of ingredients and frying the tofu before it is added gives extra flavor and a more interesting texture to the dish, as it absorbs the flavors of the tomato and vegetables.

1 cup Vegetable Stock (page 272)
Half rice recipe (page 34)
Vegetable oil for frying plus 1 tablespoon
2 3-ounce tofu cakes, halved and cut into wide strips
1 large white of leek, split, rinsed, and thinly sliced
5 large white mushrooms, sliced
1 tomato, cut into thin wedges
1 teaspoon tomato paste
1 red bell pepper, sliced 1/4 inch thick
1 green bell pepper, sliced 1/4 inch thick
1 small zucchini, cut into 1-inch chunks
1 yellow squash, cut into 1-inch chunks
1 small onion, cut into thin wedges
1 small eggplant, cut into 1-inch chunks
1 teaspoon soy sauce, or more to taste

1. Prepare the Vegetable Stock and the rice and set aside.

2. In a large skillet over medium-high heat, heat 1/4 inch oil until hot. Add the tofu and fry until crisp, about 5 minutes per side. Drain on paper towels.

3. In a large skillet or wok over high heat, heat the 1 tablespoon oil until hot. Add the leek and stir-fry. Add the mushrooms and tomato and stir-fry 1 minute. Add the tomato paste and stir well. Add the remaining vegetables, stock, and soy sauce. Cover and cook for 4 minutes. Add the fried tofu, reduce the heat to medium, cover, and cook about 10 minutes more. Serve with the rice.

WATER SPINACH SAUTÉ *(Rau Muong Xao Chao)*

MAKES 4 SIDE SERVINGS

Water spinach is one of the most pleasurable vegetables to prepare and eat for vegetarians and nonvegetarians alike. The Vietnamese prefer water spinach as the Chinese do—sautéed and finished with rich, fermented red bean paste to smooth out its slightly metallic taste.

2 tablespoons vegetable oil
1 pound water spinach, tough, lower stems removed, leaves with tender stems
    left in large sprigs
½ teaspoon sugar
2 teaspoons red bean paste, mashed

1. In a wok or large skillet over high heat, heat the oil until hot. Start adding large handfuls of water spinach, stirring to wilt them, while you add more. When all the spinach is wilted, stir in the sugar and bean paste until well blended. Serve hot.

BUDDHA RICE *(Com Chay)*

MAKES 6 TO 8 SERVINGS

Buddha rice is a vegetarian dish honored by all Vietnamese and is eaten on certain days of the month that have religious significance and during the moon's full phase. This recipe comes from Binh's aunt, one of his first cooking teachers.

> 1 coconut (or $1\frac{1}{2}$ cups canned unsweetened coconut milk mixed with $1\frac{1}{2}$ cups water)
> 3 cups long-grain rice
> 2 tablespoons vegetable oil
> 1 2-inch piece ginger, peeled, sliced very thin, stacked, and cut into thin sticks
> $\frac{1}{2}$ teaspoon salt
> 1 bay leaf
> $\frac{1}{4}$ cup soy sauce

1. To make coconut milk from a fresh coconut, take a hammer or heavy cleaver and hit the coconut over a sink all around the center, forming a circle. The coconut should break in half easily; if not, hit it a few more times. Discard the water that comes from the middle and remove the outer shell. Cut the halves into smaller pieces. Peel each piece, then grate or shred the coconut. Put the coconut meat in a medium bowl and cover with 2 cups hot water. Let stand for about 8 minutes, then pour the coconut mixture through a fine strainer placed over a bowl. Press hard to extract as much "cream" as possible. Add enough water to make 3 cups coconut liquid or combine the canned unsweetened coconut milk with water.

2. Rinse the rice in several changes of water and drain well in a colander. Let the rice dry in the colander, shaking it occasionally.

3. In a large heavy saucepan, heat the oil over medium-high heat. Add the ginger and stir-fry until fragrant, about 1 minute. Add the rice and cook, stirring to coat it well, about 2 minutes. Stir in the salt, bay leaf, coconut liquid, and soy sauce and bring to a boil. Let the rice cook, without stirring, uncovered, until the liquid settles and holes form all over the top, about 5 minutes. Reduce the heat to very low, cover tightly, and cook for 20 minutes. Remove from the heat and let the rice rest, covered, for 10 minutes. Uncover and stir the rice to fluff it up. Serve hot. The rice can sit, covered, for up to 1 hour before serving.

HOISIN DIPPING SAUCE *(Nuoc Cham Tuong)*

MAKES ABOUT ½ CUP

A thick rich satisfying dip.

1½ tablespoons vegetable oil
1 medium white of leek, split, rinsed, and finely chopped
¼ cup hoisin sauce
2 tablespoons chopped peanuts

1. In a small saucepan over high heat, heat the oil until hot. Add the leek and cook, stirring, for 1 minute. Add the hoisin sauce and ⅓ cup water and cook for 1 minute. Remove the pan from the heat, let cool to room temperature, and stir in the peanuts. The sauce will keep in a jar in the refrigerator for up to 5 days. Bring to room temperature before using.

SOY DIPPING SAUCE *(Xi Dau Cham)*

MAKES ABOUT 1 CUP

As Nuoc Cham is ubiquitous on the meat-eating Vietnamese table, this sauce is ever present at the meals of the vegetarian Buddhists.

$1/4$ *cup sugar*
$1/3$ *cup soy sauce*
1 small red chile, minced
$1^1/_2$ *tablespoons lime juice with some pulp*

1. In a small bowl, combine all the ingredients and stir in $2/3$ cup warm water. Stir and let sit to dissolve the sugar. The sauce will keep in a glass jar in the refrigerator for up to 1 week.

VEGETARIAN SALAD DRESSING *(Dau Giam)*

MAKES ABOUT $\frac{1}{2}$ CUP

Depending on the recipe, this dressing can be used as a vegetable marinade/ tenderizer, to be drained off before using another dressing; or, if the respective salad has plenty of character from its own ingredients, used as a light enhancer.

2 tablespoons white vinegar
3 tablespoons sugar
1 teaspoon freshly ground black pepper
$\frac{1}{4}$ teaspoon salt
$\frac{1}{4}$ cup plus 2 tablespoons water

1. In a small bowl, combine all the ingredients and stir to dissolve. The dressing will keep in a covered jar in the refrigerator for up to 1 week.

Coffee, Tea, and Sweets

When the French occupied Vietnam, coffeehouses became popular and lined many city streets. They were gathering places, where the French and Vietnamese lingered over pastries, newspapers, and the exceptional coffee grown in the mountains. Afternoon tea, with sweets and sandwiches served European style, was a social scene played out in the larger cities. The French also gave the Vietnamese their first taste of ice cream, which is still enjoyed, as well as crisp cookies and soft tea cakes. The French bakers are gone now and fine pastries a sweet memory, but French bread and coffee are still standards in the cafés that remain. These are tiny places, often makeshift spots, under bamboo poles that support thatched coverings or in the shade of a grove of trees. Handpainted signs sport the owners' creative spellings of their places: Café, Caffé, and Caphé.

The Vietnamese are fortunate in that they grow their own superior coffees and teas. All coffees are dark roasted. The usual brewing method is a small drip device that makes one cup at a time and is brought to the table while in the process. The end result is a strong, intensely fragrant, potent infusion, and the inch or so of viscous liquid that is your cup of coffee is plenty enough to rouse your senses. Sweetened condensed milk is similar in consistency to the coffee and makes the perfect creamer.

Jasmine tea is widely drunk in Vietnam, often with meals. It is mildly brewed to protect its flowery flavor. Artichokes, which are grown in Vietnam, are not generally eaten, but used to make a popular, soothing tea. The heart of the artichoke is sliced, then dried. Infused, it makes a very pleasant beverage, its character more distinguished if sweetened with honey.

To end a meal the Vietnamese prefer to gorge on fresh fruit. And it's amazing to see the amount of fruit they can eat. The beauty and variety of their fruits is astounding. The air is heavy with their perfume. Local mangoes have a very dense flesh that is smoky and spicy rather than sweet. Chinese lychees, spiky red rambutans, and smooth yellow loquats are abundant, and there is also the mangosteen, a highly revered and fragrant fruit. Enormous jackfruit, weighing more than twenty pounds, their scaly skins hacked open, reveal the wrinkled yellow orbs that taste like flowery candy. All kinds of bananas abound, from the tiniest finger bananas to large fat cooking types; there are dark green oranges, with bright orange insides; sweet and sour varieties of starfruit, the sweet ones for eating, the sour for Table Salad. Small apples, tart and spicy, like mini-Winesaps, are also eaten with Table Salad as well as for dessert.

While sweet pastries and confections are available commercially made, they are best prepared at home for holidays and on special occasions. The few recipes we've included in the pages that follow are desserts Binh felt strongly about because of their cultural significance. And because they are all quite good.

YELLOW BEAN–COCONUT RICE (Xoi Vo)

MAKES 6 TO 8 SERVINGS

This is a common breakfast or sweet snack food, usually bought on the street, but occasionally prepared at home for special occasions. It's a soothing, mild combination also good as a side dish to Laque Duck (page 219) or Roast Chicken with Five Spice Glaze (page 216).

3 cups short-grain sweet or glutinous rice, rinsed several times
$1\frac{1}{2}$ cups yellow mung beans
1 coconut, broken in half and grated
2 tablespoons sugar
$\frac{1}{2}$ teaspoon salt
1 tablespoon vegetable oil
$\frac{1}{2}$ cup Fried Shallots (page 62), optional

1. The day before, put the rice and mung beans in separate bowls and cover with water by 2 inches. Let soak overnight.

2. The next day, drain the rice in a colander and shake it frequently until quite dry, about 2 hours.

3. In a large bowl, cover the grated coconut with 1 cup boiling water and let stand about 3 minutes. Pass through a strainer into a bowl and press firmly to extract as much cream as possible. You should have about $\frac{1}{2}$ cup coconut "cream." Set aside. Put the coconut back in the bowl and cover with $\frac{2}{3}$ cup boiling water. Let stand a few minutes, then pass through the strainer, pressing firmly. You should have about 1 cup coconut "milk."

4. Drain the mung beans. In a medium saucepan, combine the mung beans with the coconut "milk" and bring to a boil over high heat. Reduce the heat to low, cover, and cook, until tender, about 20 minutes. (Add a few tablespoons of water if the beans get too dry.) Mash the cooked beans with a potato masher. Reserve $\frac{1}{2}$ of the bean paste.

5. In a medium bowl, mix together the rice and remaining bean paste. Form the mixture into 6 large balls and place on the rack of a large steamer. Steam for 30 minutes. Remove the lid and gently break apart the rice balls. Pour the reserved coconut "cream" evenly over the rice. Cover and steam for 5 minutes. Uncover and sprinkle the sugar and salt evenly over the rice. Cover and steam another 5 minutes.

6. Spill the rice into a very large bowl or baking pan and with 2 spoons mix in the oil and the reserved $\frac{1}{2}$ cup bean paste. Serve hot or at room temperature, sprinkled with the shallots, if you like.

COCONUT RICE CAKES FILLED WITH BANANA *(Chuoi Nuong)*

MAKES 6 CAKES

Soft, sticky coconut-infused rice surrounds a small banana, then is grilled in a fragrant banana leaf. Some of the rice gets a little crusty from the grilling. Finger bananas—very small bananas sold in clusters in Asian and Latin markets—work best for this because they are dry but sweet, and, when cooked inside the rice, turn creamy. Binh and I bought two of these cakes from a girl on a Saigon street who carried her own red-hot grill over her shoulder. They are simple to make and should be eaten hot or warm. They're wonderful with or without the coconut sauce.

1 cup long-grain sweet or glutinous rice
$\frac{1}{2}$ cup freshly grated or unsweetened shredded coconut
$1\frac{1}{2}$ teaspoons sugar
7 10×10-inch square pieces of banana leaf
6 finger bananas peeled or 6 3-inch pieces ripe banana, sliced in half lengthwise

COCONUT SAUCE
$\frac{1}{2}$ cup freshly made or canned coconut milk (page 14)
1 teaspoon sugar
Pinch salt
$\frac{1}{2}$ teaspoon cornstarch dissolved in 2 teaspoons water
3 tablespoons chopped unsalted peanuts

1. Wash the rice well in several rinses of water. Drain and put the rice in a medium saucepan. Cover the rice with 1 cup water and bring to a boil over high heat. Boil for 1 minute, then pour off about $\frac{1}{3}$ cup of the water. Reduce the heat to low, cover, and cook for 10 minutes. Remove the pan from the heat, without uncovering it, and let stand, uncovered, for 10 minutes.

2. Uncover the rice and stir to cool it a bit. Then stir in the coconut and sugar and mix well until cool enough to touch.

3. With a damp paper towel, wipe both sides of the banana leaf squares. Take 1 of the banana leaves and tear off 6 long strands to use as ties for the rice cake bundles. Take $1/3$ cup of the rice mixture and in the middle of a banana leaf form it into a 4- by 4-inch square. Put a finger banana on the rice and pull the leaf up and around the banana, rolling the rice around it like a cigar to enclose it. Fold the leaf into a neat square and tie with the leaf strand. Repeat with the remaining rice and bananas.

4. Preheat the grill or an oven to 500 degrees. Grill the rice cake bundles over a medium-hot fire until deeply charred and hot throughout, about 7 minutes per side. Or, put the cakes on a baking sheet and roast in the upper third of the oven until the leaves are crispy and the inside is very hot, about 5 minutes per side.

5. Make the Coconut Sauce: In a small saucepan heat the coconut milk with the sugar and salt over medium-high heat. When it just starts to simmer, stir in the cornstarch mixture and stir until thickened, about 30 seconds. Remove from the heat.

6. To serve: Open the banana leaf and remove the hot cake to a plate. Break it open a little and pour a small amount of warm sauce over it. Sprinkle chopped peanuts over the top and eat right away. Or let the cakes cool in their packets until warm enough to handle, then serve.

FRESH COCONUT COOKIES *(Banh Dua)*

MAKES ABOUT 65 COOKIES

Freshly grated coconut really makes a difference in these Vietnamese maca-roons, the uneven pieces of coconut providing interesting texture. If you value the delicacy of fresh coconut, the vanilla extract may be optional to you. There are two cooking times given, one for chewy cookies, another for crisp ones. They are best the day they're made, but will keep up to four days in a cookie tin.

3 cups freshly grated coconut (1 large coconut)
4 egg whites
Pinch salt
1 cup sugar
1 cup flour
1 stick butter, melted
$\frac{1}{2}$ teaspoon vanilla extract, optional

1. Preheat the oven to 400 degrees. Spread the grated coconut in an even layer on a large baking sheet. Toast on the top shelf of the oven, stirring occasionally, until the coconut is an even golden brown, about 20 minutes. If the coconut is not as fresh as it could be, reduce the toasting time a bit. Remove and let cool. Reduce the oven temperature to 375 degrees.

2. In a large bowl, using a hand-held mixer, beat the egg whites and salt until foamy, about 30 seconds. Add the sugar and beat until the whites are very shiny white and form a thick ribbon when dropped from the beaters, about 5 minutes. With a rubber spatula, fold in the flour, the butter, and vanilla, if using. Lastly, fold in the toasted coconut.

3. Grease 1 or 2 large baking sheets and drop the cookie batter by $\frac{1}{2}$ tablespoons onto the baking sheets, about 1 inch apart. Bake about 15 minutes for chewy cookies and 20 minutes for crunchy ones. Remove from the baking sheets to a rack to cool and repeat with the remaining batter. Serve warm or cooled.

JACKFRUIT ICE CREAM *(Kem Mit)*

MAKES ABOUT 2 CUPS

The jackfruit is a member of the same family as the breadfruit, the huge, starchy staple eaten throughout the Pacific. Jackfruit is quite different though, with a moist, perfumed yellow flesh. It is only available canned in this country, but its delicate, haunting flavor still comes through. For eating, buy the kind packed in light sugar water. For soft, smooth ice cream use the kind in syrup that will require no additional sugar. This ice cream has a high proportion of fruit to cream and retains its silky texture and tropical flavor for up to seven days in the freezer. Rich and exotic, one scoop after a Vietnamese meal is very soothing.

1 12-ounce jar jackfruit in syrup
$2\frac{1}{2}$ tablespoons lime juice
1 tablespoon kirsch or brandy, optional
$\frac{2}{3}$ cup half-and-half

1. Drain the jackfruit and reserve the syrup. Purée the jackfruit in a food processor, scraping down the sides of the bowl a few times, until very smooth, about 2 minutes. Put the purée in a medium bowl and stir in the syrup and remaining ingredients. Freeze in a ice-cream maker according to the manufacturer's instructions.

HOLIDAY SWEET BEAN CAKES *(Banh Xu-Xe)*

MAKES ABOUT 14 SMALL CAKES

These cakes are customarily cooked and served inside coconut leaves that have been folded into smart-looking miniature boxes. Since coconut leaves are difficult even for Binh to find, the dumplinglike sweets here are wrapped in plastic wrap, then steamed. Pandan, often called vanilla leaves, are pulverized in a blender to extract their green fragrant juice that then colors the outer tapioca layer. Though not authentic, vanilla extract added to the cooked mung bean mixture will add a similar flavor, if *pandan* leaves or paste cannot be found.

½ cup dried yellow mung beans
15 pandan *leaves, fresh or frozen, or ⅛ teaspoon* pandan *paste or 1 teaspoon*
    pure vanilla extract
1 tablespoon plus 2 teaspoons sugar
1 tablespoon grated coconut, preferably fresh
1 cup tapioca flour
¼ teaspoon salt
1 teaspoon vegetable oil

1. In a medium bowl, cover the mung beans with warm water and soak at least 1 hour or overnight. Drain the beans and put them in a medium saucepan with 1 cup water. Cover and cook over medium-low heat until tender and the water has evaporated, about 20 minutes. If the water has not evaporated completely after 20 minutes, over high heat, dry the beans, shaking the pan a few times. Set aside to cool slightly.

2. Put the *pandan* leaves in a blender with ½ cup water. Pulverize to a paste over medium speed. Put a coarse strainer over a bowl and pass the liquid through the strainer, pressing to catch all the liquid.

3. Add the 1 tablespoon sugar and the coconut to the beans. With a potato masher, smash the beans to a paste. Set aside.

4. In a large bowl, whisk together the tapioca flour, *pandan* liquid plus ½ cup water, the remaining sugar, and the salt. Mix the batter well.

5. In a large skillet over medium heat, heat the oil until hot. Pour in the tapioca batter and with chopsticks in each hand start stirring it. It will soon form a sticky mass and come together in a soft ball. Keep pulling the batter apart and turning it over to cook it well for about 1 minute. Remove the dough to a bowl and allow it to cool to the touch.

6. Pull off 14 equal-sized balls of dough, a scant tablespoon in size. Form the bean paste into 14 small forms. Oil your hands, then stretch 1 piece of the dough into a 3-inch thin disc. Put a portion of bean paste in the middle of the round, close the dough up and over it, and pinch to seal the edges. Repeat with the remaining dough and bean paste. Loosely wrap each filled cake with plastic wrap, then form them into ovals.

7. Steam the cakes, covered, in a steamer basket set over 1 inch boiling water for 10 minutes. Let cool slightly before unwrapping and eating.

ORANGE WEDDING RICE *(Xoi Gac)*

MAKES 6 SIDE DISH SERVINGS

This brilliantly colored rice is sold on the streets of Vietnam and is prepared at home for holidays and special occasions, such as banquets and weddings. The recipe comes from the north and uses an intensely orange powder ground from a dried fruit not found here. The powder can be purchased in some Asian stores that sell herbs and potions. It is called *Xoi Gat*, or carrot powder because of its color, and you may have to ask for it over the counter. It doesn't have much flavor; it is the color that is prized. Serve Orange Wedding Rice on its own, or as a side dish to Roast Chicken with Five Spice Glaze (page 216) or Pork with Fresh Tomato Sauce (page 233).

> *2 cups short-grain sweet or glutinous rice*
> *1 to 2 large banana leaves*
> *4 tablespoons butter, melted*
> *¼ teaspoon tomato paste*
> *⅛ teaspoon carrot powder, optional*
> *¼ teaspoon salt*
> *2 teaspoons sugar*
> *6* pandan *leaves, optional, or ⅛ teaspoon pure vanilla extract*

1. Wash the rice well, in several rinses of water. In a large bowl, cover the rice with water and let sit overnight. The next day, drain the rice well in a colander and allow to sit and dry, tossing it occasionally until quite dry.

2. Line a large, wide steamer rack with the banana leaves and fill the bottom of the steamer with about 3 inches of water. Bring to a boil.

3. Put the rice in a bowl and stir in the butter, tomato paste, carrot powder, salt, and sugar and vanilla extract if using. Spread the rice mixture on the banana leaves and mound it slightly in the center. Put the *pandan* leaves, if using, on top. Cover and steam over high heat until the rice is tender, about 35 minutes. You may need to add more water to the pot if it gets too quiet while cooking or if you smell it start to burn. Serve hot or at room temperature.

Entertaining in the Vietnamese Style and Spirit

The Vietnamese meal is a mix of many different dishes presented together on the table, eclectic and ever-interesting for the large group typical of the Vietnamese family. The variety of foods encourages a long, leisurely visit with loved ones. Most Vietnamese food is meant to be eaten warm or at room temperature and actually tastes better that way. Each person is given a small bowl and chopsticks. As the plates of food are passed around the table, you take what you want, then start again when the bowl is empty. It is polite to take only as much as you know you can eat.

Because of the way food is presented at the Vietnamese table, large platters and plates and salad bowls make for a beautifully set table with no individual plating needed. This is especially convenient for the cook, who can then enjoy dinner with the group. See the dessert selections if you would like to serve an unusual sweet, but otherwise the preference of serving fruit at the end of the meal gives the cook a chance to create captivating fruit displays.

Tea is usually drunk with meals. Beer is also very popular with the Vietnamese and is especially good with casually eaten dishes, like the Steamed Crabs with Chile, Black Pepper, Salt, and Lime (page 131) or Garlic Fried Crabs (page 134) and with very spicy appetizers like Sour and Spicy Bean Threads with Crab and Shrimp (page 132).

Wine, however, is an easy match with much of this food. In general, keep to the light-hearted, uncomplicated white wines, like French white wines such as Vouvray, St-Veran, and the Mâcon Chardonnays. California produces excellent Sauvignon Blancs and Chenin Blancs that are crisp and perfect with spicy, citrus-dominated sauces. Domestic chardonnays, rich and expensive, do not pair especially well with this food, except the Simi Chardonnay, which is made in the same style of the steely French Mâcons and is a great match with Vietnamese food. So is the dry white Riesling from Trefethan. Good-quality sparkling wines are a fine choice and add merriment to dinner. Try sparkling Vouvray, an Italian Brut or a well-thought-of sparkling wine from California. German wines can be a delightful surprise because their natural sweetness and floral aromas go smoothly with this food. Try a Piesporter, Riesling, Auslese, or Spätlese.

THE VIETNAMESE NEW YEAR'S DINNER

There is no more important holiday than Tet, the celebration of the coming year. The Vietnamese believe in an unbroken chain that links ancient ancestors and their spirits with the living and the unborn: the past, present, and future of the family. For two days, there is the roar of exploding fireworks and an intense air of celebration. No real cooking is done on New Year's Day; meals are kept simple and plain. Large meat-studded rice cakes wrapped in bamboo leaves have been bought or made days ago and just need reheating; they look like big, leafy salamis. People eat when and what they please. There are sweets, candies, and snacks. The big celebration dinner takes place the day after Tet. This is when holiday foods like homemade spring rolls, Silver Dollar Cakes, Caramelized Shrimp, and more are made. It's a big fuss. At Binh's mother's house, his sisters prepared a midday meal that included these dishes:

Mushroom and Leek Soup with White Tree Ears
Pork and Crab Spring Rolls
Silver Dollar Cakes with Nuoc Cham Dipping Sauce
Crispy Red Snapper with Spicy Tomato Sauce
Beef Grilled in La-Lot Leaves
Caramelized Shrimp
Table Salad and Rice

Here is a dinner I often prepare when I wish to introduce Vietnamese food to the uninitiated.

A FIRST-IMPRESSION DINNER FOR SIX TO EIGHT

Watercress-Shrimp Soup
Happy Pancakes with Nuoc Cham Dipping Sauce
Ninh Hoa Grilled Meatballs
Table Salad with Rice Noodles

Here are a number of suggestions for sit-down dinners. The dishes are simple but sophisticated. These meals could be eaten with chopsticks but knives and forks are more appropriate.

AN ELEGANT PLATED DINNER

Garlic Chive and Tofu Soup
Steamed Shrimp on Asparagus Spears
Coriander-Chile Sauce
Curried Frog Legs
Rice or French Bread
Jackfruit Ice Cream

AN EXTRAORDINARY ROAST CHICKEN DINNER

Vegetarian Tofu Soup
Mini Crab Cakes with Red Pepper Sauce
Roast Chicken with Five Spice Glaze
Orange Brandy Sauce
Water Spinach Sauté
Rice

A SUMMER DINNER ON THE GRILL

Grilled Tofu and Vegetables
Lemongrass Spareribs
Tuna with Dill and Toasted Almonds
Cool and Spicy Bean Salad

GRILLING IN AUTUMN

Shrimp on Sugar Cane with Nuoc Cham Dipping Sauce
Duck with Spicy Eggplant
Lemongrass-Scented Vegetable Sauté
Grilled Slices of French Baguette
Fresh Coconut Cookies

DO NHAU, OR ''LITTLE BITES,'' MENU

Sour and Spicy Bean Threads with Crab and Shrimp
Silver Dollar Cakes with Nouc Cham Dipping Sauce
Lemon Chicken
Tomato-Glazed Spareribs
Imperial Shrimp Rolls
Green Papaya Salad

AN IMPERIAL DINNER FROM HUE

Hue Soup with Pork and Beef
Simple Shrimp Rolls with Nuoc Cham Dipping Sauce
Broiled Quail with Preserved Prunes
Table Salad and Rice

A FULL MOON VEGETARIAN DINNER

Vegetarian Spring Rolls with Soy Dipping Sauce
Curried Tofu Sauté
Table Salad and Buddha Rice
Jasmine Tea

BEEF IN FIVE COURSES

This all-beef menu is our own choice of beef dishes, in the fashion of the classic meal of Vietnamese Beef in Seven Courses, made famous in the Saigon restaurants that specialize in serving this extravagant spread. An all-beef menu is cause for celebration, a rare treat in Vietnam, and it's a challenge to present one dish after another, which is why we feature only five courses. Serve this medley in small portions to highlight the unusual flavorings of the individual dishes and vegetable garnishes.

La-Lot Beef Soup
Grilled Curried Pepper Steak with Roasted Peppers
Beef Fondue
Pineapple Chile Sauce
Star Anise Beef Stew with Lemongrass
Shaking Beef

Mail-Order Sources for Special Ingredients and Equipment

If you live far away from an Asian market or resource, don't worry, you're not alone. Mail-order companies are established for people like you who love the food but need the basics.

Vietnam House, 191 Farmington Ave., Hartford, CT 06105; 203-524-0010. Vietnam Imports, 922 West Broad St., Route 7, Falls Church, VA 22046; 703-534-9441.
These two companies supply dry and packaged staples that are easy to mail, like jasmine rice, rice papers, rice flour, fish sauce, shrimp chips, Vietnamese bean sauce, and so on.

K. Kalustyan, 123 Lexington Ave., New York, NY 10016; 212-685-3451. This Indian merchant also carries an extensive supply of Asian ingredients, like jasmine rice, rice flour, dried lemongrass, coconut milk, curry paste, and so on.

DeWildt Imports, Fox Gap Rd., R.D.3, Bangor, PA 18013; 1-800-338-3433. A Dutch-Indonesian spice company featuring foods from all over Asia, like jasmine rice, rice papers, rice flour, dried chiles, coconut milk, dried lemongrass, soy sauce, tea, and so on. Also available is some kitchen equipment, like bamboo steamers and granite mortars and pestles.

Far East Flavors, 8547 E. Arapahoe Rd., Suite J205, Greenwood Village, CO 80111; 303-290-0575.
"The Oriental Store At Your Door" sells Asian products in particular—rice papers, rice, tapioca flour, potato flours, good Japanese Shoyu soy sauce, Vietnamese fish sauce and bean sauce, tree ears, and so on.

HERB SEEDS AND PLANTS

Nichols Garden Nursery, 1190 North Pacific Highway, Albany, OR 97321; 503-928-9280.
Their charming catalog is replete with advice, recipes, folklore, and helpful, humorous drawings. There is much for the gardener, including regular and garlic chives, lemon balm, spearmint plants as well as seeds for many different types of basil, chives, coriander, dill, red and green *perilla* leaf, and so on.

Johnny's Selected Seeds, Foss Hill Rd., Albion, ME 04910; 207-437-9294.
Red and green *perilla* leaf, garlic chives, coriander, and Thai chile seeds, among others.

The Cook's Garden, P.O. Box 65, Londonderry, VT 05148; 802-824-3400.
Red *shiso*, Thai chile seeds, and more.

Taylor's Herb Gardens Inc., 1535 Lone Oak Road, Vista, CA 92084; 619-727-3485.
Herb plants, such as basil, chives, coriander, lemongrass, and spearmint.

EQUIPMENT

Williams-Sonoma, P.O.Box 7456, San Francisco, CA 94120-7456; 415-421-4242
Mandoline slicer and grater and an electric rice steamer among many other marvelous choices.

The Chef's Catalog, 3215 Commercial Ave., Northbrook, IL 60062-1900; 1-800-338-3232.
Mandoline slicer and grater and an electric rice steamer.

Index

Salad(s) (*cont.*)
  banana blossom, 173
  bean, cool and spicy, 174–175
  beef, glazed, with roasted rice powder, 178
  chicken and grapefruit, 166–167
  Cornish hen, 163
  green papaya, 162
  pork and shrimp, classic Vietnamese, 164–165
  spaghetti squash, 170–171
  squid, with tamarind, 176–177
  table, 32–33
  vegetable, with pork, shrimp, and egg strips,
168–169
  water spinach, 172
Salad dressing
  soy vinaigrette, 51
  vegetarian, 296
Sate-Chile Oil, 58
Sauce(s), 23–25, 38
  anchovy, 23
  chile, 13
  coconut, 302
  fish, 23
  hoisin, 24
  oyster, 24
  soy, 26, 295
  Vietnamese bean, 24
  See also Dipping Sauce
Sausages, Chinese style, 25
Sauté
  curried tofu, 284
  summer seafood, with vegetables and basil, 186–187
  vegetable, lemongrass-scented, 285
  water spinach, 291
Scallion Oil, 59
Seafood, 180–204
  bass, steamed whole, with tiger lilies, 200–201
  crab farci, 126–127
  frog legs, curried, 204
  with ginger, tomato, and chiles, 190
  lobster
    coral, 194–195
    curry, light, 198–199

  scallops, shrimp and, with orange and chile, 196–197
  red snapper, crispy, with spicy tomato sauce, 188–189
  squid, stuffed, 192–193
  summer sauté, with vegetables and basil, 186–187
  trout stuffed with shrimp and scallops, 191
  tuna with dill and toasted almonds, 202–203
Sesame Oil, 25
Shaking Beef, 250
Shallots, 25
  fried, 62
Shiitake, dried, 20
Shopping, 6–7, 10
Shrimp
  artichokes stuffed with crab and, 130
  and baby taro root soup, 98
  caramelized, 183
  chips, 25–26, 67
  crunchy sweet potato nests with, 114–115
  dried, 25
  jumbo, curried grilled, 184–185
  mousse, escargots wrapped in, 120–121
  on sugar cane, 112–113
  paste, 26
  and peanut sauce, 44–45
  rolls
    imperial, with coriander and peanuts, 122–123
    simple, 110–111
    special, 116–117
  sauce, 49
  sour and spicy bean threads with crab and, 132–133
  toasts, 124–125
Silver Dollar Cakes, 142–143
Silver fungus. *See* Fungus, dried white
Simple Shrimp Rolls, 110–111
Soup(s), 70–103
  beef ball, 84–85
  bitter melon, 94–95
  cabbage roll, 92–93
  crab
    and asparagus, 88–89

About the Authors

Vietnamese-born **BINH DUONG** is the chef and owner of Truc Orient Express in Hartford, Connecticut, and La Truc in Boca Raton, Florida. **MARCIA KIESEL** is the associate director of the test kitchen and a food-writer at *Food & Wine* magazine. She lives in Connecticut.